BLACK WOMEN
NOVELISTS AND THE
NATIONALIST AESTHETIC

BLACK WOMEN NOVELISTS AND THE NATIONALIST AESTHETIC

MADHU DUBEY

INDIANA UNIVERSITY PRESS

Bloomington and Indianapolis

Library of Congress Cataloging-in-Publication Data

Dubey, Madhu.
    Black women novelists and the nationalist aesthetic / Madhu Dubey.
        p.   cm.
    Includes bibliographical references (p.) and index.
    ISBN 0-253-31841-6 (alk. paper). — ISBN 0-253-20855-6 (pbk. : alk. paper)
        1. American fiction—Afro-American authors—History and criticism.
    2. Women and literature—United States—History—20th century.
    3. American fiction—Women authors—History and criticism.
    4. American fiction—20th century—History and criticism. 5. Afro-American women in literature. 6. Black nationalism in literature.
    I. Title.
    PS374.N4D83 1994
    813'.54099287'08996073—dc20   93-14343

1 2 3 4 5   99 98 97 96 95 94

CONTENTS

BLACK WOMEN NOVELISTS AND THE NATIONALIST AESTHETIC

INTRODUCTION
BLACK FEMINIST CRITICISM

Over the last decade or so, the works of black American women novel-ists have become increasingly visible in the academy, and have engen-dered a burgeoning and vigorous black feminist critical discourse. With the exception of Zora Neale Hurston, it is black women novelists of the "second renaissance" of the 1970s who occupy the center of this critical discourse. The recent academic attention accorded to novelists such as Alice Walker and Toni Morrison makes it difficult to believe that when they first began publishing, in the heyday of the black cultural national-ist movement, their works were greeted with intense hostility from nationalist reviewers and critics. Even as black cultural nationalism and its literary program, the Black Aesthetic,[1] catalyzed the remarkable formal experimentation of black literature during the 1960s and 1970s, its race-centered aesthetic hindered a just appreciation of the works of black women novelists. While initiating a radical redefinition of liter-ary "blackness," Black Aesthetic discourse, consolidated around the sign of race, discouraged any literary exploration of gender and other differences that might complicate a unitary conception of the black experience. Black feminist literary criticism, which emerged in the wake of the Black Aesthetic movement,[2] seeks precisely to comprehend the "creative function of difference"[3] in black women's literature, and to render this literature readable in ways that both restructure and supplement the ideological program of black cultural nationalism.

Black women articulated their differences with the nationalist pro-gram in a number of manifestos, essays, and anthologies published in the 1970s.[4] These texts, containing the immediate responses of a wide range of black women to the cultural and political issues raised by the nationalist movement, along with the more explicitly academic analy-ses of the 1980s, operate throughout this book as the critical levers directing my interpretation of black nationalist discourse. While draw-ing on black feminist theory to clarify the ways in which black women novelists of the 1970s interrogated the racial discourse of nationalism, my discussion does not invest the black women's fiction of this period with a representative oppositional unity that can be uncovered by a feminist analysis. The three novelists I consider in detail—Toni Mor-rison, Gayl Jones, and Alice Walker—all variously negotiate the ideo-logical and formal priorities of black feminist criticism. Alice Walker's womanist agenda, as well as her corrective treatment of stereotypes and her celebratory appropriation of folk material, render her fiction most easily amenable to a black feminist reading. Like Walker, Toni Morrison is widely acclaimed as a "major author" of the developing black women's fictional tradition, but the distinctive formal features of her work, especially her use of nonrealist modes of characterization, unsettle the mimetic assumptions of early black feminist criticism. Gayl Jones's fiction is conspicuously absent from most black feminist works on the black women's fictional tradition, including Barbara Christian's *Black Women Novelists*, Susan Willis's *Specifying*, and Marjorie Pryse and Hortense Spillers's *Conjuring*. The critical neglect of Jones is not surprising, for her novels do not confirm the ideological aims or the formal predilections of black feminist criticism. Jones's fiction cannot be absorbed into a tradition impelled by the struggle against negative stereotypes, or into a tradition authorized by black folk practices associated with the rural South. My reading of the novels of Morrison, Jones, and Walker examines the criteria that defined a representative black woman novelist during the 1970s, and seeks to account for those elements in these writers' works that strain a nationalist or feminist reading.

As these preliminary remarks may suggest, my work directly engages two of the principal preoccupations of black feminist literary criticism: its discourse on stereotypes versus character, which bespeaks the strong political investment of black feminist critics in the notion of a whole self; and its affirmation of oral folk culture as the source of a uniquely black feminine literary authority. In this introductory chapter, I shall briefly survey these two areas of black feminist criticism, tracing their initial emergence as well as their ultimate divergence from Black Aesthetic theory.

The question of stereotypes versus full characterizations of black women in fiction forms the central concern of early black feminist critics such as Barbara Christian and Mary Helen Washington. Sketching a developmental model that is at once normative and descriptive, Christian argues that later black women novelists "create character rather than type,"[5] and "provide glimpses of reality to revise the distorted black images of the 18th and 19th centuries."[6] In her similar claim that black women's fiction has historically progressed from flat stereotypes to three-dimensional depictions of authentic black womanhood, Washington explicitly identifies black nationalism as the enabling condition for positive images of black women in fiction: contemporary black women writers are able to portray whole characters imbued with "complexity, diversity and depth" because of "the political events of the 60s and the changes resulting from the freedom movement."[7] The struggle against stereotypes in early black feminist criticism derives its initial impetus from the war of images waged in Black Aesthetic essays such as Addison Gayle's "Cultural Strangulation:

Black Literature and the White Aesthetic" and Carolyn Gerald's "The Black Writer and His Role."[8] In Gerald's famous formulation, the primary function of the black writer is to overturn the "zero image" of blackness projected in white cultural texts.[9] Early black feminist critics resume this necessary work of reversal and revision, regarding the literary stereotype as the most visible site of struggle for cultural control and self-determination.

The more recent black feminist writing on characterization in black women's fiction is also intimately connected to the Black Aesthetic agenda. In her controversial essay "Boundaries: Or Distant Relations and Close Kin," Deborah McDowell overtly places her own deconstructive move against the empowering gesture of reconstruction initiated by Black Aesthetic theorists, and indicates the two elements of the Black Aesthetic discourse on the subject that her own work attempts to challenge and surpass: its imperative that black writers should offer only positive images of black identity, and its construction of identity exclusively around the dynamics of racial difference. As McDowell suggests, the Black Aesthetic emphasis on "a 'positive' black self, always already unified, coherent, stable, and known,"[10] although remarkably liberatory when it was first articulated, later operated as a dogmatic stricture on black writers, precluding any exploration of the differences and contradictions that destabilize a monolithic conception of black identity. Further, as McDowell observes, Black Aesthetic discourse constructed race as "the sole determinant of being and identity, subsuming sexual difference."[11]

The contemporary black feminist discourse on identity is motivated by an impulse to displace the prescriptive model of black identity, unified around the sign of race, that was promoted by Black Aesthetic critics. Along with Deborah McDowell, black feminist theorists such as Hortense Spillers and Karla Holloway are insistently foregrounding the "convergences of difference," the "spaces of contradiction,"[12] the "polysemic ramifications of fracture," and the "persistence of the decentered subject"[13] in black women's fiction. Emphasizing the multiple orders of difference that constitute the black feminine subject, these theorists seek to resist the totalizing moves of other discourses on the subject, such as the definition of "man" in bourgeois humanist ideology, of "woman" in white feminist ideology, and of "black" in black nationalist ideology. In the early black feminist discourse on images of black women in literature, the term *black woman* tends to congeal into a stable and given category. It is precisely this "critical tendency to homogenize and essentialize black women"[14] that is interrogated in the writing of contemporary black feminist critics such as McDowell, Spillers, and Holloway.

While the current countermove to splinter and decenter the black feminine subject is undoubtedly productive at this particular conjuncture in black literary criticism, we cannot afford to forget the political and affective force of the early black feminist move to construct a unified, essential, and whole self. What this set of moves and countermoves clarifies is the double gesture needed in black feminist theorizations of identity: on the one hand, a continuing appreciation of the cultural history that has produced the black writer's strong investment in the model of a whole, cohesive self, and on the other, a vigilant attention to the differences within the black experience that confound any totalized, unitary definition of black identity.[15]

Recent black feminist revaluations of identity, notably Mae Henderson's "Speaking in Tongues: Dialogics, Dialectics, and the Black Woman Writer's Literary Tradition" and Deborah McDowell's "Boundaries: Or Distant Relations and Close Kin," cited earlier, take Toni Morrison's *Sula* as the exemplary fictional text that can offer, in Henderson's words, "a kind of model for the deconstructive function of black feminist literary criticism."[16] This choice in itself signals a significant departure from earlier images-of-black-women criticism, which privileged Alice Walker as the novelist who most successfully achieves complete characterizations of black women.[17] A consideration of *Sula* compels critical attention to the nonrealist modes of characterization explored in the novel, thus displacing the realist assumptions that underwrite the opposition of flat, false stereotype and whole, authentic character. The argument that stereotypes misrepresent black feminine identity presupposes a preexistent real and knowable self that fiction should mirror as accurately as possible. Such an argument unmistakably recalls the realist notion of character as the reflection of a full, coherent self.[18] One problem with installing this model of character as the goal of black women's fiction is that it disables an appreciation of the experimental, nonrealist modes of characterization deployed in so much recent black women's fiction, modes that destabilize the humanist model of identity inscribed in realist fiction.

In an attempt to situate this critical, innovative treatment of character in an indigenous cultural context, critics such as Karla Holloway and Michael Awkward have differentiated the individual self of classic realist fiction from the whole subject posited in some black women's novels,[19] such as Alice Walker's *The Third Life of Grange Copeland* and *Meridian*. Walker's womanist ideology affirms a psychological wholeness that is communally oriented and is explicitly opposed to the self-sufficient individuality of bourgeois humanist ideology. While this distinction works at an abstract, ideological level, it is often difficult to sustain at the level of fictional characterization. Communal intersubjectivity is not easy to represent in fiction, given the novel's lengthy realist legacy of individual characterization. Black women's fiction negotiates this legacy in several different ways and to varying degrees of success; as I argue in my chapter on *The Third Life*, Alice Walker inscribes her oppositional conception of the whole subject through modes of psychological character delineation that inadvertently reinstate the individual self of classic realist fiction.

The novels of Toni Morrison and Gayl Jones, in contrast, consistently employ nonrealist modes of characterization that are unreadable within the terms of images-of-black-women criticism. The realist opposition between flat stereotype and rounded character is rendered inoperative in the fictional worlds created by Morrison and Jones. *The Bluest Eye* and *Eva's Man* draw heavily upon stereotypes of black women, which, according to the evolutionary models proposed by Christian and Washington, should be obsolete by the 1970s. In *Sula* and *Corregidora*, the use of flat, projective modes of characterization serves to denaturalize the "real" and to divest subjectivity of any authentic presence. My discussion of the novels of Morrison and Jones focuses on their parody of realist forms such as the bildungsroman and their selective deployment of grotesque modes of character delineation. These strategies of characterization, even as they construct character around lack, division, and mutilation, always retain the notion of a whole and unified self as an unrepresentable, imaginary ideal. The figuration of black feminine identity in these novels, then, may best be understood as a contradictory interplay between presence and absence, wholeness and fracture.

The black woman novelist's effort to interrupt the realist legacy and to inscribe a black feminine subject other than the discrete individual self is often assisted by her appropriation of black folk cultural forms. As even the titles of so many books and essays on black women novelists indicate, black feminist critics are increasingly turning to metaphors derived from folk culture, such as conjuring, specifying, quilting, and laying on of hands, in order to theorize the distinctive literary and cultural practices of black women.[20] This recent theoretical privileging of folk cultural models may be traced back to Black Aesthetic discourse, which constructed folk forms as the origin of a uniquely black cultural practice. As I argue in the next chapter, folk (and especially oral) forms were valorized by Black Aesthetic critics as the most effective means of representing a unified and essentially black communal consciousness.

The Black Aesthetic perception of oral forms—as cultural origins that can withstand the displacement and fragmentation wrought by oppression—reappears in much of the later black feminist writing on the subject.[21] I shall consider at some length Susan Willis's *Specifying: Black Women Writing the American Experience*, which remains one of the most engaging and influential studies of the relation between oral forms and black women's fiction. Willis builds her argument around the verbal ritual of specifying, or name-calling, which she considers to be paradigmatic of the black oral tradition. Specifying, according to Willis, constitutes a "form of narrative integrity" that "speaks for a non-commodified relationship to language, a time when the slippage between words and meaning would not have obtained or been tolerated."[22] Aligning oral culture with the rural South and fiction with the urban North, and conceiving the Northern migration as the single most important development in modern black American history, Willis argues that the urban context produced new cultural forms that were marked by their distance from the oral mode. These new forms, and the novel in particular, depend on metaphorical condensation, which Willis regards as an especially apt mode of figuring historical process, of capturing the historical displacement of black culture from the South to the North.[23]

What is exceptional about Willis's book, and what distinguishes it from so many vernacular studies of black women's fiction, is its historical understanding of the different cultural contexts embedded in oral and fictional forms. Her keen attention to these differences helps Willis to avoid conflating black women's novels with the oral folk materials they strive to recall and appropriate. However, while successfully locating black women's fiction within historical processes, Willis tends to construct oral culture as a prehistorical origin. In particular, her opposition of specifying and metaphor is untenable for several reasons.[24] The first problem is with Willis's choice of specifying as the representative instance that authorizes her generalizations about the "narrative integrity" of all black oral forms. In actuality, black oral forms such as the slave songs, the blues, and the trickster tales exemplify precisely the "slippage between words and meaning," the equivocal quality of the language used by oral artists.[25] The duplicity of oral forms can itself be historically situated; through most of their history in the United States, black artists have had to negotiate the necessity of addressing a double audience. To give only one obvious example, the slave songs encoded two exactly antithetical meanings, one (expressing a religious yearning for heavenly peace) directed at the slavemaster, and the other (voicing their political desire for freedom) intended to inspire the slave community.[26] The linguistic complexities as well as the hidden political intentionalities of black oral culture must necessarily be effaced if it is to operate as a pure cultural origin.

Willis's argument, then, is hampered by its failure to acknowledge that oral culture, too, has a history. Relegating black folk culture to a static rural past, Willis's thesis implies that this culture was simply superseded by the Northern urban migration. However, the new urban conditions spawned new oral forms such as rapping, and modified earlier forms such as the dialect and the blues. As Hazel Carby observes, black writers have had to rethink the very meaning of the category "the folk" in their attempt to represent the new urban folk cultures in literature.[27] Moreover, in privileging the rural South as the foundation of a distinctively black cultural practice, critics tend to canonize Zora

Neale Hurston, Alice Walker, and Toni Morrison as exemplary black women novelists, and to marginalize compelling novelists such as Gayl Jones (whose fiction renders the urban manifestations of oral forms such as the blues) or Nella Larsen, Ann Petry, and Gloria Naylor (who convey the experience of urban dislocation without harking back to a rural Southern origin).

Without investing oral forms with any intrinsic or absolute value, my work focuses on the construction of these forms at a given ideological and literary conjuncture. During the 1960s, black folk culture was assigned a certain ideological value to make it amenable to nationalist intentions. The nationalist assertion that oral forms should authorize a uniquely black literary voice proved to be immensely productive for black women's fiction, which appropriated oral forms to serve the Black Aesthetic function of subverting the authority of white literate culture. However, as I argue in chapter 1, black women novelists were not unreservedly committed to the ideological program of black nationalism; their critical and selective adaptation of oral forms reflects their difference from the Black Aesthetic. In black women's novels of the 1970s, folk culture is subjected to a sharp scrutiny that exposes its often damaging consequences for black women. Some obvious examples of this critique, which I detail in the following chapters, are: the masculine will to power enacted in Soaphead Church's conjuring on Pecola in *The Bluest Eye;* the naturalistic folk philosophy of the Bottom community in *Sula,* which entails a reproductive definition of black femininity; the dialect in *Eva's Man,* with its relentless, derogatory naming of black women as "bitches" and "whores"; and the destructive effects on women and children of the folk figure of the badman, upon whom Brownfield, in *The Third Life of Grange Copeland,* is modeled.

The critical balance (and, at times, ambivalence) with which 1970s black women novelists approach folk forms is even more clearly visible in their representations of community. Many of the celebratory readings of folk material in black women's fiction follow Black Aesthetic theory in suggesting that the use of oral forms enables these novels not only to affirm a communal vision but also to establish a continuous and participatory relationship with their readers. Such readings—for example, Keith Byerman's *Fingering the Jagged Grain* and Michael Awkward's *Inspiriting Influences*[28]—offer an enhanced critical understanding of the ways in which folk cultural models help black women's novels to displace the fictional category of the individual protagonist, as well as the authority conventionally invested in omniscient narration. However, no novel can exactly recreate the reception context of oral forms, nor can oral modes survive intact the process of fictional appropriation. This process transmutes the fundamental attributes of oral forms, such as their assumption of an immediate, interactive relation between the artist and the black community. It is in the charged space of encounter between the oral and fictional modes that black women novelists of the 1970s conduct their explorations of community. The following chapters on the novels of Morrison, Jones, and Walker attempt a detailed formal analysis of the generic modifications, the mutually transformative interchanges produced by the induction of oral modes into this fiction.

What is perhaps most valuable about the proliferating interest in the folk orientations of black women's novels is that it has drawn attention to the remarkable formal achievement of these novels. The increasingly rigorous formal focus of current black feminist criticism supplements earlier thematic studies that sought to clarify the ideological significance of black women's fiction. These studies, such as Gloria Wade-Gayles's *No Crystal Stair* and Carol McAlpine Watson's *Prologue*, argue for the existence of a black feminine fictional tradition predicated on common thematic concerns reflecting the shared historical experience of black women. While such thematic studies supply a wealth of information about the historical contexts of black women's novels, they tend to regard these novels as informative ideological documents that faithfully reproduce historical reality.[29] One problem with applying this reflective model to black literature is that an exclusive focus on themes helps to maintain the form/content split that usually justifies a nonideological analysis of literary texts. Literary criticism has traditionally endorsed a "false dialectic of 'form' and 'content' whereby the artificially imposed terms alternate so that literature is sometimes perceived as content (ideology) and sometimes as form ('real' literature)."[30] Such an opposition between art and ideology is what frequently determines the thematic reading of black literary works as ideological tracts and, conversely, the strictly formal reading of texts that are considered truly literary. Recognizing that form is not the ideology-free domain of pure literature is the first step toward challenging the division between art and ideology. An ideological analysis of form should be particularly useful for black feminist criticism, for it questions the notion of real, nonideological literature that undergirds the formation of dominant literary traditions. These traditions dismiss the works of black writers on the grounds that their ideological nature disqualifies them from the status of true literature.[31]

In order to reverse this long history of exclusion, contemporary black feminist critics are underscoring the need for a simultaneously ideological and formal approach to black literary texts. For example, Cheryl Wall writes:

> Afro-American literature has so often been misread as mimetic representation or sociology. In other words, the verbal text has been treated as if it merely mirrored the social text. To read that way is inanely reductive, but to read black writing as if it has no relation to political reality is to vitiate its power.[32]

As Wall's comments suggest, black critics have strong reasons for investing in the category of the literary, even as they militate against the formalist definition of literature as a category that transcends politics and ideology.

In this respect, again, the theoretical project of contemporary black feminist critics is indebted to Black Aesthetic theory, which attempted to demolish the division between art and ideology. Committed to a radical revaluation of Western aesthetics, Black Aesthetic critics exposed the covert ideological agenda of formalism. Precisely because black literary texts have been historically considered deficient when judged by the aesthetic criterion of universality, some Black Aesthetic critics found it necessary to dispense altogether with the category of the aesthetic.[33] Others, however, preserved a redefined notion of art as a vehicle of ethical and political value. Their desire to assert an intimate and symbiotic connection between art and ideology motivated the Black Aestheticians' conception of literature as a direct reflection of social and cultural experience.[34] Concerned primarily with the thematic content of literary works, Black Aesthetic critics, and especially those who wrote on the novel, regarded form as a transparent medium of ideological meaning. For example, in Addison Gayle's succinct expression, "form is of less importance than the content, or . . . the message. The form is the delivery system while the message is the thing delivered."[35] Successfully challenging a formalist aesthetic at one level, by insisting that all art is ideological, Black Aesthetic theorists, by default, allowed the category of form to remain immune and peripheral to the field of ideological analysis.

Contemporary black feminist literary theory extends the Black Aesthetic gesture of challenging the dichotomy between art and ideology. Without losing sight of the ideological conditionality of all art, black feminist critics are increasingly rejecting the reflective model of Black Aesthetic and early black feminist theory. Hazel Carby, Susan Willis, Valerie Smith, and Karla Holloway, among others, emphasize the mediated status of black women's fiction[36] in an attempt to bring the category of form within the purview of ideological criticism and to reclaim it as a significant component of black literary texts. Such a critical intervention, simultaneously and inextricably formal and ideological, appears especially necessary at present, given the increasing commercial and academic appropriation of black women's fiction. Although more and more black women's novels are being reprinted in glossy new paperback editions and taught in U.S. colleges and universities, these texts are rarely subjected to the intricate formal analysis that is usually reserved for the "masterpieces" of the American literary canon. My work participates in the current black feminist effort to question the critical norms that constitute literature in opposition to ideology, and that thereby, even while admitting black women's fiction into the academy, implicitly deny this fiction the status of "true literature."

My discussion of the ways in which black women's fiction negotiates contemporary ideological discourses draws selectively (and with serious reservations) on Mikhail Bakhtin's "Discourse in the Novel," an essay explicitly intended to "overcome the divorce between an abstract 'formal' approach and an equally abstract 'ideological' approach."[37] Bakhtin's perception of novelistic language as a terrain of ideological struggle displaces the polarities of both formalism and crude Marxism, each of which gives priority either to intrinsic textual properties or to extratextual ideological contexts.[38] In Bakhtin's terms, the novel, in its fictive construction of competing social and ideological discourses, forces the recognition that "language is not a neutral medium that passes freely and easily into the private property of the speaker's intentions; it is populated—overpopulated—with the intentions of others" (p. 294).

Bakhtin's assertion that "language is always half someone else's" (p. 293) may be given special historical resonance in studies of black American narrative.[39] For the earliest slave narrators, the project of writing began as an attempt to appropriate the English language, which was "overpopulated" with the ideological intentions of the dominant white culture. Literacy, which was legally withheld from slaves, was a risky political achievement and, having achieved it, black writers had to articulate themselves in a language that denied the very possibility of black subjectivity. The impossibly ironic position of early black writers who tried to shape the master's language to suit their own intentions, cannot be smugly consigned to ancient history. More than two centuries after the inception of black narrative in America, several black women writers are still engaging the master texts of white American culture, in the form of the Dick and Jane primer in *The Bluest Eye*, the history textbook in *The Third Life*, or the toothpaste advertisement in *Sister X and the Victims of Foul Play*. These novels' explorations of black feminine identity gain their ironic edge from a dialogic parody of dominant cultural texts that produce the black woman as a sign of lack. Bakhtin's discussion of the novel's "parodic stylization" (p. 312) of reified literary and social discourses, and its appropriation of popular folk materials, can be immensely suggestive for critical inquiries into the dialogic development of the black novel. Bakhtin's work inflects my discussion of the ways in which black women novelists utilize popular folk forms and styles (such as funk, the blues, quilting, or black speech) to displace the ideological authority of white cultural texts and to refract their own oppositional intentions.

Bakhtin describes the novel's appropriation of different literary and extraliterary languages as a *dialogic* process, a term that bears a bewildering variety of meanings.[40] Without subscribing to Bakhtin's more generalized definitions of dialogia as an inherent property of all discourse,[41] I draw on his analysis of novelistic dialogia as a "critical interanimation" (p. 296), an "artistically organized" confrontation between unequally powerful social and literary languages (p. 366). In order to theorize the ways in which black women's fiction of the 1970s dialogizes the ideological discourse of black nationalism, I have appropriated and extended two of Bakhtin's more specific usages of the term *dialogia* to describe the interchanges between two utterances on the same object, and between an utterance and its contexts.

Bakhtin's theory of novelistic dialogia hinges on his assertion that all discourse responds to prior discourses and anticipates possible answering discourses of the future. His discussion of this "internal dialogism of the word" (p. 280) informs my claim that black women's fiction of the 1970s constitutes a highly mediated response to black nationalist utterances on a number of different but interrelated objects, including the black woman, the black community, the question of political change, and the function of art, among others. Black women's novels conduct a subtextual dialogue with black nationalist discourse, adopting the several strategies of directly contradicting, berating, appeasing, beguiling, and dodging an assumed and typical Black Aesthetic reader. The ideological context of black nationalism is thus internalized by these texts, constructed as the hypothetical addressee or interlocutor of their fictional discourse.

The terms *text* and *context* are further complicated and stripped of their polarized connotations of inside and outside in Bakhtin's remarks on the "contextualized (dialogizing) framing" of one discourse by another (p. 340). Arguing that an utterance may be dialogized if it is dislodged from its initial context and framed by another, alien context, Bakhtin refuses a static conception of context as single, fixed, and all-determining. Instead, his dynamic formulation of context as a "system of potentially infinite displacement and substitution"[42] opens the space for strategic misreadings and reaccentuations of a discourse in different contexts. Taking black nationalist discourse as the pre-text of black women's novels in the 1970s, I argue that some of these novels dialogize black nationalist discourse by dislocating it from its "original" context and reframing it in an alien fictional context. For example, the black nationalist discourse on reproduction and matriarchy is displaced onto the context of slavery in *Corregidora;* *Sula* displaces several supposedly radical elements of black nationalist ideology onto the deeply conservative folk vision of its Bottom community; and *The Third Life of Grange Copeland* grafts together, in the character of Grange, the ideologically incongruous figures of the mother and the nationalist. Each of these displacements produces a curious fictional and ideological hybrid that exposes the inconsistencies of black nationalist discourse.

While using some of Bakhtin's concepts to clarify the ways in which black women's novels mediate and critically misread nationalist ideology, I do not hazard any generalizations about the ideologically subversive nature of all black women's fiction. As I demonstrate in the following chapters, if the strategy of displacement used in these novels often illuminates the contradictions of nationalist discourse, it equally marks these novels' capitulation to the terms of this discourse. While much of black women's fiction subverts contemporary ideological discourses on race and gender, it just as frequently submits to the constraints of these discourses. I do not, then, concur with Bakhtin's occasionally essentialist celebration of the authentic novel, which achieves a "liberation" from ideological discourses by the very fact of turning these discourses into fictional objects (p. 348). Bracketing all essentialist definitions of good or true fiction, I seek rather to delineate the ideological construction of the category of good fiction at a specific cultural conjuncture. Through frequent references to contemporary reviews of black women's novels in journals such as *Black World, Freedomways*, and *The Black Scholar* on the one hand, and *The New York Times Book Review, The New Yorker*, and *The Chicago Tribune Book Review* on the other, I show that these works constitute themselves as novels by carefully navigating between two influential contemporary definitions of good fiction. The Black Aesthetic conception of good fiction as didactic and politically useful, and the white literary establishment's promotion of a politically neutral fiction, represent the extreme ideological poles within which black women's fiction of the 1970s was situated. I am reluctant to advance any transhistorical claims about the inherent nature of all black women's fiction, or about the relation between this fiction and contemporary ideological discourses.

Most recent theoretical work on the relation between fiction and ideology builds on Louis Althusser's essentially Bakhtinian argument that "authentic art . . . presupposes a retreat, an internal distantiation" from the ideology it engages; good novels, by Althusser's definition, expose the contradictions and limits of "the very ideology in which they are held."[43] Granting a relative autonomy to the ideological level, and refusing to "rank real art among the ideologies,"[44] Althusser's work has generated a spate of critical studies that supplant the reflective and homologous models of earlier Marxist criticism, and attempt a more modulated articulation of the unique dynamics of fiction and its complex mediation of contemporary ideologies. Given their highly productive impact on narrative studies, Althusser's pronouncements on ideology cannot, however, be unproblematically transported into the field of black feminist criticism. Neither Althusser's "theory of ideology in general" nor his "theory of particular ideologies, which, whatever their form . . . , always express class positions,"[45] can account for the simultaneous and frequently conflicting ways in which race, class, and gender discourses "interpellate" their subjects.[46] For example, the racial ideology of 1960s black nationalism was crisscrossed by the contradictory ideological interests of class and gender: the collusion of black nationalist ideology with white middle-class gender discourses significantly curtailed the radical reach of its racial discourse. Similarly, the gender identity of black women complicated their position as the racial subjects of black nationalist discourse, even as their racial identity proscribed their affiliation with the gender ideology of white feminism. The black feminine subject in the 1970s was ideologically situated in the fraught overlap between race, class, and gender discourses. My analysis of the ideological construction of black feminine subjectivity in the 1970s draws on the works of black feminist writers such as Hazel Carby, Evelyn Brooks Higginbotham, and Deborah King, who query the totalizing, additive, and analogical models of interrelating the different ideologies of race, class, and gender, and who seek to theorize instead the "multiplicative" and often contradictory relations between these ideologies.[47]

My first chapter traces the intersection of race, class, and gender interests in the black nationalist ideology of the 1960s. While liberating an oppositional racial consciousness, black nationalist ideologues defined black feminine identity within a heterosexual and reproductive frame that reinscribed the white U. S. bourgeois ideology they set out to subvert. Drawing from several black feminist essays and anthologies published during this period, I analyze the centering of the black man as the true subject of black nationalist discourse. I argue that its contradictory construction of the black woman unhinges the three central oppositions—between individual and community, oppressive past and revolutionary present, and absent and present subjectivity—that structure black nationalist discourse. The fictional mediation of these ideological oppositions forms the subject of the following chapters, which consider the novels published by Toni Morrison, Gayl Jones, and Alice Walker in the 1970s. Morrison's *The Bluest Eye* (1970) and *Sula* (1973), Jones's *Corregidora* (1975) and *Eva's Man* (1976), and Walker's *The Third Life of Grange Copeland* (1970) and *Meridian* (1976), all thematically contest, with varying degrees of success, the representation of black femininity in black nationalist discourse. In addition to exploring a black feminine identity that exceeds the nationalist definition, all these novels formally refigure the ideological oppositions of black nationalism. Employing common narrative strategies such as a structural tension between cyclic and linear time, the use of communal narrative frames and oral cultural models, and a figuration of black feminine subjectivity as absent, these novels generate a unique vision of identity, community, and historical change, a vision at once bounded by and straining against the terms of black nationalist discourse.

I

"I AM NEW MAN"
BLACK NATIONALISM AND THE
BLACK AESTHETIC

Black women's fiction in the 1970s was written, published, and received in a cultural context powerfully shaped by black nationalist ideology. Black cultural nationalists succeeded in creating a black literary community relatively independent of the white literary establishment by expanding the production and distribution network for black literature. Several autonomous black publishing houses (such as Broadside Press, Third World Press, Free Black Press, Lotus Press, and Black River Writers) and journals (such as *Freedomways, Journal of Black Studies, Soulbook*, and *The Journal of Black Poetry*) were established during the 1960s and early 1970s. Through petition campaigns, the cultural nationalists also managed to institute black studies programs at numerous U.S. universities. If, however, black cultural nationalism extended and consolidated the audience for black writing, it also demarcated this audience's horizon of literary expectations. In order to clarify how black nationalist discourse operates as both an enabling and a limiting condition for these novels, this chapter outlines some of the central elements of black nationalist discourse, and particularly those elements that contribute to its construction of black femininity.

The term "black nationalist discourse" is, of course, problematic in its conflation of various, often conflicting, strands of nationalism into a single, simplified, homogeneous ideology. In the name of clarity and convenience, historians frequently divide the many black nationalist ideologies of the 1960s into the two broad categories of revolutionary and cultural nationalism. Alphonso Pinkney, in his study of black nationalism, characterizes the ideology of revolutionary nationalism as "a combination of Black nationalism and Marxism-Leninism."[1] An emphasis on class over race is the major factor distinguishing the revolutionary from the cultural nationalists, who give priority to racial over class oppression. Cultural nationalism is based on the premises that "Black people in this country make up a cultural nation,"[2] that the distinctiveness of black culture requires an indigenous theoretical

14

framework that must be developed in absolute separation from the surrounding white culture, and that a revolution in cultural consciousness must precede the economic and political liberation of black Americans.)

Throughout this book, I focus on cultural rather than revolutionary nationalism for two related reasons. First, the cultural nationalists drew greater support from all sections of the black community; perhaps the more radical economic agenda of revolutionary nationalist ideology inhibited its wide dissemination. Second, cultural nationalism is more directly relevant to my discussion because of its palpable impact on the black literature of the 1960s and 1970s.)The Black Aesthetic program was explicitly developed as the literary arm of black cultural nationalism. Any contextual analysis of black literature in this period requires an understanding of the ideological implications of black cultural nationalism.[3])

My account of cultural nationalist discourse draws on the black feminist theory that developed out of the intersection of the black nationalist and the Women's Liberation movements of the early 1970s. Both of these movements at once catalyzed and constrained the formulation of a feminist politics centering around the black woman. Greater numbers of black women were politically active during the 1970s than at any other period in their history;[4] their experiences in the Civil Rights and nationalist movements offered them a valuable training ground for political organization. Further, although black nationalism was clearly dominant in the ideological mapping of black womanhood, it was by no means a tightly closed, self-sufficient system that precluded alternative ideological mappings. (The internal gaps and contradictions of black nationalist discourse, especially visible in its construction of black womanhood, opened the space for an alternative black feminist definition of womanhood.)

This black feminist definition was partly abetted by, but more importantly articulated against, the Women's Liberation movement of the 1970s. The close political contact between the Civil Rights and the Women's Liberation movements proved highly productive for black women; the white feminist revaluation of traditional conceptions of white femininity provided a strong impetus for black women activists to reconsider their own identities.[5] But the black feminist discourse of the 1970s makes abundantly clear that the word *woman* as used in the discourse of the Women's Liberation movement could not possibly encompass both black and white women. Toni Morrison, in her essay "What the Black Woman Thinks about Women's Lib," remarked that the difference between the bathroom signs "White Ladies" and "Colored Women" seemed to her "an eminently satisfactory one." "Ladies" signified the white middle-class female's softness, helplessness, and inactivity, as opposed to the tough, capable independence of black "women."[6]

Morrison implied that these opposed notions of femininity largely explained the inability of black and white women to find common cause as "sisters" in oppression.

Indeed, much of the skepticism of black women toward the Women's Liberation movement followed from this lady/woman opposition.[7] When, in the 1970s, white women began to seek employment as a means of escaping the confinement of middle-class domesticity, they could not possibly strike a sympathetic chord in most black women, who historically had been workers out of economic necessity rather than choice, and (whose experience of oppression in the labor market simply did not square with the white feminist conception of labor as a liberating experience for women.) Moreover, the Women's Liberation movement targeted the patriarchal family structure as the primary site of women's oppression, but for most black women, due to economic and emotional reasons, maintaining a stable family structure was a high priority.[8] Black women greeted with suspicion the Women's Liberation movement's emphasis on sexual liberation, for American patriarchal ideology, in order to preserve the white lady on her pedestal, had always typecast the black woman as a promiscuous sexual animal. Sexual conservatism often offered black women their only means of protection from sexual exploitation; only through the roles of wife and mother could they gain the social respectability that Women's Liberation advocates found so suffocating.[9]

The black feminism of the 1970s derived, then, from black women's conviction that a new black femininity "cannot be defined or demanded on our behalf by white women or Black men."[10] (The Combahee River Collective, a black feminist group established in 1974, acknowledged the debt of contemporary black feminism to the black nationalist and the Women's Liberation movements, but also stressed its difference from both: "it was our experience of disillusionment within these liberation movements . . . that led to the need to develop a politics that was anti-racist, unlike those of white women, and anti-sexist, unlike those of Black and white men."[11] In neither of these two movements could black women assume subject status; black women's sense of their exclusion from the two liberationist discourses of the period is eloquently expressed by the phrase, "all the women are white, all the Blacks are men," which forms part of the title of a well-known black feminist anthology.[12])

The black feminism of the 1970s enables an understanding not only of the racial definition of "woman" in the discourse of Women's Liberation, but also of the emphatically gendered definition of the word *black* in nationalist discourse. (The black feminist historian Paula Giddings has labeled the 1960s "the masculine decade";[13] Michele Wallace went even further in her controversial description of the black liberation movement as "a vehicle for Black Macho."[14] The centering of the black man as the true subject of black nationalist discourse, and the concomitant marginalization of the black woman, was accomplished through a variety of methods. Perhaps in its most disconcerting move, black nationalist discourse incorporated elements of the contemporary government discourse on the black family, especially as propagated by the notorious Moynihan Report (*The Negro Family: The Case for National Action*), published in 1965. An examination of the overlap between the black nationalist and the administrative discourses of the period exposes the hidden gender lines that limited what claimed to be a racial discourse representing all blacks.)

(Black nationalist writers named the black man "the number one object of racism,"[15] seconding the Moynihan Report, which isolated black men as the more acutely affected victims of racial discrimination.[16] Black nationalist leaders not only echoed this masculine emphasis, but identified the black woman as an active agent of the black man's economic and social emasculation. This move was again sanctioned by the Moynihan Report, which represented black women, statistically the most economically powerless group in the country,[17] as a dominant force that hindered the economic progress of black men. According to Moynihan, the "pathology" of ghetto blacks derived from the "deviant" matriarchal structure of the black family. At some places in his report, Moynihan acknowledged that there was no absolute reason for preferring a patriarchal over a matriarchal family structure, but that the matriarchy "seriously retards the progress" of blacks only because "it is so out of line with the rest of American society" (p. 75). Elsewhere, however, Moynihan appealed to natural instinct as a means of validating the patriarchal family: "The very essence of the male animal, from the bantam rooster to the four-star general, is to strut" (p. 62). Moynihan argued that the black male's "natural" tendency to exercise his masculinity was inhibited by the stronger social and economic position of the black woman. With the aid of highly questionable data,[18] Moynihan demonstrated that the black family was matriarchal because of its high rates of divorce, separation, husband desertion, illegitimate births, and female family heads (pp. 123–24).)

Despite their initial denunciation of the Moynihan Report, several black nationalists reproduced Moynihan's assumptions in their discourse on the black matriarch.[19] For example, Nathan Hare, in a short essay with the telling title "Will the Real Black Man Please Stand Up?," contended that "historically, the white oppressor has pitted male against female and . . . forced and seduced the female to take on his values and through her emasculated and controlled the man."[20] Similarly, Eldridge Cleaver, assuming the persona of a "Black Eunuch," argued that the black woman was the silent ally of the white man's oppression of black men: "That's why, all down through history, he has propped her up economically above you and me, to strengthen her hand against us."[21] In another essay, Cleaver, this time in his own voice, described the black woman as a strong, self-reliant, "sub-feminine" Amazon.[22] Calvin Hernton echoed Cleaver, asserting that black women display "a sort of stud-ism, which expresses itself in a strong matriarchal drive."[23]

Appropriating Moynihan's matriarchy thesis, these black nationalists seemed unaware that the government's production of a discourse that highlighted black men's lack of masculine privilege in the family served to displace and to disguise their economic oppression in the labor market.[24] The matriarchy myth effectively split the racial discourse of black nationalism along gender lines, aligning black men with white men in their common commitment to a patriarchal[25] family system. As bell hooks has argued, "by shifting responsibility for the unemployment of Black men onto Black women and away from themselves, white racist oppressors were able to establish a bond of solidarity with Black men based on mutual sexism."[26] The exchange between administrative and nationalist discourses cannot, however, be reduced to a unilateral government co-optation of black nationalist ideology. It was the investment of black male nationalists in the powerful subject position of patriarchal masculinity that motivated their collusion with administrative discourse on the matriarch.

Perhaps in an effort to contain the supposed power of the matriarch, many black nationalist organizations prescribed clearly restricted roles for black women in the movement. The Republic of New Africa, for example, advocated a return to the West African patriarchal system, in which all decision-making powers were invested in the man.[27] Amiri Baraka, in his several cultural nationalist organizations, espoused a similar reversion to traditional African gender roles, and justified patriarchy as a natural system: "Nature has made woman submissive, she must submit to man's creation in order for it to exist."[28] Robert Staples, who had earlier discredited the matriarchy thesis as an administrative ploy to diffuse the threat of black nationalism,[29] later defended male domination of the black liberation movement as a matter of "general consensus among men and women . . . that Black women had held up their men for too long and it was time for the men to take charge."[30] Such reasoning justified the marginalization of black women in the movement; black women were assigned subordinate functions, asked to "man the telephones or fix the coffee while the men wrote position papers or decided on policy."[31]

In addition to secretarial and nurturing work, the other responsibility delegated to black women was the production of male warriors for the revolution. Eldridge Cleaver eulogized the black woman as "the womb that nurtured Toussaint L'Ouverture, that warmed Nat Turner, Gabriel Prosser and Denmark Vesey."[32] In a similar vein, Robert Staples expressed his appreciation of the black woman's contribution to the black liberation struggle: "from her womb have come the revolutionary warriors of our time."[33] The black nationalists' womb-centered definition of black women was, in a sense, their strongest tribute to the Moynihan Report, for Moynihan had been dismayed primarily by black women's insufficient inscription in the patriarchal reproductive system. Black families were distinct from white middle-class families because the black man could not fully exercise his legal paternal function. Further, illegitimate births were not considered a source of stigma in the lower-class black community as they were among middle-class whites.[34] If black feminine reproduction eluded patriarchal structuring to a certain extent, both administrative and nationalist discourses sought to correct this by situating black women more firmly within white middle-class familial ideology. Black sociologists have demonstrated that the extended kinship networks typical of lower-class black families significantly modify the masculine and feminine roles typical of the white middle-class nuclear family.[35] In labeling the black woman's position as the primary economic provider for her children "matriarchal," and in decrying this usurpation of masculine privilege, black nationalist discourse endorsed the gendered division of labor and the definitions of masculine and feminine identity that characterize white middle-class familial ideology.[36]

An analysis of black women's location in black nationalist discourse thus discloses the contradictory reversion to white middle-class, masculine values in a presumably radical, gender-neutral racial discourse.[37] Their construction of black women belied not only the black nationalists' claim of absolute difference from the white middle-class standard, but also their claim of liberating a new, revolutionary black consciousness. The nationalists' attempt at a patriarchal control of black feminine reproduction was, far from being new, reminiscent of slavery. As Florynce Kennedy has remarked, "breeding revolutionaries is not too far removed from a cultural past where Black women were encouraged to be breeding machines for their masters."[38]

Denied access to the "new" revolutionary consciousness, black women repeatedly embodied the persistence of the past in black nationalist discourse. The matriarchal power imputed to the black woman was frequently traced back to her allegedly privileged status in the slavemaster's house.[39] As Margaret Walker has pointed out, the stereotype of the black matriarch recalls the nineteenth-century plantation tradition, with its image of black women as masculine, subhuman creatures capable of performing hard labor unfit for real (white) women.[40] In the black nationalist discourse of the 1960s, the black woman, as an offensive reminder of the slave past, was often represented as an obstacle between black men and their revolutionary future. Eldridge Cleaver wrote that "the white man made the Black woman a symbol of slavery and the white woman a symbol of freedom. Every time I embrace a

Black woman, I'm embracing slavery."[41] As a symbolic locus of the undesirable past, then, the black woman was excluded from the "new" political agenda of black nationalist discourse.

This peculiar positioning of the black woman in the political ideology of black nationalism was exactly reproduced in the Black Aesthetic discourse of the period. In a direct reflection of black nationalist ideology, the Black Aesthetic often constructed the revolutionary black subject in explicit opposition to the black woman. For example, the black woman was the reactionary force against which W. Keorapetse Kgositsile's Revolutionary Black Theater defined itself:

> Old decadent would-be Black woman, this theater will straighten out your mind instead of your hair. If you are too twisted and/or petrified to be straightened out, it will pulp you to death, your hideous little imitation life pungent like the stench of stale menstrual flow.[42]

The black woman here figures the dead, static past, tainted with white values, which the militant black writer must destroy before he can articulate a new revolutionary black sensibility. The Black Aesthetic figuratively trapped the black woman in the past, and barred her from participating in any new emancipatory discourse of blackness or femininity. Larry Neal, in an outline of the "neo-mythology" of the Black Aesthetic, staunchly confirmed the oldest traditional opposition between the masculine and feminine principles: "woman as primarily need / man as doer."[43]

It is hardly surprising, then, that the aesthetic program of black nationalism could not command the undivided allegiance of contemporary black women writers. These writers' attempts to escape the gender codification of Black Aesthetic discourse, and to explore black femininity in new and different guises, were vehemently denounced by Black Aesthetic critics and reviewers. Calvin Hernton has recorded the overwhelmingly negative reception of black women's literature by Black Aesthetic ideologues. Hernton writes that when black women writers such as Gayl Jones, Toni Morrison, and Alice Walker raised gender-related issues in their fiction, black nationalist critics "accuse[d] these women of being Black men-haters, bull-dykes and perverse lovers of white men and women."[44]

As Hernton's remarks imply, the works of 1970s black women writers insistently questioned, at a thematic level, the gender assumptions of black nationalist discourse. Especially in the black women's fiction of the period, elements of the black nationalist construction of black femininity directly enter the texts as thematic material. The outstanding thematic concern of black women's fiction in this period is the sexual division between black men and women that can potentially disrupt the racial unity projected in black nationalist discourse. In its exploration of a specifically feminine subject, this fiction makes visible the contradictory crisscrossing of gender and race in black nationalist discourse.

If black women novelists' thematic questioning of the nationalist construction of femininity is relatively easy to identify, far more difficult to categorize is their formal testing of the three central oppositions—between individual and community, oppressive past and revolutionary future, and absent and present subjectivity—that structure black nationalist discourse. Mediated through a feminine subject, these oppositions refuse to remain fixed in the places assigned them in black nationalist discourse. In addition to exposing the often contradictory articulation of these oppositions in black nationalist discourse, black women's novels of this period also attempt to restructure, resolve, or exceed these ideological oppositions.

The first opposition, between individual and community, is, in a sense, the founding opposition, intended to secure the radical difference of black nationalism from white U.S. capitalist ideology. The economic, political, and aesthetic program of black nationalism was authorized by its commitment to the black community,[45] which was theoretically conceived in stark contrast to the white U.S. ideology of individualism. At the economic level, Stokely Carmichael justified Black Power economic policies on the ground of their difference from U.S. capitalism. Carmichael underscored the cooperative, collective basis of Black Power, as opposed to the individualist, competitive basis of white U.S. society.[46]

Despite the separatist and collectivist rhetoric in which they were couched, it is unclear how the economic policies proposed by black nationalists provided a feasible alternative to the white U.S. capitalist system. As Charles Hamilton, one of the co-founders of the Black Power movement, conceded, a self-sufficient black economic enclave was scarcely possible, for Black Power advocates had to depend heavily on the "white power structure" for technical and financial help.[47] Most nationalist organizations, such as the Nation of Islam or Floyd B. McKissick Enterprises, advanced economic programs committed to aiding the development of black capitalist institutions.[48] The economic necessity of working within the system of U.S. capitalism, and the difficulty of implementing a viable alternative system, undermined the radical stance of black nationalist ideologues. Several black intellectuals of the period drew attention to the integrationist impulse concealed behind the separatist rhetoric of black nationalist discourse. Harold Cruse, for example, criticized the cultural nationalists for "not really fighting against the system, but against being left out of it."[49] Even a cursory analysis of black nationalist economics thus discloses the same contradiction that marks black nationalist gender and familial ideology: their rhetorical negation of the white U.S. capitalist system is betrayed by their strong, often unacknowledged investment in this system.)

Despite their inability to theorize or establish an economically separate and self-contained black community, the black cultural nationalists did succeed in promoting a powerful sense of cultural unity and independence among the black community. Stokely Carmichael and Charles Hamilton wrote that the goal of nationalist separatism from white U.S. society was to create a cohesive, distinctly black cultural community.[50] Black nationalist aesthetic theory reiterated this emphasis, declaring that black art must derive its power and meaning from the black community, and must counter the Western aesthetic privileging of the individual artist. As Etheridge Knight expressed it, the "Black artist must hasten his own dissolution as an individual."[51] Ron Karenga agreed that black art "must be collective. In a word, it must be from the people, and returned to the people."[52])

The Black Aesthetic decree that black art should address and affirm a unified black community motivated its privileging of certain literary forms over others. Drama and poetry were the preferred genres, for they facilitated direct oral communication between artist and audience. Kimberley Benston has observed that black drama in the 1960s effected a shift from "mimesis," or representation of an action, to "methexis," or communal participation in the action by all assembled.[53] A similar trend characterizes the black poetry of the period. Through informal recitals of their poems at street corners, black poets sought to recapture an oral performance context that actively engaged the black audience and that established a direct, unmediated relationship between the artist and the community.

Many black women poets writing in this period were unable or unwilling to summon this unified oral collective spirit. Despite their oral mode, the poetry of black women poets such as Sonia Sanchez and Mari Evans was less exhortative and at times sounded a tentative, contemplative note rarely found in the black masculine poetry of the period. Sonia Sanchez wondered, in her poem "blk/rhetoric": "who's gonna make all / that beautiful black rhetoric / mean something?"[54] The very private specificity of the images found in the poems of Alice Walker, Ntozake Shange, and Audre Lorde distinguished them from the direct, easily accessible imagery of Black Aesthetic poetry. The written as opposed to spoken impression often conveyed by these poets further distanced them from the oral voice that empowered Black Aesthetic poetry.

What black women poets seemed to find most constraining about the Black Aesthetic notion of community was, in Audre Lorde's words, "its tacit insistence upon some unilateral definition of what 'blackness' is."[55] Nikki Giovanni objected to the prescriptive communal vision of the Black Aesthetic because it "cuts off the questions."[56] Alice Walker, in her collection of poems *Revolutionary Petunias*, went a step further, labeling as masculine the Black Aesthetic conception of community founded on an exclusion of questions, differences, and contradictions.) In "The Old Warrior Terror," or in the verbal play of "Black Mail," Walker satirized the stern absolutism of the Black Aesthetic, as well as its construction of the black woman as its nonrevolutionary other.[57] In *nappy edges*, Ntozake Shange echoed Walker's celebration of black women's difference from the community postulated by black nationalism. Walker's petunias and Shange's five nose rings metaphorically rendered this feminine difference as the odd particular that escaped any rigid ideological system. Shange defended her need for "takin' a solo," for exploring the differences between black artists as well as within a single artist ("is this leroi jones . . . or imamu baraka"),(differences that unsettled any construction of a monolithic black identity or community.[58])

Black women writers treated the Black Aesthetic notion of community even more critically in their uses of the fictional genre. Black women's novels in this period respect the communal emphasis of Black Aesthetic theorists, but question the specific model of community propounded by these theorists. In these novels, black feminine identity is invariably located within a communal frame; employing multiple points of view and structurally interweaving various narrative strands concerning different characters, these novels formally decenter their protagonists or, more accurately,(assail the very notion of a central, individual protagonist) While retaining the communal frame, however, these novels split the black community along gender lines, thus threatening the unified racial community projected in Black Aesthetic theory. That the ideal Black Aesthetic community is predicated on a traditional, hierarchical construction of gender differences is clear from the fact that black women's fictional reworking of these differences was unanimously censured by Black Aesthetic reviewers. Black women novelists were accused of "pulling the Black male/female problem/question/ partnership out of the closet,"[59] of portraying gender divisions at a time when black nationalism required literary affirmation of a cohesive racial community.

It is not accidental that the collective vision of Black Aesthetic ideology was most seriously interrogated in black women's fiction, the genre least valued by Black Aestheticians because, lacking the oral immediacy of drama and poetry, it could not effectively transmit the collective ideology of black nationalism.[60] Yet in the 1970s the novel emerged as the predominant genre in black women's literature. Most of the black women's novels published in this period experiment with oral folk forms in an attempt to liberate a uniquely black narrative voice. For example, folk storytelling devices animate the narrative medium of Carlene Polite's *Sister X and the Victims of Foul Play* and Alice Walker's

Meridian, and the blues determines the narrative voice and structure of Gayl Jones's *Corregidora.* The use of oral modes in these and other novels is catalyzed by but not entirely commensurate with Black Aesthetic theories on the subject. Oral forms in these novels do not necessarily affirm the collective source and direction of the black writer's voice; often, the printed fictional text fails to reproduce the communication context of black oral performances. At best, the use of oral forms succeeds in intimating a novelistic vision of community represented by means of a linguistic interplay of differences. Such a community, as figured in *The Bluest Eye, Corregidora,* and *Meridian,* for example, is conspicuously at odds with the univocal oral collectivity celebrated by Black Aesthetic ideologues.

Oral forms constituted the core of Black Aesthetic theory, authorizing its vision not only of community but also of time and history. The black nationalist discourse of the 1970s was founded on an absolute temporal discontinuity between the oppressive past and the new revolutionary future. Oral forms uneasily straddled this divide, bearing an irreducibly contradictory ideological value in Black Aesthetic theory. Black Aesthetic theorists valorized oral forms because of their supposed ability to represent a new, unalloyed, and essentially black literary voice. For example, both Larry Neal and Don Lee claimed that black music voiced a uniquely black consciousness that black literary texts, dependent as they were upon the modes and styles of the Western aesthetic, had been unable to achieve.[61] Of all the black oral forms, blues music in particular was elevated by some Black Aesthetic writers as "the paradigm, . . . the outline of the Black Experience in America," and as "the essential vector of the Afro-American sensibility."[62] Yet oral forms like the blues were centuries old, originating in slavery, or perhaps even earlier, in West African culture. The historical legacy of black oral forms was acknowledged by some Black Aesthetic practitioners, such as Amiri Baraka and Larry Neal, both of whom described the blues as an expression of "racial memory."[63]

Some Black Aesthetic advocates discouraged the use of the blues in black nationalist art precisely because of its long history. Sonia Sanchez wrote, in "liberation/poem," that she would rather be black than blue because "blues aint culture/they sounds of oppression."[64] Sherley Anne Williams elaborates the reasoning supporting this rejection of the blues: "when the Black-consciousness people came along, they disavowed the blues expression . . . because of ideology, because it was supposedly 'slavery time.'"[65] The dubious status of oral forms in Black Aesthetic theory points to its inconsistent articulation of the relation between the old and the new, between the oppressive historical past and the revolutionary future. Some Black Aestheticians seemed convinced that this new future could be heralded in literature only through a denial of the prior black literary tradition. This is the basic premise of Baraka's essay, "The Myth of a Negro Literature," which, in Houston Baker's words, assumes "that the entire past of Black writing had to be jettisoned."[66] Yet, when Black Aesthetic writers tried to create a new black literature, they often found themselves relying upon past oral modes. Even their privileging of oral forms as repositories of blackness was not new, for oral modes had authorized a unique black literary voice four decades earlier, during the Harlem Renaissance of the 1920s.

This involuntary repetition of the cultural past undercuts the Black Aesthetic claim to theorize a radically new black literature. According to Baraka, the "ultimate play" of the revolutionary black theater should present not "history or memory" but "new men, new heroes."[67] But the search for these new men often reverted to a search for origins, with Africa symbolizing the "racial integrity" of this lost origin.[68] Julian Mayfield described the double direction of the nationalist quest as a "search for new spiritual quality, or the recapture of an old one, lost and buried in our African past."[69] The tension between the black cultural nationalists' return to a mythical African origin and their search for a new cultural future reveals the contradictory status of history in black nationalist discourse. As Addison Gayle expressed it, "somewhere between the landing of the first slave ship and Reconstruction, the past of black people was stolen away."[70] One of the crucial functions of black nationalist ideology was to counter this experience of cultural and temporal dispossession, and to furnish the black American community with a usable past. Often reaching back to a glorious African heritage prior to slavery, some Black Aesthetic writers underscored the value of historical reclamation for the black nationalist project: Addison Gayle, for example, counseled black artists to "return to the black past, to forge a momentary concordat with history."[71]

However, the project of historical reclamation compelled black nationalists to confront the often disturbing implications of their history in the United States. Unable to reconcile the contradictions and compromises of this history with their revolutionary program for the future, many black nationalists sought to purge black cultural history of its impurities. Preserving only those elements of their history that could pass through the ideological filter of black pride, these nationalists perforce regarded black oral culture with ambivalence, for if oral forms attest to the strength and resilience of black culture, they also bear the traces of self-hatred, double consciousness, and all the other disabling consequences of an oppressive history.[72] Their desire to forge a new cultural future free of the oppressive weight of the past motivated such consciously antihistorical postures as Larry Neal's perception of the past as the "enemy of the revolutionary,"[73] or Julian Mayfield's commitment to "wiping [history] clean from the very beginning as if it never happened."[74] These vehement disavowals of the black cultural past display the nationalists' new world repression of history, as well as their "new world belief in the linearity of new beginnings."[75]

Black nationalist discourse repeatedly figured the oppressive past through the imagery of a vicious circle or cycle. A sudden, violent rupture marked the close of this repetitive cycle, achieving a dramatic break between past and present and inaugurating the linear time of revolutionary progress. Most black nationalists hailed the urban violence of the mid-1960s as a long-awaited disruption of the "pervasive, cyclic effects" of past oppression.[76] This figuration of the oppressive past as cyclic and the revolutionary future as linear offers a way of mediating between the temporal vision of black nationalist discourse and the form of black women's fiction. An outstanding feature of this fiction is its structural tension between cyclic and linear time. In most of the black women's novels published in this period, cyclic structure enacts the repetition of the past in the present, and impedes the linear progress of the narrative. In some of these novels, such as Carlene Polite's *The Flagellants*, Toni Morrison's *The Bluest Eye*, and Gayl Jones's *Eva's Man*, a cyclic model of time entails a mythicized version of history that forecloses any possibility of revolutionary transformation. Violence in these novels (invariably sexual and domestic rather than racial and public) becomes itself a contributory part of the meaningless temporal cycle, far from heralding the liberating rupture of the cycle as envisioned in black nationalist discourse. Other novels, however, such as *Sula*, *Corregidora*, and *Meridian*, do imagine a transformation of the oppressive cycle, but this transformation is always represented in cyclic rather than linear terms. The spiral structure of *Sula*, the blues form of *Corregidora*, and the circular storytelling method of *Meridian* insist upon a continuity between past and present that alone can sustain the political changes of the future. While, therefore, none of the novels published by black women in this period can endorse the black nationalist discontinuity between oppression and liberation, past and future, all of these novels, in their interplay between cyclic and linear structures, attempt to mediate and resolve the temporal contradiction of black nationalist discourse.

The black nationalists' insistence upon a sharp cleavage between past and present is nowhere more pronounced than in their discourse on black identity. If the ghetto rebellions of the 1960s signalled a rupture of the oppressive cycle of the past, they also bespoke an extreme disaffection with the old stereotypes of black identity. Locating "the New Afro" in the "Black ghettos of America,"[77] black nationalists constructed the revolutionary black subject against the white bourgeois subject and, concomitantly, against the middle-class Negro who, as "a link between the slave and the new man,"[78] had to be destroyed. The black nationalist discourse on identity often conveys the impression that the new black subject could be conjured into being simply through an act of language. To quote Carmichael and Hamilton, "From now on we shall view ourselves as African-Americans and as Black people who are in fact energetic, determined, intelligent, beautiful."[79] Many of the essays in Floyd Barbour's book *The Black Power Revolt*, such as Jean Smith's "I Learned to Feel Black," Byron Rushing's "I Was Born," and John E. Johnson's "Super Black Man," abound in images of conversion, rebirth, and baptism into blackness. Johnson's essay, in particular, dramatically bears witness to the transformative power of naming in its repeated, incantatory declaration, "I am new man."[80] What emerges most powerfully, even from a superficial survey of black nationalist writing, is its sense of the radical newness of the black nationalist subject, and of its absolute repudiation of all past conceptions of black and white identity.

The difference of this new black subject was elaborated through the rhetoric of soul, which derived its affective power precisely from its mystique, its resistance to intellectual definition. As a condensed expression of "the unconscious energy of the Black Experience,"[81] the concept of soul was intended to name the essential, authentic, and ineffable quality of blackness. Articulated as a mode of experience alternative to the "soulless efficiency of urban industrial life,"[82] soul was evocative of emotional intensity, sexual energy, and natural vitality. If the rhetoric of soul defined blackness as a robust natural energy, whiteness in black nationalist neo-mythology was always aligned with mechanism, sterility, and effete decadence. For example, Baraka believed that "the Black man is more natural than the white,"[83] and Eldridge Cleaver argued that "Blacks, personifying the Body, and thereby in closer communion with their biological roots than other Americans, provide the saving link, the bridge between man's biology and man's machines."[84]

Nature served to validate not only the essence of the black nationalist subject, but also the means by which this subject could exercise his or her revolutionary potential. Black nationalist writers frequently took recourse to natural imagery in their rousing descriptions of the revolutionary transfer of power from whites to blacks. For example, John O'Neal thus affirmed the emergence of a "new era":

> Western culture has passed the point of its own creativity and crashes on with malevolent splendor like a mighty river rolling into a boundless desert with vigor now, but toward certain extinction in the limitless arid wasteland.[85]

This passage pictures Western civilization in a process of natural decay that will ultimately culminate in death and in the birth of a new black epoch. The momentous rhythm of O'Neal's long sentence certifies political revolution by presenting it as an ineluctable natural process, and thus runs the risk of eliding the political agency required to bring about revolutionary change. Baraka's essay "The Last Days of the American

Empire," significantly subtitled "With Some Instructions for Black People," consciously attempts to resist the temptation of metaphorically identifying revolutionary transformation with natural change. But Baraka's advice that black militants should actively and violently grasp the future is also couched in natural imagery. Baraka's erupting volcano, O'Neal's river, and Grier and Cobbs's welling tide all perform a similar ideological function: a rhetorical affirmation of violent revolution along with a natural recuperation of this violence that empties it of human agency.[86]

The black women's fiction written in the 1970s resolutely resists this tendency to naturalize the revolutionary black subject. The Bottom community in *Sula* and Ursa's foremothers in *Corregidora* unambiguously display the conservatism implicit in a naturalistic political vision. In these and other novels, the naturalization of the new black subject is shown to be a contradiction in terms: Sula, Ursa, and Meridian are all able to achieve a radically new identity only by rejecting the naturalistic philosophy that keeps their ancestors mired in the oppressive past. The nationalist conception of natural black identity appears especially troublesome when mediated through a feminine subject. As the characterizations of Sula, Ursa, and Meridian make abundantly clear, a naturalistic conception of the feminine subject inevitably demands a celebration of the "natural" feminine function of reproduction. Their attempt to exceed a reproductive definition of the black feminine subject is often visibly strained, and betrays these novels' difficulty in negotiating the nationalist notion of natural identity.

The nationalist celebration of the new black subject as a natural essence is, however, granted a certain efficacy in these novels, for it partially unfixed the notion of blackness from its traditional Western moorings. In their critiques of the "traditional color symbology of the West," nationalist writers like Stephen Henderson, Addison Gayle, and Eldridge Cleaver, among others, demonstrated the Western equation of blackness with ugliness, evil, corruption, and death.[87] The nationalist definition of blackness as an integral, beautiful, natural value was indisputably a powerful oppositional gesture against the Western construction of blackness. In most of the essays collected in Addison Gayle's anthology *The Black Aesthetic*, a new definition of blackness emerges as an inversion of the old Western definition. Carolyn Gerald, for example, urges black writers to "reverse" the "zero and negative image-myths" of blacks in white U.S. culture.[88]

Reversing white culture's zero image of blackness as absence involved investing blackness with presence, a countermove that has elicited the strong disapproval of recent critics of Black Aesthetic theory. The most famous of these is Henry Louis Gates's quarrel with the Black Aesthetic's "metaphysical concept" of blackness as presence,[89] which, instead of supplanting an essentialist notion of identity, merely

installs blackness as "another transcendent signified."[90] Seconding
Gates, Keith Byerman charges Black Aesthetic theorists with "racial
essentialism," arguing that their reversal of the Western definition of
blackness does not constitute a radical redefinition, for it necessarily
depends on the absent presence of the Western framework it sets out
to subvert.[91] Extending these critiques, we might argue that if, at one
level, the nationalist conception of the black subject as presence inver-
sively opposes Western culture, at another level, it recalls Western humanist discourses on identity, with their presupposition of "an essence
at the heart of the individual which is fixed, unique and coherent."[92]
Black Aesthetic critics took special care not to replicate the terms of
Western humanist identity, as is obvious from Ron Karenga's emphatic
opposition between Western bourgeois "individuality" and black "personality."[93] Such distinctions notwithstanding, there is no denying the
strong ideological affinity between the Western humanist definition of
man and the black nationalist construction of blackness as a unified essence.

The recent academic attack on the Black Aesthetic notion of identity,
informed as it is by the various structuralist and poststructuralist critiques of the humanist subject, has helped to clarify the theoretical
problems and contradictions attending an essentialist conception of
black identity. However, with all its theoretical limitations, in its time
the Black Aesthetic rhetoric of blackness exerted an immense emotional
and ideological influence, transforming an entire generation's perception of its racial identity. In retrospect, the Black Aesthetic discourse on
blackness takes on an almost scriptural authority, suppressing literary
explorations of the internal differences that striate black identity. But
if historical hindsight clarifies the prohibitive impact of Black Aesthetic
theory on later black writers (and on black women writers in particular), it also tends to obscure the remarkable imaginative power of the
nationalist "Will-to-Blackness" when it was initially formulated.[94] The
writing of black nationalists like Stokely Carmichael, Stephen Henderson, and Addison Gayle bristles with a sense of the sheer possibility of
blackness. The rhetorical energy of black nationalist discourse mobilizes the sign of blackness, opening it to a process of textual transfigu-
ration. The essential blackness celebrated in these writings emerges,
then, not so much as a settled, naturally given value but as a hard-won
linguistic achievement, a testament of visionary political desire.

At a first glance, black women novelists of the 1970s appear to reject
wholesale the Black Aesthetic conception of an essential, self-present
subject. The most immediately noticeable feature of many of these novels is their figuration of black feminine identity as an absence. For
example, in *Corregidora*, Ursa's desire for a new identity is incited by
her loss of a womb. Lack is also striking in *Sula*, with Eva's missing
leg and Sula's lack of a centered self. The novel's major incidents pro-

duce losses and absences, such as the sudden disappearance of Chicken Little under the rippling water, Nel's loss of Jude and Sula, and Sula's loss of Nel and Ajax. Pecola, the protagonist of *The Bluest Eye*, is conspicuously absent from the novel's narrative center. In *Sister X*, the narrator's exuberant verbal energy strives to compensate for Sister X's absence from the narrative time of the text. Many of these novels rely heavily on stereotypical and nonrealist modes of characterization, modes that assault the notion of fictional character as an unmediated reflection of an authentic, self-present subject.

It is tempting to make direct connections here, between black women's fictional stance and their positioning in contemporary ideological discourses. We might say, for example, that black women writers could not possibly represent the subjectivity of presence because black women suffered from a double ideological absence, from the categories of both "black" and "woman." But such an argument would fail to recognize the different dynamics of ideological and fictional constructions of identity. That black women were ideologically constituted as absent does not necessarily mean that their fiction will helplessly reflect this absence. And, in fact, black women's absent ideological status was fictionally manipulated in a variety of ways. For example, absence is presented as a source of freedom and power in *Sula* and *Corregidora*, but these novels do not simply controvert the Black Aesthetic conception of the subject by celebrating absence. We cannot impose the poststructuralist celebration of the absent, decentered subject upon these novels, for they are informed by a keen understanding of absence as a Western cultural imposition upon black Americans. Novels like *The Bluest Eye, Eva's Man*, and *The Third Life* strongly endorse the Black Aesthetic discourse on blackness, disclosing the destructive cultural and psychological ramifications of the Western construction of blackness as absence.

Black women's novels of the 1970s do not, then, simply oppose the contemporary nationalist discourse on black identity. While imaging black feminine identity as an absence, these novels pointedly draw attention to their production of this absence as a textual effect. All the major black women's novels of this period, and especially *Sula, The Bluest Eye, Corregidora, Eva's Man*, and *Meridian*, are elaborately structured texts that foreground their own constructedness. This narrative self-reflexivity compels the recognition that black femininity is constituted as a sign in a highly fabricated fictional sign system. In this respect, these novels take the Black Aesthetic revaluation of blackness a step further. They unsettle blackness by figuring it, not as a transcendent essence that is reflected by the fictional text but, in Gates's words, as a signifier that is "produced in the text only through a complex process of signification."⁹ This gesture is deeply indebted to the Black

Aesthetic, which, by renaming blackness as presence rather than absence, attempted to overturn through an act of linguistic will what had always been considered a fixed value. In this sense, the linguistic destabilizing of the categories of blackness and femininity in black women's fiction of the 1970s both resumes and surpasses the Black Aesthetic redefinition of identity.

The relation of black women's fiction to black nationalist discourse cannot, then, be understood in terms of simple reflection or resistance. A contextual analysis does not permit us to predict that black women's fiction in this period will always express a determinate ideological vision, nor does it help to calculate exact fictional effects. We can, however, identify the conditions of narratability specific to the cultural context in which these novels were written: use of communal frames and oral narrative modes, structural interplay between cyclic and linear time, and figuration of black feminine identity as absent. Black women's fiction in this period is bounded by these formal possibilities, but its use of these forms is not reducible to a single ideological meaning. The formal modes of black women's fiction do not always yield the ideological values these modes are intended to carry in Black Aesthetic theory. For example, the use of communal frames and oral narrative modes does not necessarily achieve a unified collective voice; cyclical structures can signify temporal transformation as well as temporal impasse; and nonrealist modes of characterization figure black feminine subjectivity as either powerful negativity or impotent absence. Dislodging forms from their ideological underpinnings in Black Aesthetic theory, this fiction exhibits a formal inventiveness that strains any univocal ideological interpretation. This refusal to fit form into a tight ideological mold is, of course, directly contrary to the Black Aesthetic perception of form as a transparent medium of ideological messages.

Precisely because its formal experimentation is so incommensurate with the functional, didactic reading norms of the Black Aesthetic, black women's fiction was read by contemporary black reviewers strictly for its thematic value. Dissociating theme from form, black reviewers either deplored the ideological ambivalence of this fiction, its resistance to a functional reading, or tried to recuperate it into the ideological requirements of the Black Aesthetic. Either kind of reading confirmed Black Aesthetic reading norms; whether these novels were ultimately labeled "good" or "bad," their value was always determined by the Black Aesthetic's functional definition of literature.

Melissa Walker's comments offer an exemplary instance of a Black Aesthetic recovery of black women's fiction. In the following passage, Walker tries to defend black women novelists from the nationalist charge that their thematic depiction of a divided community is ideologically counterproductive:

> Perhaps Black women like Maya Angelou, Toni Cade Bambara, Toni Morrison and Alice Walker asked themselves this question: how can we help people understand that social forces push them to behave in destructive ways, that they can choose to act differently, and that they can change themselves and in the process change society? For these and a number of other women, the answer was plain: they could help people understand the relation of their own lives to society. . . . They could create a literature that responds to the need of Black people to understand the social conditioning that leads them to pursue destructive behavior.[96]

Leaving aside the question of how Walker arrives at her understanding of these authors' intentions, or whether she describes these intentions accurately, what is most interesting about this passage is its assimilation of black women's fiction into the Black Aesthetic conception of literature as a corrective force that can induce social change. Walker translates these novels' apparent betrayal of Black Aesthetic ideology (their portrayal of a disunited black community) into a fulfillment of the Black Aesthetic program at a deeper level (their didactic function of strengthening and educating the black community).

Whatever these novelists' actual intentions may have been, the fact remains that their works were inserted into a culturally specific and limited set of reading practices. The Black Aesthetic definition of literature (as a means of propagating a unified black cultural consciousness) constituted the primary condition of readability for black audiences of the late 1960s and 1970s. The black women's novels published in this period inscribe within them their adjustment to the expectations of their contemporary audience (which, we must remember, was consolidated largely through the efforts of the black nationalists). This adjustment may be critically uncovered through an analysis of the management strategies,[97] such as displacement and containment, used in these novels, strategies that facilitate a kind of reformatting of these novels within the Black Aesthetic mode, such that their subversion of some aspects of this mode is rendered safely readable. The subversive elements that these novels fail or refuse to manage frequently present themselves as unreadable, or resistant to any interpretation, an unreadability that calls into question the reading norms of Black Aesthetic ideology. I shall try to elaborate, in the following discussion of the novels of Toni Morrison, Gayl Jones, and Alice Walker, the complex ways in which this fiction negotiates the terms of Black Aesthetic ideology.

II

"WHAT DID WE LACK?"
USES OF THE GROTESQUE MODE IN
THE BLUEST EYE

Frances Foster writes that the prescribed role of black women writers in the "literary revolution" of the 1960s was to destroy negative stereotypes of black women, to present the relationship between black men and women as "complementary," and to affirm the black family and community.[1] Toni Morrison's first novel, *The Bluest Eye* (1970), fails on each of these three counts. Most of the novel's characters conform to the stereotypes of earlier black fiction: Pecola is a helpless victim in the protest novel tradition,[2] Pauline is the black mammy of the plantation tradition who loves her white mistress's daughter more than her own, and Geraldine and Maureen are typical mulattas who live by white middle-class values. Relationships between black men and women in the novel are driven by violence and sexual perversion: Mr. Henry molests Frieda, Soaphead Church fondles little girls, and Cholly rapes his own daughter. The Breedlove family is a perfect illustration of the black family model portrayed in the Moynihan Report. Cholly is an unemployed alcoholic, while his wife Pauline works as a domestic servant to provide for her family. When we are first introduced to them, Cholly and Pauline are engaged in a violent physical tussle provoked by Cholly's failure to assume any familial responsibility. In short, the Breedloves are exactly the kind of family that the Black Aestheticians wished to ban from literature. The black community depicted in *The Bluest Eye* is equally out of keeping with Black Aesthetic requirements. Entirely estranged from its own cultural heritage, the novel's black community is committed to white middle-class values, and is divided by color-bias and sexism. The novel's presentation of rape, incest, and madness flagrantly flouts the black nationalist injunction that black art "must divorce itself from the sociological attempt to explain the black community in terms of pathology."[3]

Surprisingly, however, of all the novels considered here, *The Bluest Eye* has been most sympathetically received by Black Aesthetic critics. Addison Gayle, in his diatribe against the novels of Toni Morrison, Gayl

Jones, and Alice Walker, strangely exempted *The Bluest Eye*.[4] Ruby Dee, who reviewed the novel for *Freedomways*, argued that Morrison performed the crucial task of showing the black community the problems it must work through before it can "truly believe 'Black is beautiful.'"[5] According to Dellita Martin, *The Bluest Eye* helped to "propel Afro-American literature towards total liberation from the constraints of the Western aesthetic" by exposing its damaging psychological and social effects.[6] Dee and Martin are able to read the novel according to the Black Aesthetic critical mode by arguing that it performs a valuable cultural function for the black community: the novel's exposure of the destructive force of white aesthetic standards strengthens the case for the Black Aesthetic espoused by the cultural nationalists.[7]

Toni Morrison herself has encouraged such functional readings of her work. In the often-cited essay, "Rootedness: The Ancestor as Foundation," Morrison endorses the Black Aesthetic fusion of aesthetics and ethics: the novel "should be beautiful and powerful, but it should also *work*. It should have something in it that enlightens; something in it that opens the door and points the way."[8] Morrison's conception of her work also confirms the Black Aesthetic belief that art should be political and should address the black community: "if anything I do . . . isn't about the village or the community or about you, then it is not about anything, . . . which is to say, yes, the work must be political."[9]

The word *political* as used by a black woman writer in the 1970s may be interpreted in more than one sense, as referring to sexual and/or racial politics. The works of black women writers in the 1970s were denounced by black nationalist critics not because of their failure to be sufficiently political, but because of their allegedly greater attention to sexual rather than racial politics. *The Bluest Eye* succeeded in escaping Black Aesthetic censure because its exposure of black male sexism is partially displaced by its structural focus on white racism. The emphasis on racial politics is declared in the first two pages of the novel, which present three progressively distorted versions of a passage from a Dick and Jane school reader. The reader, obviously representative of the white middle-class familial norm, determines the structure of the entire novel. The chapters concerned with Geraldine, Soaphead Church, and the Breedlove family all borrow their headings and their unifying thematic motifs from the words of the Dick and Jane primer. Each unit of the primer passage—the house, the family, the mother, the father, the cat, the dog, and the friend—is elaborated into a chapter. Phrases from the Dick and Jane reader provide an interpretive lens that directs the novel's focus toward racism as the primary source of oppression for black women. The pathology and violence of the black community presented in the novel become structurally secondary to the distortions of the white middle-class standard.

The novel's ironic exposure of white middle-class values fulfills an important Black Aesthetic function; Addison Gayle argued, in "Black Literature and the White Aesthetic," that black artists must overturn the dualistic Western symbology (of white as beautiful and black as ugly) that has historically bolstered the political oppression of non-white races.[10] *The Bluest Eye* systematically undermines the white cultural and aesthetic standard represented by the Dick and Jane primer. In the very first page of the novel, where the primer passage is reprinted three times, its prescriptive language is literally deconstructed by the typographical absurdities that Morrison imposes on it. As the letters run into each other in an unpunctuated, nonsensical jumble, the sharp demarcation of its original semantic structure is blurred, and its authoritative, fixed meaning thrown into flux. This typographical play with the primer visually foregrounds the novel's subversion of white cultural authority.

The novel's treatment of the primer illustrates one of its various uses of the grotesque mode. Only by playing several different, and sometimes competing, definitions of the grotesque mode against each other can we appreciate its complex workings in *The Bluest Eye*. The novel's irreverent scrambling of the cultural master-text represented by the Dick and Jane reader fulfills one important function of the grotesque mode, traditionally considered an especially effective means of assailing middle-class values.[11] The families of Geraldine and Pauline are grotesquely lacking when measured against the primer's ideal middle-class, nuclear family. The primer, a white cultural mirror that produces black distortions, provides the pretext for a scathing critique of the apparent universality of white middle-class values. This kind of grotesque caricature would surely gain Black Aesthetic approval; in fact, Keorapetse Kgositsile recommended that black writers deploy the grotesque to precisely these ends: "the undesirable, the corrupting, the destructive, will be portrayed in a grotesque manner."[12] *The Bluest Eye* employs the grotesque as an instrument of social satire, giving rise to a defamiliarized, heightened perception of the unequal social relations naturalized by the smooth, matter-of-fact language of the reader.

As a means of satirizing white middle-class values, the grotesque mode helps gear the novel's critique of violence and pathology in the black community toward the target set by Black Aesthetic ideology. Each grotesque incident in the novel is securely linked in a causal chain that invariably leads back to racial oppression as the source of the grotesque. For example, Cholly's sexual perversion can be traced back to his experience of racism. In one of the novel's most nightmarish incidents, Cholly, while making love to a black girl, is interrupted by two white men with rifles who order him to perform for their amusement. Cholly is unable to hate the white men but his memory of this episode, "along with myriad other humiliations, defeats and emasculations" in the white world taints his perception of black women.[13] While this tracing of the origin of Cholly's sexual violence does not mitigate the horror of his rape of Pecola, the presentation of Cholly as a victim of racial oppression does partially displace his position as an agent of sexual oppression.

The tension in the novel's double focus on racial and sexual victimization leads to an interpretive impasse characteristic of the grotesque mode,[14] especially when we consider the novel's central incident, Cholly's rape of his daughter. The first discomfiting factor in this scene is the presentation of the rape from Cholly's rather than Pecola's point of view, for it restricts the reader to the rapist's angle of vision. Moreover, by showing that Cholly is motivated by an irreducibly contradictory set of emotions—revulsion, guilt, tenderness, pity, love, hatred, and lust (pp. 127–28)—the scene denies the reader the more comfortable moral option of denouncing Cholly as a rapist. One of the most difficult interpretive quandaries in *The Bluest Eye* is produced by the narrator's comment that Cholly was the only one "who loved Pecola enough to touch her" (p. 159). The word *touch* is jarring here, to say the least, for it serves as a curious euphemism for rape. The next line returns the word to its context ("his touch was fatal"), but that first unexpected usage momentarily jams our interpretive machinery and complicates our moral and emotional responses to the rape. At some moments in the scene, Cholly's role as a rapist yields primacy to his helplessness as a black man unable to assume a masculine, paternal identity: "Guilt and impotence rose in a bilious duet. . . . What could a burned out Black man say to the hunched back of his eleven year old daughter?" (p. 127). However, Pecola's paralysis and silence during the rape powerfully convey her absolute helplessness as a victim of sexual abuse. This impossible entanglement of racial and sexual victimization holds us in suspension, prevents us from resolving the ambivalent narrative presentation of the rape scene.

Most critics, however, tend to characterize Cholly as either a sexist victimizer or a victim of racial oppression. Philip Royster, for example, emphasizes Cholly's status as a victim and commends the novel's "remarkably sensitive portrait" of black men,[15] a feature that surely helped exempt the novel from Black Aesthetic censure. Other critics, who view Cholly primarily as a sexist victimizer, are unable to square the novel's treatment of Cholly with the Black Aesthetic requirement that black men be presented favorably in literature by black women.[16] One critic who succeeds in avoiding an either/or interpretation of the rape scene is Keith Byerman, who reads the scene in terms of its grotesque mode of presentation:

> On the one hand, we are repulsed by Cholly's action and sympathetic to his victim. On the other, we have been made to see that he is himself

a victim of the society that condemns him. . . . Both responses . . . are
mutually necessary for the grotesque to work in this scene.[17]

Byerman's highly sensitive analysis of the grotesque mode in *The Bluest
Eye* preserves the tension between the novel's sexual and racial perspectives. Byerman does not, however, attempt to clarify the ideological
implications of the novel's use of the grotesque. The ambivalent reader
response to Cholly that is solicited by the grotesque mode makes visible
the impossible area of overlap between sexual and racial oppression, an
area occupied by the black woman in general and Pecola in particular.

Forcing attention to the contradictory conjuncture of these two forms
of oppression, the grotesque mode helps to manage the novel's ideologically risky disclosure of sexual oppression in the black community,
while simultaneously maintaining an unwavering focus on the black
feminine subject of this oppression. This focus on the compounded effects of racial and gender oppression on the black woman is achieved
by means of an overdetermined narrative structure. Each short narrative foray leads to a single point, the suffering of Pecola. Each detail in
the novel contributes its own resonance to Pecola's tragedy, at the level
of plot or symbolism. Seemingly independent incidents, like Mr.
Henry's molesting Frieda, amplify Pecola's victimization. The stories
of Cholly's, Pauline's, Geraldine's, and Soaphead Church's pasts all culminate in their disastrous encounters with Pecola. Even the cat and dog
become unknowing agents of her suffering. The novel's highly directive
structure relentlessly pushes us in two directions: toward Pecola as a
victim, and, as we have already seen, toward the Dick and Jane reader
as the source of Pecola's victimization. The immediate (black masculine) agent of Pecola's suffering is partially obscured, becoming a middle term in the structural confrontation between the white racist
system and the black feminine victim.

The delineation of Pecola's character according to the type of the
victim is in keeping with the flat, projective characterization associated
with the grotesque mode. Michael Steig argues that the grotesque mode
offers the reader an escape route through its stereotypical character
construction, which, in its denial of full humanity to the character,
"allows us to treat him as though he were separate from our own reality, and thus unthreatening."[18] Whether Pecola's characterization as a
grotesque victim opens this kind of safety valve for the reader is important, for the issue of negative stereotypes of blacks as victims formed
a particularly vexed area of Black Aesthetic theory. Most Black Aestheticians rejected the stereotype of the helpless, inarticulate black victim
prevalent in the protest fiction of the 1940s. Hoyt Fuller, for example,
declared that the literature of protest and victims should be replaced
by a new "prose of affirmation."[19] In an interview with Robert Stepto,
Toni Morrison expressed her awareness that, according to Black Aes-

thetic dictates, black women "should not be portrayed as victims."[20] Some Black Aesthetic theorists, however, did recommend the use of the victim stereotype in black literature, but only as long as it could be made to serve a political function. Baraka argued that revolutionary black art may present victims if this presentation leads readers to recognize "that they themselves are victims."[21] Baraka's formulation of the function served by an exaggerated portrayal of the victim stereotype is exactly opposed to Steig's: according to Baraka, the stereotype must invite reader identification, and "cause the blood to rush, so that pre-revolutionary temperaments will be bathed in this blood, and it will cause their deepest souls to move."[22] In other words, black nationalist art can achieve its purpose of galvanizing the reader to action if it first draws the reader into the victim's position and then renders this position intolerable to occupy.

The overdetermined narrative structure of *The Bluest Eye* repeatedly pushes the reader into Pecola's position, yet our inability to identify fully with Pecola leaves us feeling "winged but grounded" (p. 158), a phrase that eloquently describes the reader's impossible location vis-à-vis Pecola. Her silence, madness, and complete lack of understanding of her situation distance Pecola from the reader. But the novel does not offer a definitive reading of Pecola's story that would let us categorize and thus position ourselves above her suffering. At the very end of the novel, Claudia offers an interpretation of Pecola's tragedy that she immediately withdraws with the lines, "We are wrong, of course, but it doesn't matter. It's too late" (p. 160). There is a sense at the end of the novel that the entire process of reading has been inadequate, for Pecola's suffering still remains and exceeds the bounds of the text. Pecola finally lapses into a madness that places her outside the interpretive reach of both the reader and the narrators. The novel's refusal to wring any cautionary meaning from Pecola's suffering directs us beyond the world of the text and discourages us from deriving any satisfaction from the act of reading. This uncomfortable positioning of the reader is, of course, far more consonant with Baraka's than with Steig's articulation of the grotesque stereotype.[23] In refusing to contain Pecola's suffering, the novel's use of the victim stereotype powerfully communicates to the reader the impossible subject position occupied by Pecola. However, rather than mobilizing the reader to political action, as Baraka recommended, the grotesque presentation of Pecola's character refuses to draw any functional ideological lessons, and thus produces an acute sense of unease and paralysis in the reader.

In a sense, the grotesque is the most appropriate mode for exploring the contradictory conditions of black feminine subjectivity. Grotesque characters, marked as they are by bodily lack or deformation,[24] offer a perfect means of figuring the qualities historically attached to black femininity. Even the sociological and psychological discourses on black women in the 1960s implicitly and explicitly evoked the grotesque. To give one obvious example, Grier and Cobbs described the black woman's body as "mutilated" and "grotesque."[25] Black women characters in *The Bluest Eye* are constructed around bodily lack or deformity, as with Pecola's lack of blue eyes, or Pauline's missing teeth and deformed foot. This representation of black femininity as lack clarifies the novel's divergence from the Black Aesthetic conception of the black subject as a self-present plenitude. Pecola's story is a frightening amplification of the black woman's absence from the categories of both "man" and "woman," due to her lack not only of the phallus but also of the blue eyes that signify desirable femininity. Her perception of her inadequacy as an object of desire compels Pecola to ask: "How do you get somebody to love you?" (p. 29). If "man" is the subject of desire, "white woman," not "woman," is the object; for the black woman, both the subject and the object positions are inaccessible. Unable to view herself as a desirable object, Pecola tries to imagine herself as the subject of desire, but all she can call to mind is "the no noise at all from her mother. It was as though she was not even there" (p. 49). Pecola is able to dispel this image of absence only in her brief fantasy with the Mary Jane candies: "To eat the candy is somehow to eat the eyes, to eat Mary Jane. Love Mary Jane. Be Mary Jane. Three pennies had bought her three lovely orgasms with Mary Jane" (p. 43). Confusing buying with becoming, the candy with the wrapper, the signifier with the signified, Pecola is able to grasp black femininity only by means of a hysterical collapse of the desiring subject into the object of desire.

The novel's presentation of the impossible conditions of black femininity only occasionally takes the black male as its other. There are moments in the novel when the black woman's absence is measured against the presence of the black male subject. In her erotic fantasies, Pauline imagines herself as the passive receptor of a male "Presence" (p. 90). When this presence, Cholly, finally materializes, he preserves "himself intact" by hating her (p. 37). Cholly, like Junior and Soaphead Church, is able to assert his sense of self only by "depresencing" Pauline.[26] However, the black male characters who achieve self-presence by negating black women are shown to be transferring upon these women the dehumanizing effects of their own experience of racism. After Cholly's encounter with the white men in the woods, he feels a "vacancy in his head, . . . like the space of a newly pulled tooth" (p. 119). This image of the black male subject as an absence that enables the white male subject's presence unmistakably recalls the previous chapter, in which Pauline's sense of herself as lacking is figured by her missing tooth. Imagery thus conjoins the black man and woman in a common experience of subjectivity as absence.

The presence that defines black feminine characters in the novel as deficient is represented not by the black man but by the white woman.

Pecola is acutely aware of herself as lacking not the phallus but the blue eyes, which, in her society, signify desirable femininity. Claudia, too, can answer her question, "What did we lack?" (p. 62), only with reference to the dolls that symbolize white femininity. Claudia partially succeeds in resisting the ideal of feminine desire that white middle-class society imposes on the black woman. Although "all the world had decided that a blue-eyed, golden-haired, pink-skinned doll was what every girl child treasured," Claudia has only one desire, to "dismember" the doll (p. 20). Recognizing that the doll is a cold, inanimate object, Claudia succeeds in deconstructing her society's codes of desire, but she is not able to practice a desire that exceeds these codes. She transfers her hatred of white dolls to white girls, becoming an unwitting participant in the white middle-class objectification of femininity. In a culture that iconizes Mary Jane and Shirley Temple, a black woman's desire can only run a restricted gamut, "from pristine sadism to fabricated hatred to fraudulent love" (p. 22). Each expression of black feminine desire, whether Pecola's longing for blue eyes, Frieda's love of Shirley Temple, Claudia's hatred of white dolls, Maureen's adoration of Betty Grable, or Pauline's of Jean Harlow, takes the white woman as its object. Even the title of the novel establishes the white woman rather than the black man as the other against which the black woman is judged to be grotesquely lacking. This emphasis, like the structural emphasis on the Dick and Jane reader, clarifies the complex and simultaneous interaction of racial and gender dynamics in the formation of black feminine subjectivity.

The novel's representation of black feminine identity, in accordance with Black Aesthetic theories of the subject, discloses the destructive power of the white cultural construction of blackness as absence. Thematically, as well as through its overdetermined structure, the novel clarifies how black femininity is produced and read as a sign of invisibility in the white American symbolic system. The scene in which Pecola goes to the candy store powerfully dramatizes the Western construction of black femininity as a sign of absence. The white storekeeper does not see Pecola "because for him there is nothing to see" (p. 42). Pecola is perceived as a sign that is easily read and dismissed not just by the white storekeeper, but also by most of the black characters who have internalized white middle-class values. Geraldine, for example, categorizes and dismisses Pecola with a single glance; in Pecola's physical appearance, Geraldine reads the signs of everything that is considered ugly about being black. *The Bluest Eye* insistently reminds us that the black body is not intrinsically ugly and grotesque. The ugliness of the Breedloves, for example, is bestowed on them by white culture: "It was as though some mysterious, all-knowing master had given each one a cloak of ugliness to wear, and they had accepted it without question" (p. 34). The clothing imagery used in this line emphasizes that lack and ugliness are culturally imposed rather than naturally given attributes of the black body.

So far, the novel's critique of the white cultural definition of blackness as grotesque lack is in keeping with the Black Aesthetic program. Black Aesthetic theorists, however, enjoined black writers not only to overturn the Western construction of blackness as absence, but also to replace it with a new construction of blackness as a natural, vital essence that exceeds the artificial structuring of the Western symbolic system. Whether *The Bluest Eye* offers any such alternative figuration of black femininity grounded in nature is open to question. There are moments in the novel when nature seems to provide the basis for a positive notion of black femininity. Any momentary liberation that black feminine characters achieve from the grotesque distortions of the white middle-class norm is articulated in terms of "funk," which, as Susan Willis has pointed out, recalls a natural perception of the body "prior to assimilation by bourgeois society."[27] The oppositional significance of funk as a natural mode of experience that is repressed by the white middle-class ethic is explicitly stated in the novel:

> [Middle-class black women] go to land grant colleges, normal schools, and learn how to do the white man's work with refinement. . . . The careful development of thrift, patience, high morals and good manners. In short, how to get rid of the funkiness. The dreadful funkiness of passion, the funkiness of nature. (p. 68)

Only those women, like Claudia, who enjoy the funkiness of their bodies, are able to resist the white middle-class construction of the black woman's body as an unworthy object of desire: "We felt comfortable in our skins, enjoyed the news that our senses relayed to us, admired our dirt, cultivated our scars, and could not comprehend this unworthiness" (p. 62). In this passage, funk evokes an open, receptive body marked by the materiality of life. The middle-class objectification of femininity, symbolized by the pristine, rigid body of a doll, is countered by a fluid imagery that celebrates the "lower" natural functions of the body, as, for example, when Claudia luxuriates in her puke, which "swaddles down the pillow onto the sheet—green-gray, with flecks of orange" (p. 13).

This evocation of an alternative black femininity rooted in nature seems to be supported by the novel's use of the seasonal cycle as an organizing device. The novel is divided into four sections corresponding to the four seasons. The seasonal frame vies with the frame of the Dick and Jane reader, enacting an opposition between nature and culture. The very first page of Claudia's narration establishes nature as the metaphorical ground against which the novel's action will take place: "it was because Pecola was having her father's baby that the marigolds did not sprout" (p. 9). This seeming correspondence between the natural and human realms is undermined by an equally strong emphasis on the disjunction between the two realms. For instance, Pecola becomes aware of her sexuality not in spring but, most inappropriately, in autumn. Maureen, who appears in the "Winter" section of the novel, is described as a "false spring" (p. 53). "Summer" begins with Claudia saying, "I have only to break into the tightness of a strawberry and I see summer" (p. 146). Any attentive reader will be jolted by this image, as it echoes Soaphead Church's earlier description of the breasts of little girls as "not quite ripe strawberries" (p. 141). This jarring juxtaposition of nature and human perversion illustrates the novel's presentation of culture as a grotesque distortion of the natural order.

In her discussion of the nature/culture problematic in *The Bluest Eye*, Barbara Christian writes that the novel's structure, which is "cyclical as nature, . . . defies linear analysis." Christian's detailed analysis of the "Spring" section teases out its associational, circular logic. Christian contrasts the cyclic form of the novel, sanctioned by the seasonal cycle, with the linear "march of words epitomized by the Dick and Jane prose."[28] This tension between cyclic and linear form is also apparent in the novel's use of the bildungsroman framework. The bildungsroman structure of initiation from childhood into adulthood is evoked at the beginning of the novel, when Pecola's first menstrual period initiates her into feminine sexuality.[29] The linear progression of growth and development typical of the bildungsroman is, however, disrupted as Pecola finds it impossible to gain access to her society's model of femininity. The novel's ironic evocation of the bildungsroman exposes its inability to structure the story of a black girl's sexual maturation. Pecola's story, involving rape, stunted growth, and a dead baby, is more appropriately charted by the inverted seasonal cycle, which begins with autumn and ends with summer.

This inversion of the seasonal cycle should guard us against reading the novel's cyclic form as an unqualified affirmation of nature. Several critics have viewed the novel's seasonal frame as a means of affirming a mythical vision of nature that opposes the grotesque artificialities of U.S. bourgeois culture. Barbara Christian, for example, argues that in *The Bluest Eye*, the seasons "reinforce the mythic quality of life,"[30] presenting time as a "unified entity" rather than a linear chronology.[31] Christian's argument recalls Bonnie Barthold's description of cyclic form as a means of achieving a mythic vision of temporal continuity. According to Barthold, a mythicized representation of black femininity usually involves a celebration of procreation, which ensures the continuity of the temporal cycle of nature.[32] *The Bluest Eye* begins with a black girl's entry into the procreative cycle; when Pecola first begins menstruating, Frieda reverentially informs her that she can now have a baby. Pecola's reproductive capacity, however, does not enable her to sustain the continuity of the natural cycle. We have already noted the disjunction between the movement of Pecola's story and the movement of the natural cycle: Pecola begins menstruating in autumn, is raped in spring, and gives birth to a stillborn baby in summer. Nowhere in the novel are black women celebrated as biological embodiments of the natural continuum; rather, the reproductive function of the black women characters consistently goes awry, as with Pauline's rejection of her own daughter in favor of her mistress's daughter, or Geraldine's transference of maternal love from her son to her cat. If anything, the novel's treatment of reproduction demands to be read *against* a mythical vision of femininity as a source of natural renewal. Susan Gubar has drawn attention to the traces of the Persephone myth that inform the narration of Pecola's story. Gubar argues that the novel's selective variation on the Persephone myth discourages a mythical celebration of feminine fertility; while after her rape, Persephone is "re-united with her mother and allowed to return to earth where she renews life, Pecola is rejected by her mother and remains a victim as well as a symbol of the dying land."[33] A mythical conception of fertility is further unsettled by the novel's opening and closing images of natural and feminine sterility: "The seeds shriveled and died; her baby too" (p. 9).

We may now fully appreciate the ways in which the novel's difficult treatment of nature negotiates the Black Aesthetic notion of a natural black subjectivity. *The Bluest Eye* seems to endorse the Black Aesthetic in its suggestion that "the funkiness of nature" may sanction a black femininity that resists the white middle-class objectification of women's bodies. However, the possibilities of funk are not fully developed, for a conception of black femininity as natural logically leads to a celebration of the "natural" feminine function of reproduction. This the novel cannot endorse; its deeply troubled treatment of procreation diverges from the Black Aesthetic naturalization of black subjectivity as well as from its reproductive definition of black femininity. In another contradictory move, the novel seems to affirm a mythical vision of nature in its use of a seasonal frame and a cyclic structure. But the inverted echoes of the Persephone myth render ironic any mythical conception of femininity as a source of fertility and natural renewal. The novel's inconsistent treatment of nature signals its difficulty in articulating black femininity within or outside of the ideological frame of the Black Aesthetic.

The Bluest Eye questions a mythical vision of nature not only because such a vision equates the feminine with procreation, but also because it tends to dehistoricize political oppression. At the beginning of the novel, before she has internalized her community's naturalistic world view, Claudia attempts to direct the course of natural and human events. She plants marigold seeds, hoping that if they sprout, Pecola's baby will live. The failure of her attempt convinces her that

> The earth itself might have been unyielding. We had dropped our seeds
> in our own little plot of black dirt just as Pecola's father had dropped
> his seeds in his plot of black dirt. Our innocence and faith were no more
> productive than his lust or despair. (p. 9)

Here, the adult Claudia qualifies her earlier belief that human beings
can intervene in each others' suffering as a childish, naive faith. The
disturbing comparison of a child planting seeds to a father raping his
daughter gives rise to the despairing sense that no human agency has
value, that all human acts are equally powerless against the unyielding
course of nature.

In the last paragraph of the novel, the adult Claudia's pessimistic
voice, enlarged from "I" to "we," speaks for her entire community:

> This soil is bad for certain kinds of flowers, certain fruit it will not bear,
> and when the land kills of its own volition, we acquiesce and say the
> victim had no right to live. We are wrong, of course, but it doesn't
> matter. It's too late. (p. 160)

In this passage, the black community's mythical perception of nature
leads to a dangerous fatalism. In viewing Pecola's victimization as an
irreversible fact of nature, the black community is able to find an excuse for inaction, and to absolve itself of all responsibility for Pecola's
tragedy. Claudia does question the black community's mythical naturalization of oppression ("we are wrong") but she does not posit an
alternative notion of human action that can resist fatalism ("it's too
late").

This bleak vision excludes the novel from the celebratory tradition
that Black Aesthetic theorists sought to establish. The novel's critique
of black folk values sharply departs from Black Aesthetic ideology,
which demanded literary affirmation of the black community's power
to challenge white middle-class ideology. The black community in *The
Bluest Eye* entirely lacks the resources to counter racial oppression. If
anything, the folk rituals of the novel's black community only intensify
their racial oppression.[34] Soaphead Church uses the folk practice of
conjuring on Pecola to alleviate his hatred of his own blackness. Conjuring here works as an instrument of oppression, gratifying Soaphead
Church's craving for power and confirming Pecola's powerlessness. Another example of the divisive power of folk rituals appears in the scene
in which Pecola is surrounded by a group of black boys chanting, "Black
e mo Black e mo Ya daddy sleeps nekked" (p. 55). The folk ritual quality
of this scene is established by several details. Pecola, "the victim," is
placed in the center as the boys form a circle and dance a "macabre
ballet" around her (p. 55). The boys' rhyme recalls the black folk verbal
ritual of the dozens, which involves sexual insults directed at the victim's parents. As Johanna Grimes has remarked, the boys' chant

evokes the self-hatred and the internalization of racist values expressed in the well-known black folk rhyme, "If you're white, you're right / If you're brown, stick around / If you're Black, get back."[35] The entire scene reverberates with the associations of a ritual sacrifice that will help purge the group's self-hatred. Here and elsewhere in the novel, the black community's sense of self-worth depends on their construction of Pecola as a scapegoat: "All of us—all who knew her—felt wholesome after we cleaned ourselves on her. We were so beautiful when we stood astride her ugliness" (p. 159).

We should be careful, however, not to mistake the novel's critique of a particular kind of community for a rejection of community as such. Elizabeth Schultz argues that *The Bluest Eye* opposes the communal bent of 1960s and '70s black fiction in presenting alienated protagonists who "have more in common with their white counterparts . . . than they do with other protagonists of the Afro-American novel."[36] While *The Bluest Eye* rejects a black folk community that consolidates its cultural unity by persecuting one of its most vulnerable members, the novel also renders impossible the very category of an alienated individual. The structure of *The Bluest Eye*, with its intermeshing of strands dealing with different characters, compels us to read Pecola's story in conjunction with the story of her entire community. Moreover, the novel's presentation of the black community is not entirely despairing, for it does offer an alternative vision of a positive folk community, embodied in the three prostitutes. Each of these women practices a different folk skill: China is adept at signifying, Marie tells stories, and Poland sings the blues. One of Poland's songs, celebrating a "boy who is sky-soft brown" (p. 49), partially compensates for Pecola's obsession with "blue sky eyes" (p. 40). Although they become prostitutes for economic reasons, these are the only women in the novel who are able to control and to derive some pleasure from their bodies. Their three-woman household, a relatively independent economic and ideological space, offers an alternative to the white middle-class nuclear family of the Dick and Jane reader. The fact that they are prostitutes is crucial to their positive function in the novel, for they are socially ostracized by Mrs. McTeer and the church women of the neighborhood. The prostitutes constitute a kind of feminine folk community that is marginal even to the marginal community of blacks. Perhaps it is their position at the very fringes of black society that allows them to entertain differences, as is clear from their treatment of Pecola. Even the back-and-forth, ricocheting movement of their conversation, conducted in black dialect, enacts a dynamic exchange of differences. The tone and rhythm of their talk matches Claudia's description of the speech of another feminine group, her mother's women friends: "their conversation is like a gently wicked dance. Sound meets sound, curtsies, shimmies and retires. Another sound enters but is upstaged by still another: the two circle each other and stop" (p. 16). Miss McTeer's circle of women friends and the three prostitutes constitute the novel's only intimation of a community that warmly engages and gives full play to a host of differences.

This alternative vision of community, which is only fleetingly evoked at a thematic level, is more fully developed at the level of narrative voice. Like the conversation of the prostitutes and of Mrs. McTeer's friends, the novel's narrative voice celebrates a lively interplay of differences; "sound meets sound" to create a multivocal narrative medium. This multiple voice is achieved by means of shifts between standard English and dialect, and the use of free indirect speech. These narrative strategies make it impossible to locate a central voice or a clear source of authority in the text. The novel alternates between the first-person narration of Claudia and a third-person omniscient narration. Neither of these two voices is consistent or unified in itself, so that the many-voicedness of the text is apparent not only in the difference between Claudia's and the omniscient narration, but also in the self-division of each.

In the Claudia sections of the novel, the immersed perspective of the child Claudia is often interrupted by the more detached posture of the adult Claudia. This difference between the Claudia who narrates and the Claudia who is the object of narration is evident in the very first few pages of the novel, where a memory frieze from Claudia's childhood, narrated in the present tense, is disturbed by an abrupt switch to the past tense, as the adult narrator questions the authority of her own memory: "But was it really like that? As painful as I remember?" (p. 14). The rest of Claudia's narrative continues to oscillate between the past and present tenses, an oscillation that emphasizes the gap between the two Claudias. Claudia's voice further risks its own authority through the use of slippery pronouns; the subject of Claudia's narration shifts as rapidly as her voice moves from "I" to "we." Claudia's discourse on "outdoors" is just one example of the elasticity of her voice:

> There is a difference between being put *out* and being put *outdoors*. If you are put out, you go somewhere else; if you are outdoors, there is no place to go. The distinction was subtle but final. Outdoors was the end of something, an irrevocable physical fact defining and complementing our metaphysical condition. Being a minority in both caste and class, we moved about anyway on the hem of life. (p. 18)

This passage begins in the gnomic present tense, which, aided by the absence of pronouns, is usually employed to state universal truths. The second sentence, while maintaining the same tense, specifies the utterance by attaching it to a "you" who might be any hypothetical black subject. Switching from the gnomic present tense of timeless generalizations to the past tense, the third sentence locates the question of "outdoors" in the particular moment that constitutes the setting of the novel. The unspecified "you" of the second sentence becomes a "we" in the fourth sentence, a "we" that we assume to be Claudia and Frieda. But the final sentence clarifies that this "we" refers to the entire community of poor blacks. Significantly, even in its expansion, this narrative voice does not claim the right to speak for all blacks but only for one section of the black community. This is evident in the next paragraph, when the narrating "we" of poor blacks is differentiated from the "they" of propertied blacks. Claudia's is certainly not a narrative voice that presumes to speak for all black experience.

Claudia's narrative alternates with the generalizing voice of an omniscient narrator who is usually positioned above or outside the narrative discourse. While the omniscient narrator seems to exercise great authority, a close examination reveals this voice to be vulnerable and, at every point, open to dialogue. In the Pauline Breedlove chapter, for example, the third-person narrator's version of Pauline's story is supposedly more reliable than Pauline's story of herself:

> The easiest thing would be to build a case out of her foot. That is what she herself did. But to find out the truth about how dreams die, one should never take the word of the dreamer. The end of her lovely beginning was probably the cavity in one of her front teeth. She preferred, however, to think always of her foot. (p. 88)

Even as the narrator claims to tell the truth about Pauline, the narrator's interpretation of Pauline's life is framed at both ends by Pauline's own interpretation. The last line in particular readmits Pauline's version as a valid alternative immediately after having denied it.

The narrator's initial statement of mastery over Pauline is further qualified as we continue to read the chapter. Pauline's expressive Southern dialect ("When I heerd him, shivers come on my skin" [p. 92]) often dialogizes the narrator's matter-of-fact, standard English statements ("Pauline and Cholly loved each other" [p. 92]). This linguistic dialogue unbalances the narrative hierarchy established at the beginning of the chapter, as the immediacy of Pauline's voice is often more affectively powerful than the word of the detached analyst. The omniscient narrator does not, however, always remain a neutral analyst of Pauline's dream. At times, when the narrator paraphrases Pauline's feelings in free indirect speech, the omniscient voice is charged with some of Pauline's emotional intensity, and this "stylistic contagion," as Leo Spitzer calls it,[37] taints the supposed integrity of the third-person voice.

The preceding discussion of the first- and third-person narrations as two separate, internally dialogized strands is convenient but somewhat misleading in its implication that the two voices are sealed off from each other. Usually when a novel employs both forms of narration, the first-person voice is contained within the third-person voice, enhancing the control and inclusive capacity of the omniscient narrator. *The Bluest Eye*, however, opens and closes with Claudia's first-person voice; this enclosure of the omniscient narration within the more vulnerable first-person narration contests the conventional privileging of omniscient narration as the more authoritative form. Further, the frequent alternation between the two narratives compels us continually to modify our stance according to the varying immersion and distantiation of the two voices. The dialogic principle is thus active between as well as within the two narratives. An interesting example of this is the different treatment of Marie/Maginot Line in the two narratives. We first meet Marie in the omniscient narrative, and when she later enters Claudia's narrative, we do not even know she is the same person, as in Claudia's sphere she is known as the Maginot Line. Claudia's presentation of her is acknowledged to be partial; Claudia is unable to do her justice because she has "heard too many black and red words about her" from the other townspeople (p. 64). Claudia's inability to write a narrative that is free of the voices she has heard foregrounds the novel's construction of narrative voice as a creative interplay between different, competing languages.[38]

As an overlay of several voices, *The Bluest Eye* attempts to achieve "an implied we in narration."[39] The nature of the "we" implied by the novel's narrative voices is, however, vastly different from the community posited by the Black Aesthetic. As we saw in chapter 1, the collective vision of Black Aesthetic literature was authorized by its use of an oral voice. *The Bluest Eye* is not the "talking book" that so many black writers of the 1960s and 1970s tried to write.[40] Nowhere in the novel is oral material (black dialect, storytelling, signifying, the blues) used without a standard English narrative frame. In fact, the literate quality of the narration is intrusively apparent in some places in the text, as for example in this description of Aunt Jimmy's funeral:

> The deceased was the tragic hero, the survivors the innocent victims; there was the omnipresence of the deity, strophe and antistrophe of the chorus of mourners led by the preacher. There was grief over the waste of life, the stunned wonder at the ways of God, and the restoration of order in nature at the graveyard. (p. 113)

This formal passage evocative of classical tragic drama, sharply juxtaposed with the folk funeral ritual it describes, displays the linguistic disjunctions that are produced when black oral forms are translated into a literary, novelistic medium.

Toni Morrison speaks of black oral forms as emblematic of the traditional black artist's symbiotic relation with the community. Oral forms like the church shout and the blues, according to Morrison, belong to a past when "an artist could be genuinely representative *of* the tribe and be *in* it." While lamenting the loss of this tradition, Morrison clearly acknowledges that it is irrevocably lost: "To transfer that is not possible. We don't live in places where we can hear those stories anymore."[41] Instead, Morrison conceives of the printed mode of the novel, "needed by Afro-Americans now in a way that it was not needed before," as a means of replacing the lost oral tradition.[42] "Replace" is the operative word here, for the novel, as Morrison understands it, cannot recover the oral collective heritage of the past. As a form that inscribes historical process, the novel cannot affirm a mythical temporal continuity with a pure cultural and natural origin.[43] *The Bluest Eye*'s distance from an oral folk origin is evident in its troubled treatment of myth and nature, and of oral folk material. Recognizing that she has at her disposal "only the letters of the alphabet and some punctuation,"[44] Morrison creates a heterogeneous text that cannot assume the unified communal voice associated with black oral forms. The alternative vision of community generated by *The Bluest Eye* is a uniquely novelistic one. The dialogism of the novel's several languages (the omniscient narrator's formal literary language, the Southern dialect of Pauline, Marie's storytelling, China's signifying, Poland's singing the blues, Pecola's schizophrenic conversation with herself, the dancing speech of Mrs. McTeer and her friends, and even Soaphead Church's letter to God) exemplifies a distinguishing formal feature of the novel as defined by Bakhtin, a form "populated—over-populated—with the intentions of others."[45]

Its inability to affirm a unified collectivity authorized by an oral voice constitutes the novel's sharpest point of departure from Black Aesthetic ideology. As we saw in chapter 1, the Black Aesthetic defined the black community as a cohesive monolith that could not admit differences and divisions. Black feminists like Ntozake Shange, Alice Walker, and Audre Lorde responded by exploring the stray feminine detail that escaped this codified collectivity. Despite Toni Morrison's avowed rejection of black feminism,[46] *The Bluest Eye* evokes the black feminist vision of community that was developed in the 1970s, a community galvanized by differences and contradictions. Toward the beginning of *The Bluest Eye*, Pecola, walking along the street, notices a clump of dandelions:

> Why, she wonders, do people call them weeds? She thought they were pretty. But grownups say, 'Miss Dunion keeps her yard so nice. Not a dandelion anywhere.' Hunkie women in black babushkas go into the fields with baskets to pull them up. But . . . they were real to her. She knew them. They were the codes and touchstones of the world, capable of translation and possession. (p. 41)

This passage draws into focus the novel's complex negotiation with the Black Aesthetic as well as with the white middle-class aesthetic stand-

ard, both of which construct black women like Pecola as grotesque
signs of difference. The dandelions, like Pecola, are the ugly weeds that
must be uprooted to maintain the proud and beautiful facade of a white
middle-class as well as a black nationalist community. The passage
quoted above, imaginatively possessing and translating ordinary weeds
into images of beauty, hints at a new aesthetic vision that can incorporate the stray and stubborn difference of black femininity. Like Alice
Walker's petunias and Ntozake Shange's nose rings, Morrison's dandelions open the space for a black feminine aesthetic most eloquently
described by Audre Lorde: "Difference must be not merely tolerated
but seen as a fund of necessary polarities between which our creativity
can spark like a dialectic."[47]

III

"NO BOTTOM AND NO TOP"
OPPOSITIONS IN *SULA*

While *The Bluest Eye* obliquely explores the black feminine difference from the Black Aesthetic, this difference occupies the center of Toni Morrison's second novel, *Sula* (1973). *Sula* embodies a radically new black femininity that upsets all the oppositions (between past and present, individual and community, absence and presence) that structure Black Aesthetic discourse. In a contemporary review, Jerry Bryant wrote that in *Sula*, Morrison attempts to "combine the aims of the Black Freedom Movement and Women's Liberation."[1] Rather than merely combining, *Sula* plays feminism and nationalism against each other, staging the encounter of these two ideologies as a dynamic contradiction. In a difficult double move, the novel assumes a feminist perspective to clarify the limits of nationalist ideology, but withdraws from a full development of its own feminist implications. The ideological ambivalence thus produced should discourage any programmatic political reading; *Sula* is, however, often read as a feminist novel. Barbara Jean Varga-Coley, for example, argues that *Sula* advances "the feminist argument that women are victimized in the roles society allows them."[2] Varga-Coley is right in that, unlike *The Bluest Eye*, *Sula* emphasizes the sexual rather than the racial constraints on black women. Several other elements of the novel seem to invite a feminist reading, such as its depiction of black men and its critique of the institutions of heterosexuality and reproduction. However, a closer consideration of these elements reveals the counterpressure exerted by black nationalist ideology on a feminist articulation of black femininity.

Predictably, black nationalist critics denounced the feminist elements of *Sula*, focusing their critique on the novel's extremely unflattering portrayal of black men. Addison Gayle argued that the novel's feminist intentions necessarily fail because

> You can't very well do a hatchet job on Black men without also doing a hatchet job on Black women. Therefore, if you read *Sula* . . . , the images of both the men and the women are equally nauseating.[3]

Other critics, while not sharing Gayle's strongly censorious tone, emphasized that the novel's feminist focus involves a "severe symbolic mutilation of the Black male psyche" and is "psychologically devastating for the collective male ego."[4] It is true that, with the exception of Ajax, all the black male characters in *Sula* fit the type that the Black Aestheticians wished to ban from black literature. The very names of characters like Chicken Little, Boy Boy, and the Deweys evoke an image of black men as frozen in a state of perpetual, irresponsible childhood. The stunted physical growth of the Deweys, who remain boys forever, is paralleled by Plum's psychological refusal of adulthood. The emasculation of black male characters in the novel seems to be counterbalanced by the strength of some of the novel's black women characters, such as Eva and Sula. Asked by Robert Stepto to respond to "the feeling in certain literary circles" that black women should not be portrayed as emasculators, Toni Morrison remarked that "everybody knows, deep down, that Black men were emasculated by white men, period. And that Black women didn't take any part in that."[5] The presentation of Jude's character in *Sula* clearly pinpoints racial oppression rather than black female dominance as the cause of black male emasculation. Jude's failure to attain adult masculinity derives from his forced employment as a waiter, his inability to find any other meaningful work. As with Cholly in *The Bluest Eye*, Jude's humiliation in the white man's world directly colors his perception of black women. Jude's position as head of the household compensates for his humiliation in the workplace; only by viewing his wife as the hem of his garment is Jude able to reclaim "some posture of adulthood."[6]

However, unlike the presentation of Cholly in *The Bluest Eye*, Jude's status as a victim of racism does not in any way extenuate his responsibility for his treatment of women. His narrative of himself as a pathetic victim of racism is mocked by the narrator as "a whiney tale that peaked somewhere between anger and a lapping desire for comfort" (p. 103). Sula exposes Jude's complicity in his victimization, and offers a startling perspective on the black man as "the envy of the world" (p. 104), which defamiliarizes the contemporary nationalist discourse on the black man initiated by the Moynihan Report. This discourse, constructing the black man as "the number one object of racism,"[7] assigned the black woman the subsidiary role of healing the black man's damaged masculinity. Unlike Nel, who willingly fulfills this prescribed feminine function, Sula refuses to offer "milkwarm commiseration" (p. 103) for the woes of the black man. Rejecting the image of the black man as the prime victim of racism and its concomitant image of the black woman as nurturer, Sula brackets the issue of racism and opens the space for a new articulation of black masculinity and femininity. Sula's deliberate misreading of Jude's narrative is a double-edged gesture: her refusal to be the hem of the black man's garment displaces the

[handwritten marginalia: feminist challenge to false new blk / misc. slant but calls for any / BBM music the revolutionary subject]

masculinist emphasis of black nationalist discourse, but her negation of Jude's victim identity accords with the black nationalist goal of fashioning a new black identity free of the oppressive past. In this instance, the novel first employs a black feminist perspective to undo one element of black nationalist ideology (its masculine emphasis), and then aligns this feminist critique with another element of black nationalist ideology (its denial of the black victim type and its affirmation of a new black subject). This double move exposes the contradictory construction of the black male in black nationalist discourse, as both the helpless victim of racism and the new revolutionary subject.

The novel's treatment of black male-female relationships exhibits a similar uneasy adjustment to the terms of black nationalist discourse. All the major black male-female unions in *Sula* end with male desertion, and with a bleak vision of heterosexual femininity as characterized by loss and absence. For example, during his brief marriage with Eva, Boy Boy is rarely home, and when he ultimately abandons Eva, her attempt to rebuild her life without him mysteriously involves a lost leg. This pattern of desertion and loss is repeated in the narratives of Nel and Sula. Jude leaves Nel with "no thighs and no heart" (p. 111), and Ajax leaves Sula with "nothing but his stunning absence" (p. 134). Heterosexuality in the novel is insistently associated not just with loss, but with death. Reflecting upon the lives of the women in her community, Sula observes that "those with husbands had folded themselves into starched coffins" (p. 122). Sula's own heterosexual experiences cause her to weep "for the deaths of the littlest things" (p. 123). The description of Nel and Sula's adolescent erotic play powerfully establishes the symbolic connection between the vagina and the grave, between heterosexuality and defilement:

> Each then looked around for more debris to throw into the hole: paper, bits of glass, butts of cigarettes, until all of the small defiling things they could find were collected there. Carefully they replaced the soil and covered the entire grave with uprooted grass. (p. 59)

The novel's critique of heterosexuality converges in its representation of the three-woman Peace household. Eva Peace meets men entirely on her own terms, feeling no compulsion to support their perception of themselves. Eva's sexual abstinence is exactly opposed to Hannah's promiscuity, but although Hannah craves masculine attention, she attaches no great value to her sexual encounters with men, which are "pleasant and frequent but otherwise unremarkable" (p. 44). Hannah challenges the possessive ethic of heterosexuality; wholly incapable of loyalty or jealousy, she disregards other women's marital ties by sleeping with their husbands. Sula's sexual promiscuity poses an even greater threat to her community, for, unlike Hannah, Sula bruises the "pride and vanity" of the men whom she tries out and discards (p. 115).

This description of the Peace women's subversion of heterosexuality is only partially accurate, for it conveniently omits, as do most readings of *Sula* as a feminist novel, an opposing strand in the Peace women's characterization that squarely aligns them with heterosexual ideology. The narrator insistently reiterates that the Peace women "loved all men" (p. 41) and then anticipates the argument (an argument actually offered by Susan Willis) that the three-woman Peace household, a space that escapes a male-dominated structuring of the family, allows these women to "exercise heterosexuality on their own terms."[8] The narrator rejects this argument, emphasizing the Peace women's unconditional affirmation of heterosexuality: "It was manlove that Eva bequeathed to her daughters. Probably, people said, because there were no men in the house, no men to run it. But actually that was not true. The Peace women simply loved maleness, for its own sake" (p. 41). Not only do the Peace women love all men, they help hold the structures of heterosexuality firmly in place. Eva fusses interminably with newly wed women who neglect the wifely duties of cooking their husbands' suppers on time, laundering their shirts, and so on. Hannah, too, serves the traditional feminine function of enhancing the man's sense of his self; she makes the man "feel as though he were complete and wonderful just as he was—he didn't need fixing—and so he relaxed and swooned in the Hannah-light that shone on him simply because he was" (p. 43).

Sula is somewhat different from Hannah and Eva for, through most of the novel, she maintains a far more radical stance against heterosexuality. Sula's frequent heterosexual encounters convince her that a lover can never be a friend (p. 121). However, a close analysis of Sula's experience of sexual intercourse discloses an irreducibly contradictory sequence of responses. Heterosexuality appears to be all-important for Sula, being the "only place where she could find what she was looking for" (p. 122). This statement is puzzling, for we are told, a page earlier, that Sula is looking for the "other half of her equation" (p. 121), and that this desire is not satisfied by her male lovers. On the contrary, orgasm with these men makes Sula aware of a profound loneliness in which she fuses not with her masculine lovers but with herself (p. 123). If sex does not unify Sula with her male lovers, it does provide her only means of achieving a strong, centered self: "particles of strength gathered in her like steel shavings drawn to a spacious center, forming a tight cluster that nothing, it seemed, could break" (p. 123). This cluster does, however, fall apart, confirming Sula's sense of solitude. Every moment of this sequence undoes the previous moment, vacillating between two contradictory perceptions of heterosexuality as the most meaningful and the most disappointing experience in Sula's quest for self.

Barbara Smith relies heavily on this scene in her reading of *Sula* as "an exceedingly lesbian novel."[9] Smith uncovers an important and usually overlooked layer of the novel, but her reading elides all the passages that present heterosexual intercourse as the medium of Sula's epiphanic encounter with herself. A further problem with Smith's reading is not that a lesbian analysis of *Sula* is reductive, as some critics have claimed,[10] but that Smith does not clearly define her use of the term *lesbian novel*. Smith argues that *Sula* "works as a lesbian novel not only because of the passionate friendship between Nel and Sula, but because of Morrison's consistently critical stance toward the heterosexual institutions of male/female relationships, marriage and the family."[11] This definition does not sufficiently clarify the difference between a feminist and a lesbian critique of heterosexuality. Despite its problems,[12] however, Smith's essay does help to account for the novel's ambivalent treatment of Nel and Sula's relationship and of heterosexuality. Far from being reductive, Smith's was one of the first essays on *Sula* to acknowledge that the novel's reversion to a conventional heterosexual plot diverts attention from the subversive potential of the Nel-Sula relationship.[13]

Nel and Sula's union constitutes the novel's strongest challenge to Black Aesthetic discourse. As we have already seen, one of the functions of black women writers, as prescribed by the Black Aesthetic, was to depict black male-female relationships as necessary, complementary unions. *Sula* often summons the heterosexual cliché of men and women as the two halves of each others' equations. Sula's "craving for the other half of her equation" (p. 121) is occasionally placed in a heterosexual context, as, for example, when she describes herself through the traditional metaphor of the feminine as an empty space filled by a man: "There was this space in front of me, behind me, in my head. Some space. And Jude filled it up" (p. 144). More frequently, it is a woman, Nel, who constitutes the other half of Sula's equation: for Sula, Nel is "the closest thing to both an other and a self" (p. 119). The Nel-Sula union significantly but not entirely displaces the heterosexual formula of a man and a woman forming a complete person. Nel and Sula's first meeting is structured like a typical romantic, heterosexual encounter. The very fact that their fantasies are described as "Technicolored visions" (p. 51) indicates their conventional nature. Nel imagines herself in a fairy-tale heroine's posture of waiting passively for a prince. Sula, as the active prince galloping on a horse, completes the heterosexual union of the active and the passive, the masculine and the feminine principles. This romantic fantasy is, however, disrupted by the simple fact that it is a female, Sula, who occupies the masculine place. Even more significantly, the heterosexual union of prince and princess yields primacy to the union of two female friends who can share the delight of the same dream. This scene certainly supports Barbara Smith's observation that, set within a heterosexual frame, Nel and Sula's erotic fantasies betray their hidden desire for a feminine rather than a masculine lover.[14]

In the first part of the novel, Nel and Sula's complementary union is explicitly distinguished from the oneness of the heterosexual couple, Nel and Jude. Whereas Sula helps Nel to define herself and to see old things with new eyes, Jude likes to "see himself taking shape in her eyes" (p. 83). While the Nel-Sula union preserves the difference of each, in the Nel-Jude union, "both of them together would make one Jude" (p. 83). The friendship of Nel and Sula is ruptured in the second part of the novel, which deals predominantly with the heterosexual conflicts between Nel and Jude, Sula and Ajax. Sula's affair with Ajax provides the most striking instance of the novel's capitulation to heterosexual conventions. With Ajax, Sula becomes "like all of her sisters before her" and lapses into the expected role of the black woman as nurturer when she asks Ajax to lean on her (p. 133). The Ajax incident simply cannot be made to cohere with the presentation of Sula's character in the rest of the novel. Her affair with Ajax drastically reduces Sula's feminist difference from the heterosexual women of her community. Precisely because it lacks any plot preparation or psychological plausibility, the Ajax episode appears to be a compromise gesture that gives heterosexuality its due. The whole sequence of events from Sula's first meeting with Ajax to her death seems to square her down to size, to render her transgressive character readable according to an acceptable fictional code of feminine characterization. The uncomfortable nature of this compromise is evident in the incoherent resolution of the Ajax incident. In an abruptly linked causal chain, Ajax's desertion of Sula leads to her awareness that there are no more new experiences in store for her, which leads to her death. Maureen Reddy remarks that Sula's death, of a mysterious wasting disease, is reminiscent of the deaths with which unconventional nineteenth-century fictional heroines were punished.[15] While evoking this conventional ending, however, the novel plays a significant variation on it. Sula does not feel the shame and contrition of her literary predecessors; she dies proudly, convinced that it is she rather than the conventional women of her community who is really "good" (p. 146). In her conversation with Nel just before she dies, Sula herself points out the difference between the ending of her own unusual plot and the endings of most conventional black women's plots: "I know what every Black woman in this country is doing. Dying. Just like me. But the difference is, they dying like a stump. Me, I'm going down like one of those redwoods" (p. 143).

Readings of *Sula* as a feminist novel emphasize that Sula's characterization seems sharply discontinuous from earlier representations of the black woman in fiction.[16] Most of these readings are silent on the Ajax incident, for it seems to detract from the novel's presentation of Sula as the embodiment of a radically new black femininity. That most readers are baffled by Sula's inconsistency is apparent from the strenuous critical attempts to translate her character into a familiar ideological format, whether feminist or nationalist. Roseann Bell, for example, turns to nationalist ideology to clarify the radical newness of Sula's characterization: "It should not be surprising that *Sula* is regarded as an important statement in contemporary discussions on the Black Aesthetic," for Sula's character "suggests a positive way of freeing our fettered minds from the oppressive tentacles of a past which . . . prevents us from progressing and projecting a new vision."[17] Bell is partially right, in that the newness of Sula's character cannot be fully appreciated without reference to Black Aesthetic theories of the radical black subject. However, the contradictory newness of Sula is not fully readable within an exclusively nationalist or feminist ideological frame; instead it provides yet another example of the novel's selective and critical appropriation of both ideologies.

As Bell's comment indicates, Sula does share one central emphasis of black nationalist discourse: its affirmation of the newness of the ideal black subject. As we have already seen, Sula rejects the old image of blacks as victims and reaches for an identity free of the past of racial oppression. In fact, the temporal opposition of black nationalist discourse is enacted in the novel's opposition of Sula and the black community. While Sula perceives the present moment as pure possibility, the black community of the Bottom clings to an absolute, static vision of the past. In a contemporary review of *Sula*, Sara Blackburn observed that the setting of the novel "seems somehow frozen, stylized" and "refuses to invade our present."[18] The novel's opening chapter, in particular, conveys this frozen impression by situating the Bottom in a remote, inaccessible past: "In that place, where they tore the nightshade and blackberry patches from their roots to make room for the Medallion City Golf Course, there was once a neighborhood" (p. 3). This impression of temporal distance is strengthened by the "nigger joke" that traces the origin of the Bottom all the way back to slavery. Encapsulating the folk philosophy of the Bottom community, the nigger joke perpetuates the history of racial exploitation, casting the white slavemaster as an omnipotent manipulator and blacks as his innocent dupes. The black community in *Sula* is deeply invested in this image of themselves, for the role of the victim offers them a way of safe resignation. Preserving their victim status protects them from the rigors of creating a new identity free of their oppressive past: "They were merely victims and knew how to behave in that role. . . . But the free fall, oh no, that required—demanded—invention" (p. 120). The black community's tenacious attachment to a static past is perfectly expressed in Nel's statement, "Hell is change" (p. 108).

Exactly contrary to her community's philosophy is Sula's conviction that "the real hell of Hell is that it is forever" (p. 107). Sula's conception of time as a medium of ceaseless change gives rise to her sense of self as sheer risk and imaginative possibility; Sula dares "the free fall," creates herself anew every moment. The temporal continuity valued by her community appears, through Sula's eyes, to be nothing but repetitive sameness: "Nothing was ever different. They were all the same" (p. 147). Sula's entire life challenges this sense of sameness; even her death seems to result from her awareness that she has exhausted all new possibilities: "There aren't any more new songs and I have sung all the ones there are" (p. 137). Shadrack, mistaking Sula for a typical member of her community, offers her the promising word "'always' to convince her, assure her, of permanency" (p. 157), but the only "always" that Sula ultimately accepts is the finality of death (p. 149).

The opposition between Sula and the black folk community of the Bottom cannot, however, be read in staightforward Black Aesthetic terms as an opposition between a new present and an oppressive past. While privileging newness and change, Sula embodies a specifically feminine newness that cannot be easily assimilated into Black Aesthetic ideology. Sula rejects the reproductive function so valued by her community: when Eva advises her to become a mother, Sula replies, "I don't want to make somebody else. I want to make myself" (p. 92). This emphasis on feminine self-creation at the expense of nurturance of children is crucial to a correct understanding of Sula's radical newness. In *Sula*, an important element of black nationalist discourse—its natural, reproductive definition of black femininity—is displaced from the "new" Sula to the black community, which otherwise represents an ideology tied to the oppressive past and resistant to change. This incongruous yoking of the old and the new, of elements both essential and inimical to black nationalist ideology, exposes the limits of the newness valorized by this ideology. Employing a black feminist perspective on reproduction, the novel makes visible the point at which the "new" black nationalist discourse regresses into the past.

Sula's refusal of reproduction is her greatest point of difference from her community; it is what renders her evil and unnatural to the people of the Bottom. Sula's return to the Bottom is heralded by an unnatural plague of robins, and her death is followed by an untimely frost in October and a false spring in January. These natural disorders symbolically parallel the disorder that Sula's "unnatural" refusal to be a mother unleashes on her community. Barbara Christian persuasively argues that the problem of physical survival faced by the novel's black community determines their definition of women as mothers, as guarantors of temporal and natural continuity.[19] On the barren topsoil that the white slavemaster gives his slave, and where the Bottom is established, the black community daily confronts the malevolence of the natural elements. Their struggle for survival against natural disaster and their consequent, obsessive fear of death, explain the community's perception of Sula as an unnatural witch. Sula's subversion of motherhood and her commitment to temporal discontinuity cause the black community to construct her as a scapegoat and to defend with renewed vigor their conception of motherhood as the primary feminine function.

The novel's critique of reproductive ideology is accomplished not only through Sula's character, but also through several portraits of black women who live by their community's valuation of reproduction as the sole outlet for feminine creativity. Helene Wright, whose daughter, Nel, is her sole purpose for living, supervises Nel's upbringing so closely that she drives her daughter's imagination underground (p. 18). Her obsessive preoccupation with her children twists her maternal love into "something so thick and monstrous she was afraid to show it lest it break loose and smother them with its heavy paw" (p. 138). Eva Peace, in the early part of the novel, is the stereotypical strong black mother whose life is entirely dictated by her concern for her children's survival. When Eva finds that her excessive maternal love has led her to a cold, dark, stinking outhouse, using her last piece of food to relieve her son's constipation, she abandons the role of mother altogether, leaves her children with a neighbor, and goes away to find a better life for herself. Upon her return, Eva maintains a careful distance from her children, and burns her son because he expects her to nurture him again. That Eva chooses to kill her son rather than play mother all her life powerfully dramatizes the unhealthy consequences of the Bottom community's prescription that black women center their lives around reproduction.

However, if the novel critiques the black community's commitment to a reproductive definition of femininity, it does not unreservedly endorse Sula's absolute rejection of motherhood.[20] To an extent, Sula's refusal to be a mother is a liberating feminist gesture that initiates a new exploration of black femininity outside reproductive parameters. But Sula's radical redefinition of herself also depends on her denial of her mother. It is her accidental discovery of the failure of the maternal bond (Hannah's remark that she does not like Sula) that motivates Sula's invention of herself: "Hers was an experimental life—ever since her mother's remarks sent her flying up the stairs" (p. 118). This statement of a direct causality between Sula's rejection of her mother and her creation of a new self is reminiscent of the black nationalist discourse on the mother. While conceiving reproduction as the black woman's primary revolutionary contribution, black nationalist discourse constructed the mother as "the undisputed enemy of all revolutionary ideas."[21] Sula's rejection of reproduction is problematic precisely because it repeats the black nationalist gesture of constructing a new and free identity in explicit opposition to the mother. The novel's treatment of reproduction thus produces a contradictory interlocking of black feminist and nationalist ideologies. *Sula's* feminist critique of the institution of motherhood exposes the limits of black nationalist "newness"; this feminist critique is then itself questioned because, when taken to its logical conclusion, it demands a denial of the mother that disturbingly recalls black nationalist discourse. Black nationalism and feminism are both distinguished from and folded back into each other, in a difficult dialectic that clarifies the troubling implications of both ideologies.

In a similar set of double moves, the novel questions both the black community's affirmation of reproduction as a means of ensuring temporal continuity, and the temporal discontinuity that results from Sula's rejection of reproduction. Sula's new identity entails a complete disregard for her ancestors, as, for example, when she enjoys watching her mother burn or when she shocks the sentiments of her community by sending her grandmother away to an old people's home. In her essay "Rootedness: The Ancestor as Foundation," Toni Morrison writes:

> If we don't keep in touch with the ancestor, . . . we are, in fact, lost. . . . When you kill the ancestor, you kill yourself. I want to point out the dangers, to show that nice things don't happen to the totally self-reliant if there is no conscious historical connection.[22]

Morrison's remarks may be almost exactly applied to Sula, whose total self-reliance is suicidal because it lacks a historical connection with the ancestor. With no grounding roots in the past, Sula's radical difference proves to be meaningless and is ultimately reduced to the very sameness she tries to challenge: "If I live a hundred years my urine will flow the same way, my armpits and breath will smell the same. My hair will grow from the same holes. I didn't mean anything. I never meant anything" (p. 147). Sula's newness so sharply departs from the past that it cannot revitalize her community's old ways; the encounter between the new (Sula) and the old (the community), far from producing a dynamic exchange, remains locked in a state of absolute contradiction. We are told that the black community's exposure to Sula "changed them in accountable yet mysterious ways" (p. 117), but this change paradoxically works against change, only confirming the black community's adherence to their old, conservative ways.

The sterile confrontation between Sula and her community obliquely discloses the inadequacy of the nationalist conception of the radically new black subject. Showing that such a subject cannot be politically effective, the novel questions the absolute dichotomy between the oppressive past and the revolutionary future in black nationalist discourse. Sula elaborates but fails to choose between two antithetical views of historical change: the black community's passive fatalism and the black nationalists' belief in sudden, stark historical change. The narrator mocks the black community's hope that their condition will change on its own, a hope that keeps them mired in their oppression.

The first time that the entire Bottom community joins Shadrack's Suicide Day procession, they are driven by "the same hope that kept them picking beans for other farmers; . . . kept them convinced that some magic 'government' was going to lift them up" (p. 160). However, if this passive hope is suicidal, so is the black community's single act of rebellion against their oppression: their expression of anger at their exclusion from productive labor (the construction of the tunnel) results in collective suicide. The construction of the River Road in 1927 holds out the false promise of black employment, but is eventually built entirely by white labor. The same pattern is exactly repeated in 1937 with the construction of the tunnel. This presentation of history as circular repetition compels a critical reconsideration of the black nationalist vision of historical change as a clean, decisive break from the past cycle.

The novel directly engages the black nationalist conception of the 1960s as a period of unprecedented advancement for black Americans. The chapter "1965" opens with the lines, "Things were so much better in 1965. Or so it seemed" (p. 164). The narrator concedes that some progress has taken place: more black Americans are integrated into white society and hold better jobs. This appearance of change is, however, thrown into doubt by the contradictory statement, "The young people had a look about them that everybody said was new but which reminded Nel of the deweys" (p. 164). This puzzling comparison of the new young people of the 1960s with the deweys is not developed or explained. The only possible overlap between the two is that they both embody a "plural name" (p. 68). Perhaps it would be overworking this brief, incidental comparison to suggest that the new people of the 1960s share the deweys' commitment to a plural, collective identity that erases all singularities and differences. The mention of the deweys in the context of the 1960s is even more startling because the deweys' stunted growth is utterly incongruous with the black nationalists' conception of the 1960s as a period of remarkable progress for blacks.

We must, of course, remember that the connection between the deweys and the new people of the 1960s is drawn by Nel, and we know that Nel is unlikely to appreciate even real changes, given her conviction that "Hell is change." Although the narrator's stance cannot be exactly identified with Nel's, the narrator unmistakably shares Nel's skepticism and regret about some of the changes that occurred in the 1960s:[23]

> The Black people, for all their new look, seemed awfully anxious to get to the valley, or leave town, and abandon the hills to whoever was interested. It was sad, because the Bottom had been a real place. These young ones kept talking about the community, but they left the hills to the poor, the old and the stubborn—and the rich white folks. Maybe it hadn't been a community, but it had been a place. (p. 166)

This passage brings into sharp focus the novel's interrogation of both the temporal and communal visions of black nationalist ideology. The value of community, which the black nationalists claimed as a distinctive feature of their new vision, is here displaced to the past, presented as one of the casualties of the changes of the 1960s. By means of this displacement, the novel suggests that temporal discontinuity, so strongly valorized in black nationalist discourse, inevitably produces a rupture of community.

By Black Aesthetic standards, the novel's inability to represent a new, revolutionary black community would certainly constitute an imaginative and political failure. The black community presented in the novel is moored to the oppressive past and is, therefore, problematic from a Black Aesthetic standpoint. When we are first introduced to the Bottom neighborhood, in the beginning of the novel, it has already become a thing of the past. The narrator's description of the Time and a Half Pool Hall, Irene's Palace of Cosmetology, Reba's Grill, and singing and dancing in the streets, vividly conveys the sense of a "real place" that Nel finds so lacking in the Bottom of the 1960s. Susan Willis argues that the social practices of the Bottom community "have little or nothing to do with the economics of exchange and everything to do with the exchange of social life." Willis seems to read the novel's presentation of the Bottom in entirely positive terms: "for the Bottom, the impossibility of being a part of production and trade ... creates a space for the generation of community."[24] The novel does make this connection between exclusion from economic production and development of a black community. In fact, racial and economic oppression appear to be the necessary conditions for the existence of a distinctive black folk culture. In the chapter "1965," the communal practices that characterized the earlier black neighborhood have disappeared as a result of the increasing economic integration of blacks into the white U.S. economic system. However, the novel does not uncritically affirm this kind of community contingent upon oppression and segregation. If the forced exclusion of blacks from labor and production generates a distinctive folk culture, it also precipitates their collective suicide at the end of the novel.

Moreover, the folk culture of the Bottom, like the folk culture presented in *The Bluest Eye*, keeps the black community trapped in its oppressed condition. The nigger joke, a folk survival mechanism, helps the community tolerate their difficult predicament but it does not offer any means of resistance or transformation. That the folk culture of the Bottom is geared toward survival rather than change is also apparent in the community's perception of evil as an uncontrollable natural phenomenon that must be allowed to run its course. This black folk philosophy, explicitly justified by the narrator as "a full recognition of the legitimacy of forces other than good ones" (p. 90), can be read either positively, as resilience, or negatively, as slackness. The novel characteristically balances both interpretations in tension, and disallows our

choosing between them. The black community's philosophy of evil results in an admirable acceptance of difference, evident in their treatment of Sula: they regard Sula's difference as evil, as a natural
aberration, but they allow her to survive. The naturalistic philosophy
of the Bottom folk, however, fails to discriminate between different
kinds of evil, placing racial oppression in the same class of phenomena
as floods and disease (p. 90). They greet all "evil days"—whether caused
by Sula, a natural disaster, or political factors—with "an acceptance
bordering on welcome" (p. 89). Such a world view inevitably keeps the
community mired in its oppressive situation and obstructs the development of a new political creed directed at change and resistance.

If the black folk community of the Bottom is both celebrated and
criticized, so is the radical, new identity of Sula. Kimberley Benston
writes that the new black subject of the 1960s, based as it is on absolute
temporal discontinuity, necessarily "defaces communal reality."[25]
Sula's character clearly demonstrates that a wholesale rejection of the
past can only produce a singular individual alienated from the community. Throughout the novel, Sula verbally constructs and satirizes several collective "they's," such as her discourses on black men
(pp. 103–104), on the black community of the Bottom (p. 120), and on
conventional black women (pp. 142–45). Sula's vision of her community as "a drawn-out disease" (p. 96) is certainly liberating, in that it
allows her to explore her own self outside all the constraining racial
and sexual conditions that determine her community's construction of
identity. However, Sula's denial of her community is countered by the
novel's structure and mode of narration, which, beginning and ending
with the Bottom community and intertwining the stories of Shadrack,
Nel, and the Peace family, forces us to read Sula's story as part of the
story of an entire community. Even if Sula sees herself as a distinctive
individual pitted against her community, the reader is compelled to
read her story "sometimes against but always because of the group
experience which provides the frame of reference."[26] Sula's singular
conception of herself also has been thematically criticized for its lack
of social grounding. As Adrienne Munich asks, in her analysis of Sula's
narrative about black men: "Where is Sula in this story? Is she outside
the world of which Jude is the envy? How would one analyze her voice?"
That her story "gives its teller no place"[27] is both Sula's strength and
weakness. Her complete lack of social positioning allows her to defami-
liarize and flout her community's conventions, but it also prohibits her
from effective political intervention in the life of her community.

The opposition between Sula and her community thus plays havoc
with the black nationalist articulation of the opposed terms of individual and community, past and present. In black nationalist discourse,
the individual and the past are absolutely negated, while the community and the present are absolutely affirmed. In *Sula*, these oppositions

refuse to remain in the places that black nationalist discourse allots them: the undesirable term "past" is aligned with the valued term "community," and the temporal discontinuity celebrated in black nationalist discourse is shown to produce the singular individuality decried by black nationalists.

The characterization of Sula in opposition to her community also topples the one remaining opposition, between absence and presence, that structures Black Aesthetic discourse. While the black nationalists celebrated the new black subject as presence, *Sula* figures the new black subject as absence, and attaches the value of presence to the static world view of the novel's black community. The folk rituals of the Bottom are calculated to assuage the community's fear of process. An example of this is provided in Chicken Little's funeral, which is the community's resounding statement against the "stupidity of loss" (p. 107). As Keith Byerman expresses it, the funeral "transforms an absence into a presence" by asserting the permanence of communal structures and rituals.[28] This need for public rituals that confirm temporal and communal stability explains the black community's easy acceptance of National Suicide Day, a ritual that meets the community's need to control their fear of death.

That a notion of identity as presence helps to ensure temporal continuity and guards against the "stupidity of loss" is evident in the account of Shadrack's process of self-recognition. Shadrack's traumatic experience of the violence of World War I causes his grotesque perception of his own body; he wakes up in an army hospital room to find his hand "growing in higgledy-piggledy fashion like Jack's beanstalk all over the tray and the bed" (p. 9). The war also strips Shadrack of all the signs of a positive identity: he has "no past, no language, no tribe, no source, no address book" (p. 12). Shadrack's fear of his body's mobility and his self's absence is not alleviated by the hospital nurse's attempt to bind him with physical cords as well as with the figurative fixity of a name. Shadrack's speculation on the title "Private," confusing the proper noun with the adjective, unnames the institutional identity that is imposed on him by white society. Shadrack finally quells his fear through an affirmation of blackness as pure self-presence:

> A black so definite, so unequivocal, it astonished him. He had been harboring a skittish apprehension that he was not real—that he did not exist at all. But when the blackness greeted him with its indisputable presence, he wanted nothing more. (p. 13)

Shadrack's vision of blackness, obviously evocative of the Black Aesthetic notion of blackness as presence,[29] depends on a fearful repression of the indeterminacy of the self and the body.

Shadrack's process of self-definition provides a standard for the black community's construction of identity as presence. Nel, who is a representative member of her community, parallels Shadrack in her resolution to "be on guard—always" against the fluidity of her body (p. 22). As with Shadrack, Nel's perception of the grotesque formlessness of the body arises from an encounter with white society. The lacing and binding imagery introduced in the Shadrack chapter reappears as Nel watches her mother humiliated by a white conductor: "the hooks and eyes in the placket of the dress had come undone and exposed the custard colored skin underneath" (p. 22). Like Shadrack, Nel counters her fear of this vulnerable body by affirming the sheer presence of her self: "Each time she said the word *me* there was a gathering in her like power" (p. 28). Nel's "newfound me-ness" (p. 29) resembles Shadrack's in its denial of process and indeterminacy. As Shadrack tries to banish his fear of absence by instituting the public ritual of National Suicide Day, so Nel clings to a stable identity through her dedication to the institutionalized roles of wife and mother. The narratives of the two characters disclose the stasis that accompanies a perception of the self as presence. Both Nel and Shadrack evade change by relying on the safety and security of institutional structures, and by affirming blackness and femininity as fixed, unchanging essences.

Eva's identity at first appears to be different from Nel's and Shadrack's, in that it converges not around presence but around the absence of her missing leg. Eva's search for a new self is initiated by her repudiation of the socially prescribed role of mother. The very process by which Eva arrives at a new self is an absence in the text: we are not told how she loses her leg or acquires her powerful new identity. Whereas Shadrack had been frightened of the sudden growth of his hands, Eva tells "fearful" stories about "how she had a corn on her toe and it just grew and grew and grew" (p. 30). Eva's narrative about the growth and mobility of her missing leg reveals the imaginative power and freedom that derive from an acceptance of bodily process. A similar sense of creative play is evident in Eva's disregard for the fixity of names. She mischievously names a man with fair skin and blond hair Tar Baby; this ironic gesture foregrounds the arbitrary nature of the signifiers "black" and "white," which do not necessarily correspond to physical colors, and unsettles Shadrack's vision of blackness as a definite, fixed essence. However, Eva's construction of herself around absence is not very different from her community's celebration of presence, for both achieve the ultimate effect of negating change and process. Although Eva's missing leg frees her to "literally invent herself,"[30] it also literally constricts her mobility; crippled and paralyzed, she spends her entire life confined to a wheelchair. Eva's naming of the deweys, too, restricts their bodily growth and prevents them from developing beyond the limits set by their name. Her naming of them robs the deweys of all specificity and difference, binds them into a sameness vividly figured by the image of the three deweys entangled in each others' shoelaces.

It is not Eva but Sula who represents the liberating potentialities of a self conceived as pure absence. The process of Sula's self-definition is catalyzed by two incidents that expose her to the "stupidity of loss." The death of Chicken Little impresses upon Sula the sense of "something newly missing" (p. 61), but instead of clutching at Shadrack's promise of "always," Sula decides to accept the fundamental absence of the self. She has "no ego," "no center," "no compulsion to verify herself" (p. 119). If the Chicken Little incident teaches Sula that there is "no self to count on" (p. 119), her realization that her mother does not like her teaches her the second crucial lesson that "there was no other that you could count on" (pp. 118–19). Unlike the other characters in the novel, Sula does not attempt to allay her fear of absence by grasping at an established social identity. Her sense of identity as an inconsistent, heterogeneous, temporally discontinuous process is figured by her birthmark, which is variously interpreted by different members of her community as a stemmed rose or a tadpole or the devil's ashes. This bodily mark of indeterminacy distinguishes Sula even from Eva, whose bodily lack still allows her a powerful, definite sense of presence and identity.

The necessary interdependence, in Sula's character, of temporal discontinuity and absence exposes the incoherence of the black nationalist articulation of these terms. In black nationalist discourse, temporal discontinuity impossibly supports a celebration of the black subject as presence. *Sula* not only makes visible this ideological contradiction by yoking together the disjunct values of presence and stasis, but also offers a model of black identity that more effectively displaces the Western humanist model of the subject. The representation of Sula's identity as a temporally discontinuous process undermines the notion of unified, coherent individuality implicit in realist fictional forms like the bildungsroman. *Sula* deliberately summons the bildungsroman by its structural use of years as the temporal markers that chart Sula's growth into adulthood. The linear expectations of the bildungsroman are frustrated, however, by the large gaps between years, gaps that elide the most significant moments in the development of Sula's self. For example, the years of Sula's absence from Medallion, when she presumably arrives at her new identity, constitute one of the more conspicuous temporal gaps in the novel.

The representation of Sula's self as temporally discontinuous not only denies the unified, developmental model of the bildungsroman; it also places Sula's character within an alternative fictional rhetoric—of the grotesque—that partly subverts the self-present individuality assumed in classic realist fiction. The grotesque mode in *Sula* (clearly distinct from the grotesque mode in *The Bluest Eye*, which represents black identity as inauthentic, distorted mimicry) is rich with transgressive and creative, rather than merely parodic, possibilities. This function of the grotesque mode has been most fully formulated in feminist appropriations of Bakhtin's concept of the grotesque body. Mary Russo, in her essay, "Female Grotesques: Carnival and Theory," offers a concise definition:

> The grotesque body is . . . the body of becoming, process and change. The grotesque body is opposed to the classical body, which is monumental, static, closed and sleek, corresponding to the aspirations of bourgeois individualism.[31]

Sula's processual identity and bodily indeterminacy allow us to read her character within this Bakhtinian articulation of the grotesque as a fictional mode that opposes the centered, closed, static individuality of classic realist fiction.

Sula's character does not, however, fully realize the transformative potential of the grotesque body, which, in Bakhtin's terms, is an emphatically communal body, "always already part of a throng."[32] Sula's grotesque body enacts a purely individual transgression that is tolerated by her community as a taboo spectacle, a form of licensed play. Although the grotesque figuration of Sula's body firmly refuses the model of self-sufficient individuality inscribed in realist fiction, the stridently individualistic rhetoric in which Sula expresses her singular difference from her community forecloses the liberatory possibilities of the grotesque vision of a transformed body politic. This disjunction—between the novel's thematic articulation of Sula's exceptional individuality and its formal reliance on a mode of fictional characterization that challenges the very notion of individuality—constitutes yet another instance of the irreducibly contradictory presentation of Sula's character. The novel's refusal to resolve its own contradictory articulation of the categories of individuality and community indirectly clarifies the similarly unresolved contradiction in black nationalist discourse.

Recombining the terms presence, stasis, and community, as opposed to absence, temporal rupture, and individuality, *Sula* upsets the seemingly clear and absolute polarization of these terms in black nationalist discourse. The novel not only redistributes, but also attempts to synthesize these opposed terms through the device of the split protagonist, Nel and Sula, each of whom embodies one side of the three sets of oppositions. Nel is aligned with the values of presence, stasis, and community, and Sula with absence, newness, and individuality. A fusion of these antithetical terms is suggested by the novel's conclusion:

> "All that time, all that time, I thought I was missing Jude." And the loss pressed down on her chest and came up into her throat. "We was

girls together," she said as though explaining something. "O Lord, Sula," she cried, "girl, girl, girlgirlgirl." (p. 174)

The imaginary reunion of Nel and Sula only partly succeeds in resolving the division between the two characters that complicates the second part of the novel. This division, caused by the girls' initiation into heterosexuality, is merely circumvented at the end of the novel, for Nel's cry involves a return to girlhood, to a moment prior to Nel and Sula's enlistment into heterosexual ideology. Bypassed rather than fully resolved, heterosexual conflict remains to trouble the novel's conclusion.
(Moreover, Nel and Sula's union does not entirely compensate for the loss associated with heterosexual femininity, for Nel is able to invoke Sula's presence only by mourning her absence, only by recalling a past moment that is already lost. The ambiguous place of Sula in the resolution, both present and absent, should guard against a reading of the novel's conclusion as a reinstatement of full, self-present identity. Yet critics frequently interpret the novel's ending as a successful synthesis of Nel and Sula's opposing qualities into a single, "complete picture of the hero."[33] Morrison herself encouraged such a reading in her comments on Nel and Sula in an interview with Robert Stepto: "There was a little bit of both in each of these two women, and . . . if they had been one person, I suppose they would have been a rather marvelous person." Stepto's response, "But these two characters are nevertheless fractured into Nel and Sula,"[34] points to the difficulty of regarding the novel's split protagonist as an image of a whole, unified feminine subject.[35] Even the symbolic reunion at the end of the novel cannot overwrite the sense of fracture, the division between Nel and Sula's characters as they are presented through most of the novel.)
Precarious as the reunion of Nel and Sula may be, it produces an image that suggests a possible formal resolution of the novel's thematic contradictions. Nel's cry for Sula is described as "a fine cry" that has "no bottom and no top, just circles and circles of sorrow" (p. 174). This final sentence of the novel not only uses the image of a circle; it effects a complex circular return to the beginning of the novel. The statement that Nel's cry has no top or bottom unmistakably recalls the second page of the novel, which recounts the nigger joke of the Bottom on top of a hill. The linear hierarchy of tops and bottoms is displaced by Nel's circular cry. Nel's cry also circles back to her girlhood with Sula in the early part of the novel. This circular return to a past event, which produces a transformed, new understanding of this event, characterizes the structure of the entire novel. The novel's chapters, each titled by a year, create the misleading impression that the novel defers to a strict linear chronology. But, as Barbara Christian has pointed out, each of these years/chapters is "but the focus of intertwining circles of other times, other events."[36] For example, only three of the eighteen pages of

the chapter "1921" are actually set in the year 1921; the beginning of the chapter goes back eleven years, to describe Eva's marriage with Boy Boy and her struggle as a mother, and most of the rest of the chapter freely moves backward and forward from 1910 to 1921. Linear chronology is most conspicuously askew in the chapter "1923," as Eva unsuccessfully tries to remember the exact linear sequence of the five strange omens that prefigured Hannah's death.

While it clearly derails a linear movement of time, the novel does not unreservedly endorse a cyclic temporal vision. If the oppressed condition of the Bottom community originates with the linear hierarchy of tops and bottoms, the circular repetition of history keeps them trapped in this condition. One example already cited is the River Road that raises and defeats hopes of black employment in 1927, followed by an exactly repetitive pattern in 1937, with the construction of the river tunnel. To give another example, the nigger joke of the beginning of the novel comes full circle by the end: the topsoil of the Bottom actually becomes more valuable than valley land, in an ironic fulfillment of the slavemaster's false promise. But this circular reversion of value works against the black community, for the value of Bottom land begins to increase just as the black residents of the Bottom begin to move down to the valley.

This circular repetition of history, which reinforces the economic and racial exploitation of the black community is not, however, identical to the circular movement of the novel's structure. Toni Morrison has suggestively characterized the structure of *Sula* as "more spiral than circular."[37] As opposed to the tightly closed circles that structure *The Bluest Eye*, the circular movement of *Sula* is accumulative rather than exactly repetitive. The beginning and closing points of the novel's spiral do not quite overlap, thus leaving open the possibility of transformation. The novel at first offers an incomplete rendering of an event, withholding its meaning from the reader. Later chapters curve back to the earlier event, filling out its implications. The reader is almost always refused interpretive access to the novel's major events the first time they are narrated. For example, Eva's burning of Plum is incomprehensible when it is first presented, in "1921." We discover Eva's motivation two years later, in the chapter "1923." Similarly, Sula's slashing her fingertip puzzles the reader in "1922," and is partially explained in "1937." This circular movement, spiraling back to transform past incidents and to add new layers of meaning, resolves, at the level of narrative structure, the novel's thematic opposition between past and present.

Along with its temporal synthesis, the novel's structure also stages an interplay of absence and presence, individuality and community. *Sula* is structured around a series of events that not only speak of absence, but actually create an absence of meaning in the text that is later filled by several different interpretations. For example, Shadrack's baffling utterance of the word "always" in "1922" continues to resonate throughout the novel; Sula's and Shadrack's competing perceptions of the word are presented later, in "1940" and "1941." Another example is Chicken Little's drowning, which creates a "something newly missing," a space for meaning that is not filled until the last few pages of the novel, when Eva offers a startling new perspective that jars with Nel's earlier perception of the drowning. These two cases exemplify the novel's construction of meaning not only as a dialectic of absence and presence, but also as a collective exercise involving narrator, characters, and readers. Toni Morrison explains the use of structural absences in her fiction as a means of soliciting the reader's active participation in the text: "My language has to have holes and spaces so the reader can come into it."[38] The novel's spiral structure ensures that meaning is not authoritatively handed down from author to reader. Instead, the structural absences, meant to be filled by the competing interpretations of different characters and readers, throw the text open to a process of collective production.

The collective construction of meaning elicited by Sula's spiral structure is clearly contrasted with the authoritative transmission of meaning that the novel attributes to white American culture. The nigger joke illustrates the slaveowner's monopoly on meaning; the white master possesses the sole right to assign values in a dualistic, hierarchical scheme that bolsters his own politically powerful position. Perhaps less obviously, Sula suggests that the structural dualities of black nationalist discourse endorse a similar hierarchical construction of values. That the oppositions of black nationalist ideology are fundamentally top/bottom oppositions is clear in that each privileged term derives its value from an absolute negation of its other. Sula undermines this hierarchical binary structuring by refusing to valorize any one term of an opposition at the cost of devaluing its opposed other.[39] Individuality and community, past and present, absence and presence: all these terms are both preserved and canceled in Sula. The attempted synthesis of these terms, at the level of narrative structure, does not erase the novel's thematic contradictions. Instead, as I have tried to elaborate throughout this chapter, all the double meanings generated by Sula install unresolved contradiction as the central designing principle of the novel.

In this respect, Sula exhibits its own complicity with the binary structuring of black nationalist discourse: even as it dislocates, the novel does depend on these very dualities to structure its own vision. Even the novel's central structuring device, the opposition of Nel and Sula, reflects and refigures the black nationalist opposition of community and individuality, past and present, absence and presence. That all these oppositions are subsumed in the Nel-Sula pair signals both the novel's containment within and transgression of the boundaries of black nationalist discourse. As we saw in chapter 1, the gender construction of black nationalist discourse retains intact the white middle-class definitions of masculinity and femininity. The feminine pair of Nel and Sula unbalances, even as it cannot fully dismantle, the hierarchical gender opposition of black nationalist as well as white U.S. middle-class ideology.

IV

"A NEW WORLD SONG"
THE BLUES FORM OF *CORREGIDORA*

Toni Morrison described Gayl Jones's first novel, *Corregidora* (1975), as a "story that thought the unthinkable," a radical break in fictional representations of black women:

> No novel about any Black woman could ever be the same after this. [*Corregidora*] had changed the terms, the definitions of the whole enterprise. . . . Ursa Corregidora is not possible. Neither is Gayl Jones. But they exist.[1]

Morrison did not acknowledge the extent to which Ursa Corregidora was made possible by her own changing of "the terms, the definitions of the whole enterprise" in *Sula*. *Corregidora* shares with *Sula* a scathing critique of heterosexuality that concludes with a strained compromise, an exploration of black feminine sexuality outside a reproductive frame, an affirmation of the powers of subjectivity conceived as absence, and a cyclical structure that intimates the possibility of temporal transformation. *Sula*'s shifting and unsettling of the terms of black nationalist discourse surely enabled *Corregidora*'s success in imagining a black femininity unthinkable within these terms.

The remarkable continuities between *Corregidora* and *Sula* should not, however, disguise the fact that *Corregidora* more seriously challenges the reading codes of Black Aesthetic ideology than does *Sula*. While Morrison's insistence on the political function of her work[2] confirms the Black Aesthetic fusion of art and politics, Gayl Jones, in her emphatic dissociation of art and politics, intentionally disqualifies her work from the Black Aesthetic definition of good art.[3] In an interview with Mari Evans, Jones said:

> I think sometimes you just have to be "wrong"; there's a lot of imaginative territory that you have to be "wrong" in order to enter. I'm not sure one can be a creative writer and a politician—not a "good" politician.[4]

Jones went on to acknowledge that she had "an unfortunate public image" because she failed to write the didactic, "politically correct" literature required by the Black Aesthetic.[5] When *Corregidora* was first published, black reviewers castigated its "politically incorrect" presentation of "sexual warfare" in the black community.[6]

Corregidora is, however, more amenable to a Black Aesthetic reading than is Jones's second novel, *Eva's Man*. While Black Aesthetic critics reviled *Eva's Man* for its absolute negation of Black Aesthetic ideology, they attempted, however unsuccessfully, to recover *Corregidora* into the functional reading norms of the Black Aesthetic. To the Black Aesthetic reader looking for detachable ideological messages, the novel's representation of the Corregidora matriarchy, in particular, would seem to overlap at key points with the black nationalist discourse on matriarchy. An important element in this discourse is the contention (in the works of Grier and Cobbs, Billingsley, and others) that the contemporary black matriarchy is a legacy of slavery. In *Corregidora*, the matriarchy constituted by Ursa's great-grandmother, grandmother, and mother also has its origins in slavery. Scholars of the black family in the 1960s and early 1970s traced the black woman's supposed dominance back to the slave woman's privileged position in the slavemaster's house. In Jones's novel, Ursa's great-grandmother is one of the slaveowner Corregidora's favored slaves. He sells her male children but keeps her only girl child, thus perpetuating the Corregidora women's dependence on him. As a result of this dependence, Ursa's foremothers internalize the values of the white power structure as the male slaves presented in the novel do not. An example of this is the young slave boy who escapes from Corregidora's plantation to fulfill his dream of joining a renegade slave community in Palmares, at the very moment that Ursa's great-grandmother (Great Gram) is raped by Corregidora.

In fact, the matriarchy presented in the novel seems to feed directly into the Black Aesthetic discourse on the black mother/matriarch as an oppressive figure who keeps the black community bound to its slave heritage. According to Larry Neal, the antagonism toward the "strong Black mother" in the new literature derives from the fact that her "aspirations and values are closely tied to those of the white power structure and not to those of her man."[7] The mothers in the new black literature represent the "Old Spirituality" and must be denounced for their unquestioning acceptance of their oppressor's values.[8] The matriarchs in *Corregidora*, too, embody the force of past oppression, as their ideology remains locked within the framework of slavery. Significantly, it is a male character, Tadpole McCormick, who points out that the Corregidora women's procreative creed "could also be a slavebreeder's way of thinking."[9]

A final area of coincidence between the novel and nonfictional discourses on matriarchy is that both hold the matriarchy responsible for the "pathological" relationships between black men and women. The Corregidora women devalue black men except as a means of reproduction; Ursa's mother, as a result, has no use for her husband after he impregnates her. Even the relationship of Ursa and her husband, Mutt, is haunted and distorted by Ursa's obsession with her foremothers. In each case, the matriarchy obstructs the development of healthy relationships between black men and women; the women's primary allegiance is to the maintenance of the matriarchy rather than to marriage. As we saw in chapter 1, contemporary discourses on matriarchy exhorted black women to liberate themselves from the matriarchal family and to align themselves with black men. The same ideological message may be crudely extracted from *Corregidora*: the end of the novel affirms Ursa's freedom from her matriarchal past and her reconciliation with Mutt, thus satisfying the ideological requirements of the Black Aesthetic.[10]

The above Black Aesthetic analysis of *Corregidora* is, of course, problematic in several respects, not least in its recovery of the novel into the heterosexual parameters of Black Aesthetic ideology. Further, such a reading, based on the assumption that fiction reflects contemporary ideological discourses in unmediated ways, necessarily leads to a reductive functional analysis that precludes an understanding of the novel's complex transformation of these discourses. Several important elements of the novel's representation of the Corregidora matriarchy must be elided in order to support a functional reading, and these are precisely the elements that do not coincide with the contemporary ideological discourse on black matriarchy. For example, the Corregidora matriarchy is the novel's only evocation of a collectivity, a collectivity sustained by oral cultural transmission. The Corregidora women's experience of slavery is literally erased when the slaveowner burns all written records. The women resist their exclusion from official history by means of oral narrative: "We were suppose to pass it down like that from generation to generation so we'd never forget" (p. 9). The Corregidora women must produce generations who will carry their version of history into the future: "The important thing is making generations. They can burn the papers but they can't burn conscious, Ursa. And that's what makes the evidence" (p. 22). As a means of making generations, the womb becomes the site of these women's political resistance, and of their definition of themselves and their value. Clearly, for the Corregidora women to claim the power of their wombs is an important oppositional strategy, for it is precisely this power that Corregidora's peculiar sexual exploitation of them had denied. Their inversive ideology is apparent also in their oral narrative, which serves the function of keeping alive their hatred of their white oppressor. Keith Byerman has remarked on the allegorical, dualistic universe projected by the oral matriarchal text;[11] this didactic narrative characterizes Corregidora as an absolute, unmitigated villain.

The matriarchal Corregidora narrative is, therefore, a collective, didactic, oral text that serves an inversive political function. This set of semes[12] associated with the Corregidora matriarchy is remarkably evocative of Black Aesthetic discourse, which conceived art in exactly these terms. A careful consideration of the novel's representation of the matriarchy thus produces a contradictory ideological construct. On the one hand, we find a set of negative semes consonant with contemporary discourses on matriarchy as an oppressive force that keeps black women locked in the white power structure and prohibits a new articulation of black femininity. On the other, we find all the outstanding attributes of Black Aesthetic ideology displaced onto the matriarchy.

This configuration of inconsistent semes alerts us against reading characters in the novel as transparent reflections of social types such as the matriarch, and compels attention to the fictionality of character constructs. The disparate semic status of the Corregidora women may be more fully understood as a fictional displacement rather than a direct reflection of contemporary ideological discourse. Of the several semes of black nationalist discourse that are displaced onto the matriarchy, reproductive ideology is perhaps the most striking. As we have seen in chapter 1, black nationalist discourse defined the black woman in reproductive terms; her primary political function was to create babies for the revolution. In *Corregidora*, this reproductive ideology is displaced, not, as we might have expected, onto the slaveowner Corregidora. Such a displacement would have been authorized by historical fact, as slavemasters did assess black women's economic worth primarily by their breeding capacity.[13] Further, a displacement of 1960s reproductive ideology to the slave past would have conveyed the connection, made by several black feminists, between slaveowners' and black male nationalists' discourses on black women. *Corregidora*, however, resists scoring this easy ideological point and, in fact, deviates from most fictional accounts of slavery in presenting a slaveowner who forbids his slave women to breed, hence giving rise to their inversive reproductive ideology. One function served by this surprising displacement is that it renders controversial ideological material safely readable. Under the guise of exposing the oppressive matriarchal structure (an ideological intention sanctioned by black nationalist and aesthetic discourse), the novel is able to explore more freely the repressive implications of a reproductive definition of black women. Displacement here serves as a textual mechanism that both veils and enables the novel's elaboration of black feminine sexuality outside a reproductive frame.

Corregidora attempts to discover a clitoral feminine sexuality that exceeds the reproductive definition of black femininity in the discourses of both slavery and black nationalism. The novel begins with a hysterectomy that forces a thorough revaluation of feminine identity and sexuality. Ursa feels "as if something more than the womb had been taken out" (p. 6); she finds, in fact, that she has lost all her previous grounds for self-definition. Ursa's body excludes her from the Corregidora women's reproductive narrative of desire. At the beginning of the novel, we know that Ursa has to find a new story for herself that can account for her lack of a womb, and a new conception of feminine desire that is not centered around reproduction. Ursa's hysterectomy loosens her desire from the narrative frame that previously fixed it, and the plot of the rest of the novel is constituted by a series of attempts to articulate Ursa's desire in a new text.

The first choice Ursa makes after she leaves the hospital is marriage, with Tadpole McCormick. That Tadpole is a false choice is frequently signaled through Ursa's friend, Catherine, who points out that Ursa's relationship with Tadpole is motivated by fear (p. 26). Afraid that her hysterectomy has defeminized her, Ursa attempts to quell this fear by reaffirming her heterosexuality. But, in bed with Tadpole, Ursa realizes that she can no longer feel any sexual pleasure; she does, however, have a few moments with Tadpole when she begins to glimpse a new possibility: "I was struggling against him, trying to feel what I wasn't feeling. Then he reached down and fingered my clitoris, which made me feel more" (p. 75). Ursa's nascent awareness of clitoral pleasure offers her a possible space outside the reproductive system, but the potentiality of this "more" that Ursa feels is not developed at this point in the novel. She is unwilling to admit this new sexual awareness to Tadpole, quite rightly, as we later learn that for him any woman who is outside the reproductive system is no longer a woman. Ursa cannot articulate this desire even to herself: "What I felt didn't have words" (p. 75).

The unspeakable nature of a desire that is outside of the reproductive system is further explored in the middle section of the novel dealing with Ursa's lesbian friend, Cat Lawson. Lesbianism is a choice we expect to encounter in a plot that is impelled by the quest for a nonreproductive feminine sexuality. When Ursa first discovers that Cat is lesbian, she leaves Cat's apartment in disgust, and is unable to think or speak about the issue. In a later scene, Cat is obliged to explain and justify her lesbianism; Cat's husband's frequent sexual rejection of her and her sense of humiliation at her job are the factors that drive her to lesbianism. Lesbianism, as it is spoken of in the novel, is entirely an inversive reaction and seems to need an excuse in failed heterosexual relationships. For this reason, a critic like Keith Byerman can argue that lesbianism in this novel is "a form of narcissistic evasion . . . marked by absence and negation rather than by creative assertion. It is a space of not-men rather than of women."[14] Byerman's interpretation is fully supported by whatever little is said of lesbianism in the novel, but it fails to attend to the silences that mark all the scenes involving Cat. The only scene in which Ursa and Cat explicitly discuss lesbianism begins with the following lines: "She scarcely said anything before the ceremony, and then when we were driving back, she didn't say a word" (p. 62). In the next three pages, there are twelve statements informing us that either Cat or Ursa did not speak. Their conversation, which writes off lesbianism as an evasion of heterosexuality, is insistently punctuated by silences that draw attention to all that the novel does not say about lesbianism. The entire scene is narrated in terms of negatives that acknowledge, by the very force of their denial, the appeal of lesbianism as a possible plot choice for Ursa. Ursa's posture throughout the scene is of tense refusal: she refuses to look at Cat, she refuses to reassure Cat that she will not tell Tadpole, and she refuses to show that she understands Cat. The scene ends with Cat waiting for an embrace that Ursa refuses to give.

Cat does not directly enter the novel again but, in a later scene, when Ursa realizes that using Tadpole to compensate for her lack of a womb was a mistaken choice, she is surprised to find herself echoing Cat's words (p. 87). And when she finally leaves Tadpole, Ursa expresses her confusion about her sexuality in an internal monologue addressed to Cat, in which she finally admits what she would not say earlier, her fear that the failure of heterosexual relationships threatens to dissolve her very sense of herself: "Afraid only of what I'll become, because those times he didn't touch the clit, I couldn't feel anything" (p. 89). Significantly, Ursa is able to mention her clitoral pleasure only to Cat, albeit in an imagined conversation. Clitoral sexuality remains an undeveloped possibility outside the reproductive system, a possibility that the text does not entertain again after Ursa's internal monologue.

However, before Ursa's plot can be resolved, the novel disposes of Cat by means of a particularly brutal gesture. Toward the end of the novel, Ursa learns that Cat has lost all her hair in a factory accident. Cat's lesbian friend, Jeffy, who recounts the incident to Ursa, says: "That kind of thing makes you don't feel like a woman" (p. 177). As Ursa is about to regain her feminine identity with Mutt, Cat is placed in the position of not-woman that Ursa had occupied at the beginning of the novel. The resolution of Cat's plot seems to confirm the equation of nonreproductive sexuality and lack of femininity, but the very violence of the resolution unbalances this equation. There is something gratuitous about the plot's punishment of Cat, an unnecessary added emphasis[15] that signals the powerful appeal of what must be contained before the novel can find its heterosexual resolution.

Gloria Wade-Gayles has commented on the novel's uncertain treatment of lesbianism:

> Jones treats two lesbian characters with sensitivity but she steps back from developing them or making clear use of them in the novel. Our failure to get a handle on the novel that does justice to Jones's vision demonstrates the need for clearly defined and tested approaches to les-

bian criticism. With such approaches we might find that *Corregidora* belongs to the tradition of latent lesbian fiction.[16]

Our "failure to get a handle" on the novel's treatment of lesbianism obliquely directs us to the ideological context in which the novel was written. Gloria Joseph has described lesbianism in the black community as a "story with silences and denials as its most salient features."[17] Joseph explains black women's resistance to lesbianism as a result of its vehement denunciation in black nationalist discourses, which castigated lesbians as man-haters who had no role in a movement that needed men and women to work together against racism. According to another faulty argument, if all black women were to become lesbians, the race would dwindle from lack of reproduction.[18]

Because of the powerful cultural authority of black nationalist discourse in the 1960s and early 1970s, black women writers who included overt lesbian material in their fiction found it difficult to gain access to black publications. For example, when Alexis DeVeaux submitted stories with lesbian themes to black journals, she was questioned about the legitimacy of such themes in black literature, for lesbianism was widely perceived as a threat to "the whole concept of the Black family or the Black community or the Black male-female relationship."[19] These strictures against representing lesbianism as a positive alternative may suggest one possible reason for its ambivalent treatment in *Corregidora*. As the novel's critique of reproductive ideology had to be displaced, so the possibility of lesbianism must be contained to satisfy contemporary conditions of publication and readability.

Although *Corregidora* withdraws from a full exploration of lesbian and clitoral sexuality, it does, like *The Bluest Eye* and *Sula*, conduct a thorough critique of reproductive sexuality, a critique that hinges on the Corregidora women's obsession with "making generations" (p. 22). Bonnie Barthold argues that the Corregidora women's narrative mythically recovers the traditional African celebration of procreation as a means of ensuring temporal continuity. Making generations allows these women to counter the fragmentation of time that is caused by the degradation of childbirth during slavery and by the slaveowners' repudiation of history. Barthold reads the Corregidora women's narrative, authorized by the African celebration of reproduction, as a successful synthesis of myth and history.[20] The myth-making power of the Corregidora women's text is easily granted, but this mythical vision is precisely what keeps them trapped in the historical past of slavery. Like the Bottom community in *Sula*, the Corregidora women mythicize their oppressive history, and are thus unable to perceive it as history, or to envision a future untainted by the slavery creed.

The Corregidora women's mythical narrative constructs reproduction as a natural desire; this naturalization of reproduction is relentlessly questioned in the second and third chapters of the novel. Chapter 2 deals with Ursa's mother, in whom the desire to reproduce has been so deeply instilled that it appears to be instinctive rather than conscious: "It was like my whole body knew. Just knew what it wanted" (p. 114). Ursa's mother repeatedly asserts the bodily basis of reproductive desire in an unsuccessful effort to naturalize her ancestors' ideology of reproduction. As she herself admits to Ursa later in the scene: "I know it was something my body wanted. Naw. It just seem like I keep telling myself that, and it's got to be something else. It's always something else but it's easier if it's just that" (p. 116). Her suspicion that the desire for reproduction is not necessarily a natural desire based in the woman's body opens the way for an understanding of the psychological and social constitution of this desire.

The denaturalization of her ancestors' reproductive myth enables Ursa to perceive what this myth represses. Her mother's deepest and most inchoate desires cannot be expressed within this reproductive economy:

> Something she kept not to be given. As if she'd already given. There was things left, yes. It wasn't the kind of giving where there's nothing left. It's where what's left is something you keep with you, something you don't give. I mean, the first giving made what's left. (p. 102)

Ursa's mother's first giving of herself in childbirth, far from exhausting all that she has to give, instead creates a residue that cannot be given within the terms of the reproductive system. Ursa's visit to her mother is motivated primarily by her wish to recover this superfluous, excessive feminine desire that the Corregidora women's reproductive myth cannot contain.

The novel completes its demythicizing of reproductive ideology in chapter 3, which narrates Ursa's childhood memories of May Alice and the Melrose woman. May Alice is ruined when her boyfriend, Harold, impregnates and then abandons her, and the Melrose woman commits suicide because she suspects she is pregnant. Both women react to their pregnancies with guilt: the Melrose woman kills herself, and May Alice insists that Ursa apologize to Harold, "like it was her fault" (p. 141). Ursa's memories of these two women, when juxtaposed with her ancestors' pride in their reproductive capacity, betray the contradictory nature of her society's ideology of motherhood: at once a source of pride and of shame. Ursa's childhood memories also clarify the insistent channeling of a young girl's sexual desire toward reproduction; as Harold keeps repeating, "Let us in so we can give you a baby. Don't you want a baby?" (p. 138). In narrating her memories of the pain and confinement associated with motherhood, Ursa is finally able to accept her own loss of a womb, which she now sees as a source of oppression as well as of limited power.

The novel's conclusion, returning Ursa to her husband, attempts a nonreproductive but heterosexual adjustment of Ursa's desire. In the final scene of reconciliation, as Ursa performs fellatio on Mutt, she exercises a feminine power outside the reproductive system: "A moment of pleasure and excruciating pain at the same time, a moment of broken skin but not sexlessness, a moment that stops just before it breaks the skin: 'I could kill you'" (p. 184). The resolution of Ursa's plot, like Cat's, depends upon a latent violence that troubles, even as it establishes, the return to heterosexuality. The lesbian and clitoral possibilities that the novel's middle had made fleetingly available are partially but not entirely displaced by the heterosexual conclusion. The choice of fellatio rather than cunnilingus displaces the clitoral site of feminine sexuality in favor of the phallus. However, fellatio, as a sexual act that is superfluous to a reproductive exchange of energy, situates Ursa at the very margins of heterosexuality (at a moment that stops just short of "sexlessness"). This boundary is perhaps the only space where an exercise of feminine power is possible. For the woman fully enclosed within the heterosexual, reproductive system (May Alice, the Melrose woman), power is entirely inaccessible. And the woman who finds her pleasure outside this system (Cat) is divested of all power. Ursa's position, both inside and outside, invests her with a sexual power, which, in a heterosexual context, is necessarily a power of potential violence ("a moment that stops just before it breaks the skin"). The precarious nature of this heterosexual adjustment is italicized by a conspicuous lack of plot or psychological motivation. As Ursa decides to go back to Mutt, she admits that she has not forgiven him (p. 182) and that she still hates him (p. 183). She explains (or rather fails to explain) her reconciliation with Mutt in highly uncertain language: "I don't know what he saw in my eyes. His were different now. I can't explain how" (p. 183).

The very last lines of the novel present a dialogue between Mutt and Ursa that follows the repetition-with-variation structure of a blues stanza:

> He came and I swallowed. He leaned back, pulling me up by the shoulders.
> "I don't want a kind of woman that hurt you," he said.
> "Then you don't want me."
> "I don't want a kind of woman that hurt you."
> "Then you don't want me."
> "I don't want a kind of woman that hurt you."
> "Then you don't want me."
> He shook me till I fell against him crying. "I don't want a kind of man that'll hurt me neither," I said.
> He held me tight. (p. 185)

The tight formal symmetry of this passage conveys a deceptive sense of closure. The first and last lines, with their images of sexual containment, suggest that the mobile energy of the beginning of the novel has finally found its proper frame. The placing of the final line in a blues stanza usually carries a sense of culmination, completion, and release. Ursa's statement, "I don't want a kind of man that'll hurt me neither," seems to serve this structural function here, but it does not quite provide an adequate articulation of Ursa's desire. Even at the very end, Ursa can only say what she does not want in a heterosexual relationship ("I don't want a kind of man . . ."). Anything beyond this negative desire remains unspoken. The repetitive rhythms of Mutt and Ursa's blues stanza suggest a dialogic structure in which the opposing terms (man and woman) are equal. But the two terms are also mutually exclusive: Mutt does not want a woman who will hurt him, and Ursa is precisely that woman. Their exchange, then, dramatizes the incommensurability of their desires. On a thematic level, the novel's end does not mark a progression from the beginning; Ursa's and Mutt's desires are as incompatible at the end as they were at the beginning.

But the end of the novel does achieve a formal progression from the beginning, in that the impossibility of heterosexual desire is expressed in a different mode at the end. The blues structure of the final dialogue is so aesthetically gratifying because it constitutes a perfect formal medium for the novel's contradictory representation of heterosexuality. Several commentators on the blues have observed that heterosexual conflict is one of the major themes of blues music.[21] While Charles Keil considers the blues vision of heterosexual relations to be fundamentally masculine, *Corregidora* draws on a feminine tradition of the blues established by such singers as Bessie Smith, Billie Holiday, and Ma Rainey, who, as Michele Russell and Hazel Carby have argued, enabled black women to speak of themselves as sexual subjects.[22] The blues form in *Corregidora* balances the terms *man* and *woman* in a state of charged contradiction. The novel's refusal to resolve its heterosexual conflict exemplifies a distinguishing formal feature of the blues: as a "model of disequilibrium," the blues presents "conflict as a norm,"[23] as an ongoing process rather than a problem to be resolved.

The blues mode allows *Corregidora* to contain, not only the contradictory terms "man" and "woman," but also all the other thematic oppositions that structure the text, such as individual and community, and past and present. We have already seen how the novel's figuration of the Corregidora matriarchy combines past and present in a single character construct. The Corregidora matriarchy is a contradictory textual figure that includes elements of slavery that are to be discarded as well as elements of 1970s ideology that supposedly represent a new black consciousness. The contiguity of these opposed semes draws attention to the incoherent coexistence in the 1970s of the (past, regressive) discourse on black matriarchy with the (new, liberatory) discourse of black nationalism. While the characterization of the Corregidora women exposes the ideological contradictions of black nationalist discourse, the novel's blues form attempts a formal containment of these contradictions.

Jones said, in an interview, that *Corregidora* was her attempt "to make some kind of relationship between history and autobiography."[24] If, then, her project in this novel is to mediate between past and present, collective and individual experience, blues is certainly the form most appropriate to this project. Houston Baker characterizes the blues as a form situated at the boundary between dualities, a place of "productive transit" crisscrossed by contradictions: "place betwixt and between, the juncture is the way station of the blues."[25] The distinctive formal feature of the blues is its ability to contain several sets of oppositions, such as tears and laughter, limits and possibilities, immersion and transcendence, past and present, individual and community. The blues form of *Corregidora* promotes a non-binary structuring of these oppositional categories and liberates a black narrative voice that is at once old and new, oppressed and free, anonymous and singular—a blues voice that is unique in its ability to contain such contradictions in a state of creative tension.

Ralph Ellison describes the relation of the individual blues musician to the prior group tradition as a "delicate balance": "this tradition insisted that each artist achieve his creativity within its frame. He must learn the best of the past, and add to it his personal vision."[26] *Corregidora* is certainly structured on a dialogue, if not a "delicate balance," between the past and the present, between collective and individual experience. Ursa's first-person story is interpenetrated by the collective text of her maternal ancestors, which is typographically distinguished from Ursa's narrative by the use of italics. The cyclic, repetitive structure of the matriarchal narrative seems to impede the linear forward movement of the plot. As Ursa tries to recover from her hysterectomy and to create a new story of her sexual desire, the old story of the Corregidora women inexorably carries her back into the past. The vacillating forward and backward movements between the two stories give rise to an acute sense of temporal impasse.

A progressive, developmental plot model is most seriously undermined by the novel's use of the blues structural device of repetition with variation. Ursa's narration of her story, through verbal echoes, establishes the similarity between Corregidora's treatment of his slave women and Mutt's treatment of Ursa. Like Corregidora, Mutt teaches Ursa to use obscene language. Corregidora had called Great Gram "his little gold piece" and sent her out as a prostitute to make money for him. Likewise, in a repetitive variation, Mutt calls Ursa "his piece of shit" (p. 165) and threatens to put her up for sale. Even Ursa's reconciliation with Mutt at the end of the novel involves a recursion into her matriarchal past; Ursa finally discovers, in the act of fellatio, the mysterious source of Great Gram's sexual power over Corregidora. Is the configuration of Ursa's power at the end of the novel a development from her position at the beginning? The last two chapters remind us that the plot has indeed been moving forward in a linear direction, as twenty years have passed since the first chapter. But in the final scene, Ursa reenacts the past, does what Great Gram did to Corregidora.

Earlier in the novel, Ursa states that "everything said in the beginning must be said better than in the beginning" (p. 54). There seem, impossibly, to be two simultaneous beginnings here, one of which must follow the other in order to improve upon it, suggesting a circular structure of repetition with difference. The difference of the novel's blues structure from linear narrative models such as the bildungsroman may be better appreciated with reference to the "cut," a black musical device discussed in James Snead's essay, "Repetition as a Figure of Black Culture." Snead writes that in black oral forms, if there is a linear goal, "it is always deferred; it continually cuts back to the start, in the musical meaning of 'cut' as an abrupt, seemingly unmotivated break with a series already in progress, and a willed return to a prior series." Snead goes on to write that the cut, instead of covering over differences, simply accommodates them within the system.[27] The plot of *Corregidora* throughout exemplifies the workings of the cut: various linear forward drives of the plot, such as Ursa's relationship with Tad, are abruptly suspended as the novel cuts back to the prior narrative series concerning Ursa's female ancestors. In a narrative structured by the cut, it becomes irrelevant to ask the bildungsroman question of whether, at the end of the novel, Ursa succeeds in articulating a radically new identity that ruptures her ancestral heritage. The movement of her plot is, rather, a process of accumulation and variation on her foremothers' stories. Any notion of the present as a new and decisive break from the past (precisely the temporal model valorized by Black Aesthetic discourse) is simply incongruent with the novel's structure and temporal vision. The device of the cut achieves a sense of structural and temporal continuity, and allows a formal containment of the potentially discontinuous terms, past and present. This formal containment must be distinguished from the problem-solving impetus of classic linear plots; the blues structure of *Corregidora*, like the spiral structure of *Sula*, formally accommodates rather than erases the text's thematic contradiction between past and present.

The complex temporal vision facilitated by the blues form of *Corregidora* both reflects and reworks the contradictions in the contemporary nationalist discourse on the blues. The Black Aestheticians assigned the blues a rather paradoxical ideological status. For some black nationalist critics, like Amiri Baraka, the blues is the only black cultural form that is free of white ideology; it communicates, therefore, an authentic black voice that literary texts have been unable to achieve. Only in the blues mode did black artists maintain "their essential identities" as blacks;[28] the world projected in blues music is "the Blackest and potentially the strongest."[29] In an exactly opposite interpretation, Ron Karenga, another prominent Black Aesthetic advocate, describes the blues as the black cultural form most deeply mired in the past and, hence, an ineffective vehicle for black nationalist ideology:

> We say the blues are invalid, for they teach resignation, in a word, acceptance of reality—and we have come to change reality. . . . [The blues] are not functional because they do not commit us to the struggle of today and tomorrow, but keep us in the past.[30]

By Karenga's reasoning, the blues, which originated in the spirituals and work songs of slaves, is a mode of historical compromise that cannot serve the black nationalist's intent to express a new black consciousness untainted by the slave creed. This denial of black cultural history leads most Black Aestheticians to a theoretical impasse: if all past cultural forms are invalid, what is the source of the new unalloyed black voice, and what renders it distinctively black? Houston Baker writes that "what is genuinely new in contemporary works of Black American literature" is their use of folklore as the foundation of a uniquely black cultural tradition.[31] Nothing in Black Aesthetic theory reconciles these mutually exclusive formulations of Karenga on the one hand, and Baraka and Baker on the other. In the 1960s and early 1970s, the blues emits two exactly antithetical ideological messages: at once the resigned voice of the old Negro who must be destroyed, and the empowered voice of the new black nationalist.

This very ideological confusion enables *Corregidora*'s complex formal negotiation with the temporal vision of black nationalist discourse. In a difficult double move, Ursa's blues voice allows her to express a feminine sensibility that is at least partially free of the oppressed and repressive collective tradition represented by the Corregidora women's narrative. In appropriating the blues form, *Corregidora* satisfies the Black Aesthetic injunction that black writers should use oral forms to express a distinctly black consciousness. But we cannot ask the Black Aesthetic question of whether the novel liberates a new black voice because the very question of newness is obviated by the blues mode, which inevitably carries traces of the black cultural past. The novel's structure of incremental repetition refuses the possibility or even the desirability of linear rupture, and institutes instead a processual model of change that contains the terms past and present in a state of productive disequilibrium.

If, at the level of narrative structure, the blues form mediates the temporal contradiction of black nationalist discourse, the novel's thematic affirmation of a blues voice unsettles the black nationalist conception of subjectivity. The blues voice in *Corregidora* does not express the full, self-present, unified subject affirmed in black nationalist discourse. The very beginning of *Corregidora* refuses the notion of an immediately present black voice; Ursa's hysterectomy does away with the fullness of voice she previously possessed when she sang her blues songs to Mutt "out of [her] whole body" (p. 46). After the hysterectomy, when her body is marked by loss and absence, Ursa's blues voice, too, is ruptured and doubled; she can no longer sing her ancestral past with her earlier simplicity. Instead, she must now sing a song that can express both her sameness and difference from her ancestors: "I wanted a song that would touch me, touch my life and theirs. A Portuguese song, but not a Portuguese song. A new world song" (p. 59). This song should contain both past and future, collective and personal experience, should accommodate the deliberate duplicities of the phrase "new world song": is it the New World of America that the Portuguese slaveowners came to centuries ago, or is it a utopian new world in the future? The form that can best express this double vision is the blues, which is, as Ralph Ellison calls it, an "art of ambiguity."[32]

Ellison also underscores the suggestive as opposed to the declarative mode of the blues, which "imply far more than they state outright" and "make us constantly aware of the meanings which shimmer just beyond the limits of the lyrics."[33] This implicit power of the blues that seems to reside somewhere behind or beyond language, is put to uniquely feminine uses in *Corregidora*. Ursa's blues voice expresses the "more" of feminine identity that cannot be verbally communicated: "I was trying to explain it, in blues, without words, the explanation somewhere behind the words" (p. 66). The blues voice does not name but only intimates, through breath and rhythm and intonation, what slips through language: "Oh I don't mean in the words, I wouldn't have done that. I mean in the tune, in the whole way I drew out a song. In the way my breath moved" (p. 103). Ursa's double-voiced song cannot render her feminine identity immediately present in language, and is founded, in fact, on the absence of what the Corregidora women's narrative constructs as the prime marker of black femininity, the womb: "The center of a woman's being. Is it? No seeds. Is that what snaps away my music, a harp string broken, guitar string, string of my banjo belly. Strain in my voice" (p. 46).

This strain in the voice, this recognition of a split and an absence within the feminine subject, is what distinguish Ursa's blues from the Corregidora women's oral text, some of whose semes (oral, collective, functional) are evocative of the Black Aesthetic. The Corregidora narrative not only erases Ursa's difference from a collective femininity centered around reproduction, but also represses the fundamental ambivalence of feminine sexual desire. The Corregidora women express, at a manifest level, their absolute hatred of Corregidora, but this hatred masks the intensity of their deeply repressed, unconscious desire for him. Unlike the Corregidora women's story, Ursa's blues, accommodating as it does the contrary emotions of pleasure and pain, tenderness and violence, desire and hatred, constitutes an alternative narrative form that can represent the contradictory nature of black feminine sexuality. Challenging the univocal oral collectivity postulated by the Black Aesthetic, Ursa's blues voice signifies black feminine subjectivity as the "more" that exceeds the reproductive terms of the nationalist discourse on black women.

The blues mode of *Corregidora*, then, opens a radically innovative formal space for black women's fiction and, in fact, so powerfully transfigures the form of the novel that, paradoxically, *Corregidora*'s remarkable achievement *as a novel* often escapes critical appreciation. Most vernacular theories of black American fiction tend to collapse the novels into the oral tradition; Jones's own novels have often been described as blues songs or performances.[34] Jones's recent book *Liberating Voices: Oral Tradition in African American Literature* is a valuable contribution to the recent spate of vernacular theories of black fiction, for it rigorously attends to the stylistic transformations entailed in any literary appropriation of oral forms. In her discussion of the blues poetry of Langston Hughes, Jones argues against "mere duplications of folk forms," underlining instead the "imaginative intensity and complexity that a creative writer should have when making literary use of any folk . . . form." While pointing to the inadequacy of literary works that "laboriously adhere" to oral forms,[35] Jones does not acknowledge that such literary procedures are not merely undesirable but impossible. However fully a literary text may appropriate an oral form, it can never reproduce the conditions of production and reception that mark traditional oral forms and that generate a distinctive set of context-bound assumptions about the relation between performer and audience. To state the obvious, a novel, unlike an oral performance, is consumed by a single reader in silent privacy.[36] This difference has a crucial bearing on the manner in which novels address their hypothetical readers. In analyzing how a novel adapts and transmutes oral material, we might bear Robert Hemenway's questions in mind: "What performance aesthetics characterized the original folklore event? Do these aesthetics carry over into the literary artifact?"[37]

The performance context of the blues is characterized by a call-and-response interaction that establishes an immediate, participative relationship between solo performer and audience.[38] Keith Byerman has argued that a fictional text that relies on the blues mode opens up a call-and-response dialectic between author and audience.[39] The narrative discourse of *Corregidora* undoubtedly subverts a monological transmission of meaning from author to reader (as might be the case, for example, with the omniscient narrator of classic realist fiction[40]). Whatever narrative authority and control Ursa's story might possess is scattered by the continual incursion of other narrative addresses and contexts into her text.

However, although narrative meaning in *Corregidora* is greatly a matter of negotiation between narrator and characters, the novel does not establish a dialogic relationship between narrator and reader that might approximate the call-and-response pattern of black oral performances. *Corregidora* does not actively solicit the reader into the text as do other novels that attempt to recreate an oral communication context, such as Carlene Polite's *Sister X and the Victims of Foul Play*. In fact, in *Corregidora*, the reader's position is frequently usurped by characters whom the narrative directly addresses, without the use of quotation marks to demarcate these utterances as quoted speech. Examples of this abound especially in the first two chapters, in which the narrative voice is frequently addressed to a "you" who is either Mutt, Cat, Ursa's foremothers, even Tadpole, but never the reader.

The reader seems especially uncomfortably situated in those instances when Ursa's unconscious fantasies and memories disrupt her conscious narrative. In these passages, the reader voyeuristically consumes Ursa's fantasized dialogues with Mutt. Despite their dialogic construction, these conversations create a disquieting sense of silence and exclusion, as we know that Mutt's speaking and listening place is a locus of imaginary, impossible desire that cannot be occupied by either the character Mutt or the reader. The reader's position as an intruder in Ursa's deeply private fantasy spaces is, of course, characteristic of the fictional reception context and is incompatible with the situation of the listener in an oral call-and-response framework. This tension between the oral and fictional modes is dramatized in a dialogue between Gayl Jones and Claudia Tate. Jones said that in *Corregidora* she draws on black oral traditions of storytelling, which always emphasize the "importance of the hearer, even in the internal monologue where the storyteller becomes her own hearer." Tate responded that when she read the novel, she felt that she was "hearing a very private story, one not to be shared with everyone."[41] Tate's remark clarifies how, despite authorial intentions, the novel cannot exactly reproduce the communication context of oral forms.

That we are reading a novel rather than listening to a blues performance is most obviously apparent in the extremely opaque imagery used in the novel.[42] Again, this is particularly true of the expressionistic images of the dream sections, for example: "I am the daughter of the daughter of the daughter of Ursa of currents, steel wool and electric wire for hair" (p. 67). Ursa's dream images all obsessively mark her difference from the feminine collective—her lack of a womb: "Vinegar and water. Barbed wire where a womb should be. Curdled milk" (p. 76).

An exploration of Ursa's unconscious and of her ambivalent relationship with the oral collectivity can be best conducted within the genre of the blues novel, a mixed genre that subjects both the blues and the fictional modes to a process of mutual enhancement and modification. Fictional techniques of character delineation (such as the eavesdropping strategy so characteristic of the novel's access to psychological knowledge) help to develop the "self-assertive motives," the "subjective territory" peculiar to the blues.[43] The blues mode, in turn, revises the fictional category of the distinctive individual protagonist, inflecting the novelistic "I" with the intersubjective "we" of black oral forms.[44]

The fictional appropriation of oral materials thus dialogizes both forms, clarifying their limits and their capabilities.[45] Despite its strong oral accentuation, *Corregidora* does not securely locate the reader within a call-and-response framework, nor does it represent collectivity in unproblematic terms. However, the novel's psychological elaboration of Ursa's individuality is itself dialogized by the blues voice and structure of the text, which reinscribe collective history and tradition. This dynamic relationship between the oral and novelistic modes enables *Corregidora* to traverse temporal, subjective, and generic boundaries with remarkable ease and flexibility. In *Liberating Voices*, Gayl Jones remarks that "most African American oral forms tend to avoid simple dualities."[46] The blues form of *Corregidora* (like the spiral structure of *Sula*) reconfigures the categories of past and present, individual and community, innovation and tradition, oral and literary, into a complex narrative mode that transcends the simple dualities of Black Aesthetic discourse.

V

"DON'T YOU EXPLAIN ME"
THE UNREADABILITY OF *EVA'S MAN*

Unlike *Corregidora*, Gayl Jones's *Eva's Man* (1976) cannot be even partially recovered into the Black Aesthetic critical mode. Each of the novel's salient thematic and formal features, such as its treatment of castration and lesbianism, and its use of stereotypes, first-person narration, and black dialect, resists a Black Aesthetic reading. This defiance of the contemporary conditions of readability produces a visible sense of strain in the text. The most subversive moments of *Eva's Man* are shrouded in an incoherence that seriously jeopardizes the reader's interpretive function, and prevents us from distilling any clear meaning from the text. It seems almost as if the novel must disclaim its right to meaning altogether if it cannot posit the clear, didactic meaning required by the Black Aesthetic. *Eva's Man* renders itself unreadable, as it were, in order both to escape the functional reading codes of the Black Aesthetic and to obscure its own refusal of these codes.

Predictably, then, the contemporary critical reception of *Eva's Man* was almost unanimously unfavorable.[1] The rare favorable review commended the novel precisely for its divergence from Black Aesthetic literature. For example, Richard Stookey of *The Chicago Tribune Book Review* found *Eva's Man* "refreshing" because unlike Stookey's conception of the typical contemporary black novel, *Eva's Man* did not aim its anger and violence against racial oppression. Stookey went on to state that *Eva's Man* "goes about its business wholly without explicit reference to the dimension of racial oppression and in so doing elevates itself out of the supposed genre known as the 'black novel' and into the realm of universal art." Stookey's review dismisses racial oppression as a narrow, parochial concern, and explicitly states that the dynamics of sexual oppression constitute a literary theme of universal interest.[2] A reading such as Stookey's lends credence to the black nationalist argument that black feminist literature was actively promoted by the white literary establishment primarily because it deflected attention away from white racism to black sexism.[3] Loyle Hairston, a prominent

Black Aesthetic critic, wrote that *Eva's Man* was accepted by white reviewers because of its critique of black men rather than of white society. While Hairston defended *Corregidora* because it was "far from being a feminist tract," he castigated *Eva's Man* for being "a study in male hostility."[4] However, the contemporary critical furor over *Eva's Man* cannot be fully accounted for by the novel's feminist focus and its emphasis on sexual rather than racial oppression. As we have already seen, *Sula*, too, was denounced by Black Aesthetic critics as a feminist novel that diverted attention away from white racism toward black sexism. But the Black Aestheticians' disapproval of *Eva's Man* was pitched considerably higher than their critique of *Sula*. While Black Aesthetic critics debated the thematics and the sexual politics of *Sula*, *Eva's Man* seemed to represent such a powerful threat to black nationalist ideology that the very legitimacy of its publication was contested. Keith Mano, writing in *Esquire*, argued that *Eva's Man* lacks any artistic merit and if it had been written by a white or a black male novelist, "it would still be in manuscript."[5] Insinuating that *Eva's Man* was published only because Toni Morrison, as the editor at Random House, agreed to publish it, Mano deplored the fact that "more and more of late, publishing has become a transaction between women, for women."[6]

Toni Morrison was fully cognizant of the ideological implications of her decision to publish *Eva's Man*. Morrison described the novel as a "considered editorial risk" because "someone might say, 'Gee, all her [Jones's] novels are about women tearing up men.'"[7] Morrison's comment points to the one feature of *Eva's Man* that drew the most extreme negative reaction from contemporary critics—Eva's castration of Davis, which constitutes the climax of the novel. Unlike the other novels considered here, *Eva's Man* does not even attempt a resolution within the heterosexual parameters of Black Aesthetic ideology. The novel presents no black male character equivalent to Ajax in *Sula*, Mutt in *Corregidora*, Grange in *The Third Life of Grange Copeland*, or Truman in *Meridian*. While Mutt could be regarded as the liberator of a new black heterosexual femininity, the representation of black male characters in *Eva's Man* admits no possibility of a heterosexual compromise. Eva's castration of Davis and her consequent imprisonment appear to be the only logical conclusion to the novel, for each of Eva's heterosexual encounters results in violence and imprisonment. Eva's first heterosexual experience, with Freddy Smoot, initiates her into violence: after molesting her with a dirty popsicle stick (one of the many objects in the novel that stands in for the penis), Freddy presents Eva with a pocket knife. Eva threatens to use this pocket knife when Alfonso tries to molest her, and actually uses it when Moses Tripp takes her for a whore. Eva's stabbing of Moses Tripp leads to her first imprisonment in the novel, an imprisonment that is later replicated when her husband,

James Hunn, keeps her locked in his home, and when Davis confines her to his apartment.

Eva's literal, physical imprisonment parallels her psychological imprisonment in the male-created stereotypes of black women as whores and bitches. These stereotypes serve the double function of constructing black women as a powerful, dangerous force, and of justifying the black masculine attempt to contain this force. The stereotype of the black woman as a whore, for example, invests black women with an excessive, disorderly sexual energy, which then becomes the object of masculine regulation. Similarly, the bitch stereotype endows the black woman with destructive power and strength; the subjugation of black women by black men is then rationalized as an attempt to curb this destructive power. However, stereotypes in the novel do not enact a simple exchange of power originating in the oppressor and directed at a helpless victim. Stereotypes are not merely imposed upon black women by black men; black women characters in the novel often appropriate the stereotype because it offers them their only means of exercising power. For example, when Eva occupies the position of greatest power over Davis, as she kills and castrates him, she is actually submitting to the images through which Davis has perceived her. Soon after they meet, Davis misnames Eva Medina as Eve and Medusa, thus remaking her in the traditional conception of women as evil corrupters and destroyers of men. Eva seems to acquiesce to Davis's naming of her even at her moment of greatest resistance. Biting Davis's penis, she casts herself in the role that Davis assigned her, of Eve biting the apple: "I bit down hard. My teeth in an apple."[8] Immediately after the castration, Eva assumes Davis's second image of her: "I'm Medusa, I was thinking. Men look at me and get hard-ons. I turn their dicks to stone. I laughed" (p. 130). Eva's laugh is only one of the many details that complicate the novel's treatment of stereotypes: Eva is both laughing the powerful laugh of the Medusa and laughing at Davis's conception of her as Medusa.

The novel's presentation of the stereotype as the site of ambivalent exchanges of power is most clearly apparent in its treatment of the Queen Bee, the community's name for a woman who takes on a series of lovers, each of whom dies soon after his encounter with her. The image of the Queen Bee, created by the black women of the community, reveals these women's internalization of the conception of black women as whores and bitches. However, this image does not merely reflect the women's passive acceptance of masculine stereotypes; the Queen Bee stereotype is manipulated by the novel's black female characters to serve a number of different uses. Miss Billie and Eva's mother turn the type into a subject, humanize the Queen Bee by looking at her from the inside rather than the outside. Eva's mother feels that "she would be more scared to be the Queen Bee than to be any of the men" (p. 41) because the Queen Bee cannot love whom she wants. Miss Billie, receptive to this entirely new perception of the Queen Bee, admits that "she hadn't never looked at it that way, but it must be hard on the Queen Bee too" (p. 41). Eva's appropriation of the Queen Bee stereotype plays yet another variation on it. While the original Queen Bee commits suicide, helplessly accepting the guilt for her involuntary destructive power over men, Eva actively exercises this power when she murders Davis. Eva's assumption of the Queen Bee stereotype transforms it into a symbol of vengeance, but even this articulation does not finally fix the type's potential meaning. The Queen Bee type continues to transform itself, accruing new and even contradictory layers of meaning with each configuration. Toward the end of the novel, Eva's madness mobilizes the stereotype beyond recognition, as Eva becomes both the Queen Bee and the victim of the bee's sting (p. 151). Eva's insane play with the stereotype finally divests it even of the gender specificity that originally motivated the type; Eva imagines herself as a feminine flower stung by a masculine Queen Bee: "He stings me between my breasts, the bud between my legs. My flower" (p. 151).

The novel's treatment of the Queen Bee and of other sexual stereotypes is markedly at odds with the theorization of the stereotype in Black Aesthetic and early black feminist criticism, both of which construed the stereotype as a false image imposed on the oppressed by the oppressor, and enjoined black writers to counter the stereotype with the authentic, actual experience of black men and women. The black writer should thus invoke the authority of realism to challenge and correct the falsity of the stereotype. In his diatribe against *Sula*, *Corregidora*, and *Eva's Man*, Addison Gayle urges readers to censure these novels' distorted, stereotypical presentation of blacks and to demand, instead, more "realistic paradigms" of black experience.[9] In a black feminist reading that only superficially differs from Gayle's, Gloria Wade-Gayles justifies *Eva's Man* on the grounds of its realism: "Jones's fictive world mirrors the real world Ladner and other sociologists have studied."[10] In their common appeal to realism, both Addison Gayle and Gloria Wade-Gayles overlook the complex status of "reality" in *Eva's Man*. The novel not only eschews the authority of narrative realism; it also thematically poses the question of the "real" in terms entirely incommensurate with Gayle's and Wade-Gayles's opposition of stereotype and reality.

Eva's Man provides no authentic black femininity against which we might measure the truth or falsity of a particular stereotype. Characters in the novel are entirely constructed by the distorted perceptions of others; the novel presents no original, essential selfhood that escapes this stereotypical structuring. Eva's character, for example, is first introduced to us through the words and images of others: the newspaper portrays Eva as a "wild woman" (p. 3), and the general public perceives her as a whore (p. 4). Nowhere in the novel are these images revised or superseded, as Eva never articulates her sense of difference from these stereotypical constructions. We are given no reason to believe that she possesses a hidden, integral self that resists or precedes the stereotype; on the contrary, Eva consistently validates the stereotypical expectations of male characters in the novel. To give one example, Moses Tripp tells Eva, "One of these days you going to meet a man, and go somewhere and sleep with him. I know a woman like you" (p. 166). Eva's encounter with Davis, to all appearances, confirms Tripp's perception of her as a whore. Even while the novel militates against the stereotypical perception of black women as whores and bitches, it does not offer any alternative, authentic definition of black femininity that exceeds these stereotypes.

The novel's exclusive reliance on stereotypical characterization refuses the realist model of character as the reflection of a knowable real subject. Not only the characters in the novel, but the novel itself relentlessly constructs identity in stereotypical terms.[11] Characterization in *Eva's Man* is a random yoking of names and attributes. Especially in the second half of the novel, traits are so arbitrarily shuffled from one name to another that the difference between names ceases to signify, and the realist notion of character—as a distinctive collection of physical and psychological traits—loses all functional value. The displacement of character traits along a chain of different names is so pervasive that it is difficult to isolate particular examples; character fragments double and triple each other in a hollow mirroring that complicates any conception of the subject as a coherent, unified entity. Eva and Elvira, Charlotte and Joanne double each other. In an imagined scene with Mr. Logan, Eva substitutes herself for Miss Billie, James Hunn substitutes for Freddy Smoot, for Eva's father, and for Davis. The prison psychiatrist (who shares Freddy Smoot's last name and reminds Eva of Tyrone) tries to fix the process of character substitution around the name of Davis, suggesting that he represents all the men who had ever abused Eva. Eva's response to the psychiatrist's suggestion— "Who?" (p. 81)—indicates that the chain of substitutions lacks any end or origin; characters ceaselessly displace and replace each other in a process of empty reflection that denies any access to the real nature of identity. Far from the authentic, self-present subject of black nationalist discourse, the novel's use of stereotypes figures the black subject as fragmented, absent,[12] and lacking any ground in reality.

The novel's failure to posit an authentic black subject is not, however, its most serious point of difference from contemporary black articulations of the stereotype. While Black Aesthetic and feminist critics invoked the authority of realism, their equally strong emphasis on positive images exposed the limits of this realism. According to these theorists, the black writer must not only contest stereotypes with the

truth; more importantly, the black writer must replace negative stereotypes with positive images.[13] The contradiction between realism and
positive images apparently went unnoticed; in the same essay, Addison
Gayle advised black writers to present "realistic paradigms" and to
"create images, symbols and metaphors of positive import from the
black experience."[14] Some of the most critical contemporary reviews of
Eva's Man focused on the novel's failure to present positive, politically
functional images of blacks. June Jordan, for example, begins her review of the novel with the familiar opposition of stereotype and reality,
describing *Eva's Man* as a book of "sinister misinformation" that fails
to revise the existing stereotypes of black women.[15] Further in Jordan's
review, however, it becomes clear that the real problem with *Eva's Man*
is not that it perpetuates stereotypes, but that these stereotypes are
negative and do not serve a clear moral or political function:

> I fear for the meaning of this novel. What does it mean when a young
> Black woman sits down to compose a universe of Black people limited
> to animal dynamics? And what will such testimony, such perverse am-
> bivalence contribute to the understanding of young girls in need of res-
> cue and protection?[16]

Jordan's comments identify the two features of the novel's use of negative stereotypes that cannot be reconciled with Black Aesthetic or early
black feminist theory: the novel's presentation of blacks through time-
worn sexual stereotypes ("people limited to animal dynamics"), and its
refusal to offer a clear, didactic judgment of these stereotypes ("perverse ambivalence").

Eva's Man provides more than enough support for the first of Jordan's
objections, in its narrow presentation of blacks as entirely sexual creatures. All of the novel's characters are driven by a sexual appetite that
seems absolutely beyond the control of reason. Eva learns to view herself and other blacks as sexual animals through the education she re-
ceives from Miss Billie and her mother. Miss Billie repeatedly uses
animal imagery to describe black males: Freddy Smoot is a "banny
rooster" (p. 14) and the other black boys in the neighborhood are "a
bunch of wild horses" (p. 20). Miss Billie's repetition of the words, "Once
you open your legs, . . . it seem like you caint close them" (p. 15), impresses upon Eva her society's perception of black feminine sexuality
as an uncontrollable natural urge. The rest of the novel sustains this
association of sexual, natural, and animal by means of frequent metaphorical overlaps between food, sex, and defecation. When Eva rejects
Elvira's sexual propositioning, Elvira describes Eva as "sitting right on
a pot, but afraid to shit" (p. 40). Mustard reminds Davis of "baby's turd"
(p. 8) and vinegar and egg of feminine sexuality. As the man with no
thumb refers to Eva as "sweetmeat" (p. 68), Eva's gaze persistently
returns to the plate of pigfeet in front of him. Alfonso mocks Eva's

virginity, repeating, "Most girls your age had the meat *and* the gravy" (p. 57). After sex with Davis, Eva feels "like an egg sucked hollow and then filled with raw oysters" (p. 66). The metaphorical identification of food and sex culminates in Eva's castration of Davis: "I raised blood, slime from cabbage, blood sausage" (p. 128).

Confining its characters to this restricted orbit of food, sex, and defecation, *Eva's Man* seems to support the age-old racist stereotype of blacks as primitive and animalistic. The novel's apparent adherence to this stereotype drew the most extreme negative reactions from Black Aesthetic critics. In his caustic review of *Eva's Man*, Addison Gayle wrote that the novel remains trapped in negative myths "borrowed from a racist society." According to Gayle, *Eva's Man* envisions blacks as "a primitive people defined totally in terms of our sexuality; . . . ours is the world of instinctual gratification—where sex, not power, not humanity, reigns supreme."[17] Gayle's comment is accurate in the sense that *Eva's Man* does not overtly or thematically reject the primitive black stereotype.[18] On a formal level, however, the novel's tight enclosure of the reader as well as the characters within the sexual stereotype implicitly conveys the limitations of this stereotype. The novel's obsessive emphasis on the natural, instinctual functions paradoxically achieves the effect of denaturalizing these functions. *Eva's Man* repeats and recycles a limited number of sexual stereotypes in a stylized manner that forces us to regard black sexuality as a textual fabrication rather than a natural essence. The problem with *Eva's Man*, then, is not that it fails to critique the stereotype of the primitive black, but that this critique is not explicit enough to meet the Black Aesthetic demand for a clear, didactic literature. Gayl Jones herself was aware that her ambivalent use of stereotypes could not be reconciled with the contemporary concern with "positive race images."[19] The "perverse ambivalence" of *Eva's Man* derives from its reluctance to pass unequivocal thematic judgments on the racist and sexist stereotypes of the past, and its failure to offer a new set of positive and politically useful images of blacks.

The question of negative stereotypes versus positive images of blacks intersects with another important area of Black Aesthetic theory: its opposition of the oppressive past and the free future. Black Aestheticians optimistically relegated negative stereotypes of blacks to the historical past; Larry Neal, for example, declared that "there are no stereotypes any more. History has killed Uncle Tom."[20] Only through a repression of the oppressive historical past could Black Aesthetic writers liberate a new, revolutionary consciousness. The temporal vision of *Eva's Man* fails to respect this dichotomy between old and new, past and present. Toward the beginning of the novel, Eva states that "the past is still as hard on me as the present" (p. 5). The novel's structure insistently enacts the repetition of the past in the present. The entire narrative is a desperate act of memory: Eva obsessively remembers her past in an unsuccessful attempt to order and transcend it. Eva's conception of time as a repetitive sameness erases any difference between the past, present, and future. This sameness, however, does not constitute a vision of temporal continuity. The fragmented structure of the novel presents time as a series of shattered moments linked to each other by sheer, random repetition.

Of all the novels considered here, *Eva's Man* most radically disrupts the bildungsroman structuring of time as a medium of change, progress, and development. It is possible to detect a submerged linear strand in the first part of the novel, which presents Eva's life in a roughly chronological fashion. In chapter 1, the eight-year-old Eva has her first sexual encounter with Freddy Smoot. Chapter 2, the only chapter in the novel that preserves a clear linear focus, deals with the twelve-year-old Eva's perception of her mother, father, and Tyrone. Subsequent chapters present the key incidents in Eva's life, from her stabbing of Moses Tripp to her marriage with James Hunn. Part 1 ends with Eva's desertion of James Hunn and her decision to work at P. Lorillard Tobacco Company. The next three sections of the novel abandon linear chronology altogether; Eva's earliest memories of Freddy Smoot and her encounters with Elvira and the psychiatrist in the narrative present merge into the same meaningless cycle.

The cyclic structure of *Eva's Man* offers no possibility of redemption, unlike the spiral structure of *Sula* or the blues form of *Corregidora*. The structure of *Eva's Man* is more akin to the tightly closed circles that structure *The Bluest Eye*. In both novels, circular repetition creates a sense of suffocation for the reader; the thematic entrapment of the protagonists of the two novels is replicated by the reader's imprisonment in the novels' repetitive structures.[21] The circular repetition of both novels installs a deterministic vision of time and history that allows no possibility of change or transformation.[22] *Eva's Man*, even more so than *The Bluest Eye*, bears out Roger Rosenblatt's thesis that circular form in black American fiction frequently figures history as an overdetermined, inescapable destiny.[23] This despairing vision of history is, of course, exactly opposed to the black nationalist belief in new beginnings, in a revolutionary future that can obliterate the oppressive past.

Eva does seek an escape from her own oppressive past, but her search for temporal redemption does not direct her toward the future-oriented goal of black nationalist discourse. Eva's attempt to counter her sense of the fragmentation of time involves a recursion into her ancestral past. Contrary to the nationalist affirmation of temporal discontinuity, *Eva's Man* implies that only a recovery of ancestral continuity can redeem the senseless temporal cycle that imprisons Eva. Early in the novel, Miss Billie gives Eva one of her "ancestors bracelets," and impresses upon Eva the importance of being "true to one's ancestors. She said there were two people you had to be true to—those people who came before you and those people who came after you" (p. 22). Eva's alienation from the ancestral cycle is signaled by her loss of Miss Billie's bracelet when she is eight years old. The bracelet seems to symbolize a temporal continuity dependent upon reproduction: Miss Billie with-holds the bracelet from her daughter, Charlotte, until she decides to get married and have children. Charlotte and Eva—like Joanne Riley, who doubles Charlotte and Eva in several ways—refuse to have any children; this refusal does not seem to be liberating, as it is for Sula or Ursa. For Eva, at least, a liberation from the temporal cycle seems possible only through a recovery of generational continuity.

The redemptive possibilities of Eva's lost ancestral past are embodied in the gypsy Medina, after whom Eva and her great-grandmother are named. Medina's character is rich with inchoate possibilities that Eva (or the novel) fails to realize. Medina intersects only obliquely with Eva's ancestral past: she is a white gypsy whose incoherent promise is filtered to Eva though the memories of her great-grandmother. Me-dina's race is crucial to her function in the novel; as a white woman, she cannot represent a pure racial or ancestral origin for Eva. Moreover, Medina speaks deprecatingly of peckerwoods, seemingly unaware that she herself falls into this stereotypical category. When Eva's great-grandfather tries to reduce Medina to the stereotype, Eva's great-grand-mother points out that Medina is not a peckerwood simply because she does not see herself as one. Medina's perception of herself provides Eva's sole glimpse of a psychological freedom that escapes the constric-tion of racial stereotyping.

Medina offers a possible release not only from Eva's imprisonment in stereotypes, but also from her imprisonment in time and in hetero-sexuality:

> The gypsy Medina, Great-Grandmama said, had time in the palm of her hand. She told Great-Grandfather, "She told me to look in the palm of her hand and she had time in it."
>
> Great-Grandfather said, "What did she want you to do, put a little piece of silver over top of the time."
>
> Great-Grandmother said, "No." Then she looked embarrassed. Then she said, "She wanted me to kiss her inside her hand."
>
> Great-Grandfather started laughing. (p. 48)

The image of Medina holding time in the palm of her hand exemplifies her control over time, as opposed to Eva's helpless entrapment in it. Meditating on her own sense of time as an inevitable, uncontrollable force that denies human choice, Eva repeatedly recalls Medina, and asks, "Do you think there are some things we can't help from letting happen?" (p. 49). Eva tries to recover Medina's secret power over time by kissing the palm of Davis's hand, but Eva's heterosexual variation on Medina's latently lesbian gesture robs it of all meaning. In the passage quoted above, Eva's great-grandmother's embarrassment at mentioning the kiss to her husband suggests its unspoken erotic implications. Eva's great-grandfather's laughter and his cynical interpretation of Medina as a typical gypsy who wants nothing but money, imply that Medina's mysterious promise is not accessible to men. That Medina represents a distinctly feminine possibility is confirmed in the scene when Eva tells Davis about Medina, and he, like Eva's great-grandfather, "laughed hard" and "said he didn't know what I meant" (p. 49).

Throughout the novel, Eva tries to affirm her continuity with her namesake. When Davis misnames her Medusa, Eva fiercely defends her ancestral name. Wandering from town to town, Eva attempts to recover the mobility of the gypsy, and repeatedly draws attention to her own wild hair, reminiscent of the thick hair of Medina. However, Eva's continuity with Medina does not go beyond the external details of name, appearance, and physical mobility. Eva holds only sweat in the palms of her hands, failing to recapture Medina's grasp of time. The redemptive possibility suggested by Medina becomes increasingly obscure and inaccessible as the novel progresses: "I licked the palms of my hands. I bit shadows" (p. 157). Soon after Eva kills and castrates Davis, she imagines Medina telling her to "toss his blood into the wind and it will dry" (p. 138). Medina's advice does not help to absolve Eva's sense of guilt, as is clear from the blood imagery that pervades the last two sections of the novel.

The very end of the novel, however, seems to suggest that Eva has succeeded in realizing some of the possibilities figured by Medina: Eva's acceptance of Elvira as a lover implies that Eva has escaped the heterosexual pattern of violence and imprisonment. The novel's conclusion also suggests that with Elvira, Eva has finally liberated herself from the past, as this is the only time in the novel that Eva is able to live in and affirm the present moment:

> "Tell me when it feels sweet, Eva. Tell me when it feels sweet, honey."
> I leaned back, squeezing her face between my legs, and told her, "*Now*."
> (p. 177, emphasis mine)

It is questionable, however, whether Elvira actually represents a viable alternative to Eva's earlier imprisonment in heterosexual relationships. For one thing, the very physical setting of their relationship, a prison cell, detracts from its liberatory possibilities. Darryl Pinckney argues that the lesbian encounter of Eva and Elvira is "not prison rape, the articulation of power. It is an indication of emotional requirements still unsatisfied."[24] Eva's acceptance of Elvira, however, seems to be motivated not by emotional but by purely sexual requirements. An earlier conversation between the two women, in which Elvira complains that female prisoners are not allowed male "sex visits" (p. 149), suggests that Eva and Elvira come together only because heterosexual relationships are not permitted in prison.

Further, Elvira pursues Eva as aggressively as do the men in the novel, and her propositioning of Eva is couched in the language of heterosexual seduction. Frequently, it is impossible to distinguish between Elvira's words and the words of Eva's male lovers. For example, Elvira's "You hard, why you have to be so hard?" (p. 158) recalls Davis's "You a hard woman, too, ain't you?" (p. 8). In some passages in the novel, Elvira's words exactly echo the words of male characters who probe or violate the privacy of women:

> "How did it feel?" Elvira asked.
> "How did you feel?" the psychiatrist asked.
> "How did it feel?" Elvira asked.
> "How do it feel, Mizz Canada?" the man asked my mama. (p. 77)

This passage, along with many others, reduces Elvira's lesbian difference to the repetitive sameness of all the heterosexual encounters in the novel. It is not the radical difference of lesbianism from heterosexuality, but a mere fact of circumstance (the unavailability of men in prison) that leads Eva to Elvira.

However, if the lesbian encounter of Eva and Elvira is no different from Eva's heterosexual encounters, why is it made to carry the burden of resolving the novel's heterosexual conflicts? The very placing of the Eva-Elvira scene, at the end of the novel, invites us to read it with the special emphasis that fictional conclusions conventionally require. Simply through its placing at the end of the plot, lesbianism is invested with a significance that the novel otherwise refuses to develop. This ambivalent treatment of lesbianism is also evident in other details, such as the brevity of the scene, as well as its absolute lack of preparation. Immediately before Eva succumbs to Elvira, the narrative directly addresses Davis: "Last night she got in the bed with me, Davis. I knocked her out, but I don't know how long I'm going to keep knocking her out" (p. 176). This is, significantly, the only instance in the novel where Eva's narrative directly addresses another character; this address achieves the effect of reasserting Eva's heterosexual desire for Davis and diminishing the value of her lesbian encounter with Elvira. Eva's address to Davis further strips the lesbian scene of all significance by suggesting that Eva is motivated by the sheer tedium of resisting Elvira's persistent advances.

The novel's incoherent treatment of lesbianism is not surprising, given the contemporary hostility to positive portrayals of lesbian characters in black fiction.[25] As we have already seen in the chapters on *Sula* and *Corregidora*, the ambivalent presentation of lesbianism in black women's fiction of the 1970s marks these novels' adjustment to the heterosexual emphasis of black nationalist discourse. *Eva's Man* goes further than *Sula* or *Corregidora* in pushing the resolution of its protagonist's plot outside a heterosexual frame. This uncompromising refusal of heterosexuality logically leads to a consideration of lesbianism as a probable point of resolution. *Eva's Man* does admit the full implications of its critique of heterosexuality, presenting lesbianism as the only remaining plot choice for its protagonist. Having gone so far, however, the novel withdraws meaning from its own conclusion, as if in a belated effort to appease its contemporary reading public. The necessity of this self-protective gesture becomes evident through even a superficial glance at contemporary reviews of *Eva's Man*; the judgment expressed in *Publishers Weekly*, that Eva "descends into the ultimate corruption in prison,"[26] is typical of the contemporary response to the novel's lesbian conclusion.

The novel's treatment of castration is even more fraught with ambivalence than its treatment of lesbianism. Lesbianism and castration are the two thematic elements of *Eva's Man* that pose the most serious threat to the heterosexual assumptions of Black Aesthetic ideology; hence, the severely strained treatment of these two elements. Like lesbianism, castration occupies a highly privileged place in the novel's plot: as the climax, the castration inevitably bears a heavy interpretive weight. The castration scene is marked by the sudden appearance of italics, and by a symbolic and metaphorical overload that further encourages the reader to attach extra emphasis to the scene. The very language of the narration thickens as Eva remembers her castration of Davis. Almost as if to compensate for the castration, Eva offers a series of metaphorical substitutes for the penis, such as sausage, apple, plum, and milkweed. In later chapters, this metaphorical substitution extends to include owl, eel, cock, and lemon. The strain in the novel's presentation of the castration is apparent in that the scene seems unable to bear the burden of meaning that it is made to carry. For example, Eva's comparison of the castration to Eve's biting the apple opens up a possibly rich symbolic field. However, the immediately following comparison of the penis to another fruit, the plum, denies the symbolic potential of the apple by returning us to a literal level of meaning, where the apple is merely a fruit.

This simultaneous arousal and withdrawal of meaning exemplifies the difficult interpretive access that the castration scene provides the reader. In this scene, Eva directly addresses the reader for the first and only time in the novel: "What would you do if you bit down and your teeth raised blood from an apple? Flesh from an apple? What would you do? Flesh and blood from an apple? What would you do with the apple? How would you feel?" (p. 128). While this direct address appears to solicit the reader's active participation in the scene, Eva's questions actually deflect the reader's interpretive activity. Instead of answering the reader's question, "How did it feel?"—a question obsessively posed to Eva by the other characters in the novel—Eva simply throws this question back at the reader. She further complicates the reader's function in this scene by suggesting that she killed and castrated Davis because he did not tell her about his wife (p. 129). The reader cannot, however, accept the explanation Eva offers here, for we have been told earlier that "there were also people saying I did it because I found out about his wife. That's what they tried to say at the trial because that was the easiest answer they could get" (p. 4). Pushing us toward an interpretation that has been discredited earlier, the novel makes it impossible for us to answer the question, "How did it feel?"—the question that, in a sense, motivates the entire narrative. Michael Cooke has described *Eva's Man* as "a curt, elided whydunit."[27] The novel offers several possible reasons for Eva's castration of Davis: his silence about his wife, his physical imprisonment of Eva, his refusal to commit himself to her, his stereotypical perception of her as a whore. All these answers are true to a certain extent, but they do not seem to answer adequately the question of Eva's motivation. The novel anticipates all the explanations the reader is likely to entertain and robs them of validity by showing that they were imposed upon Eva at the trial, by the psychiatrist and by a curious, sensation-seeking press and public. Eva herself remains conspicuously silent about her motive, refusing to provide an authoritative interpretation of the castration.

The castration, then, seems to mean everything and nothing; the novel surrounds its climactic incident with an obscurity and density that discourage the reader from extracting any clear meanings or ideological messages from the incident. This incoherence, like the incoherent treatment of lesbianism, partially obscures the novel's uncompromising refusal to cater to the heterosexual expectations of its contemporary reading public. Again, a mere glance at the contemporary critical response to *Eva's Man* allows us to understand the novel's contradictory treatment of the castration as a necessary defensive gesture. Black Aesthetic criticism of *Eva's Man* rises to a shrill and almost paranoid pitch when it confronts the novel's presentation of castration. In Addison Gayle's review of the novel, for example, literary and even political judgments give way to sheer personal vilification of the author. According to Gayle, it is Jones and not Eva who seeks "a personal release from pain, a private catharsis, which could be achieved only when the Black man had been rendered impotent."[28] In a discussion with Roseann Bell, Gayle goes even further: "If Gayl Jones believes that Black men are what she says they are, she ought to get a white man."[29]

Perhaps it was precisely in order to protect herself from such criticism that Gayl Jones repeatedly tried to curtail the scope of the novel's meaning. Jones said, in an interview: "I'm sure people will ask me if that's the way I see the essential relationship between men and women. But that man and woman don't stand for men and women—they stand for themselves, really."[30] Jones partly succeeded in her attempt to restrict the meaning of *Eva's Man* to a particular story of a particular man and woman. Several critics, such as Margo Jefferson and Larry McMurtry, have read the novel as a narrow, concentrated exploration of a single life that is not representative of the lives of black men and women in general.[31] Jones also tried to delimit the political significance of *Eva's Man* by emphasizing the difference between the author and the narrator, and directly linking this difference to the absence of political messages in her work:

> There are moments in my literature, as in any literature, that have aesthetic, social, and political implications but I don't think that I can be a "responsible" writer in the sense that those things are meant because I'm too interested in contradictory character and ambivalent character and I like to explore them without judgements entering the work—without a point of view entering.[32]

The use of first-person narration in *Eva's Man* works to distance the author from the risky ideological implications of the novel. The complete absence of authorial intervention closes us within Eva's mind, and compels us to read the novel as an effect of a particular character's restricted vision.[33] The first-person narration of *Eva's Man* thus helps to contain the novel's controversial thematic material.

This containment is facilitated by the unreliability of the novel's first-person narrator. It is impossible to assign any truth value to Eva's narration because, as the psychiatrist tells her at the beginning of the novel, she does not know how "to separate the imagined memories from the real ones" (p. 10). Eva insistently tries to convince us of the truth of her narrative at precisely those moments when the reader most seriously doubts her: "Naw, I'm not lying. He [James] said, 'Act like a whore, I'll fuck you like a whore.' *Naw, I'm not lying*" (p. 163). We know, however, that Eva is lying, for she attributes to James the exact words that her father spoke to her mother. The very exactness of the repetition, here and elsewhere, robs Eva's narrative of the authority of realism.[34] Eva's unreliability permeates every detail of the novel, including her castration of Davis. The police report and the prison psychiatrist inform Eva that she did not bite off Davis's penis, as she believes; the very truth of the novel's central incident is thus thrown into doubt.

The unreliability of Eva's narration is, of course, a result of her madness. Eva's madness functions as a kind of safety valve, allowing readers to dismiss the more uncomfortable moments of the novel as the distorted fabrications of an insane mind. The use of a mad narrator serves to distance not only the reader, but also the author, from the ideological implications of the work. Keith Byerman, in fact, discounts a reading of *Eva's Man* as a feminist novel precisely on the grounds of Eva's madness, emphasizing that "the ideology, the madness are Eva's, not Gayl Jones'."[35] The peculiar ideological function performed by madness in *Eva's Man* may be better appreciated by means of a comparison with *The Bluest Eye*. Pecola's madness serves as an instrument of social satire, strengthening the novel's powerful critique of the violence, racism, and sexism of American society. The novel's relentless tracing of the causality of Pecola's madness gives this madness a social dimension, and constructs Pecola as a helpless victim of her society. That Pecola's madness is narrated by Claudia and the omniscient narrator allows the reader to place her madness in some kind of relation to a sane, "real" world. *Eva's Man* provides the reader no directions, no clues to a correct reading of Eva's madness. The novel's kaleidoscopic jumbling of time (itself an effect of Eva's madness) makes it impossible to establish a causality, an origin for Eva's madness. We have no means of judging whether the repetition of events in Eva's life caused her insanity or whether Eva's insanity is the source of the repetition of events in her narrative. All we have is Eva's madness, unmediated by a sane narrator; we are given no relatively real fictional world that might help us place Eva's madness in perspective. This unmooring of Eva's madness from any "real" narrative context greatly complicates the reader's interpretive function. We cannot identify with Eva, or take away any clear meaning from her madness. Eva's madness contributes, as it were, to the impression of self-containment conveyed by *Eva's Man*. Eva's unfiltered, insane, first-person narration serves to lock meaning inside the text, and to diminish the text's power to illuminate the reader's world.

Our sense of the self-containment of the text is intensified by the narrator's vehement denial of the very acts of reading and interpretation. The novel presents a supposedly qualified reader of Eva's madness in the prison psychiatrist, who anticipates most of the reader's possible explanations for Eva's madness. At the end, Eva effectively stalls the psychiatrist's and the reader's interpretive activity: "Don't explain me. Don't you explain me. Don't you explain me" (p. 173). It is difficult to disregard Eva's plea, considering that all the reader surrogates in the novel (the lawyers, the police, the journalists, and the general public) assault Eva's integrity with their sexist, stereotypical readings. Eva tells the psychiatrist, "Don't look at me. Don't make people look at me" (p. 168). Throughout the novel, Eva is defined by male characters looking at her and interpreting her. In her attempt to explain to the prison psychiatrist why she killed Davis, Eva keeps repeating, "The way he was looking at me . . . , the way he was looking at me. . . . Every man could look at me the way he was looking. They all would" (p. 171). The acts of looking and interpretation are invariably acts of masculine power in *Eva's Man*; the novel offers no possibility of a looking, a reading that can respect the integrity of the feminine object. Any kind of interpretation appears to be a violation of the text's privacy. *Eva's Man* preserves its own integrity by refusing the reader's function, and constituting itself as an unreadable, inviolable text.

The opaque surface of *Eva's Man* works as a kind of protective device, and achieves a formal containment of the novel's subversive treatment of contemporary ideological material. This use of first-person narration also challenges the formal requirements of Black Aesthetic ideology, although the first-person voice in itself is not inimical to the collective, oral emphasis of the Black Aesthetic. As Charles Rowell points out, "the first person as a narrative device is . . . a preferred form in the oral tradition." Gayl Jones agrees that the "subjective testimony" of first-person oral storytelling establishes a continuity between the speaker and the listener.[36] In *Eva's Man*, however, the first-person mode serves the exactly opposite function of sealing off the narrator from the reader. Eva announces, "I didn't want to tell my story" (p. 77); her resistance to the act of narration, her view of interpretation as violation, and her distrust of her audience,[37] controvert the Black Aesthetic celebration of the oral artist's untroubled relation to the community. As Jones herself pointed out, *Eva's Man* poses "a kind of challenge to the listener."[38] While the novel employs the first-person mode privileged in the oral tradition, its use of this mode achieves an effect of self-enclosure that denies the collective emphasis of Black Aesthetic ideology.

A similar contradiction characterizes the novel's presentation of black speech, another formal feature valorized in Black Aesthetic theory. *Eva's Man* seems in accord with the Black Aesthetic in its exclusive reliance on black speech (or dialect) as the medium of narration. Unlike *The Bluest Eye, Sula,* and *Corregidora, Eva's Man* does not use standard English to mediate the dialect spoken by its characters. In an influential essay on the development of black dialect as a literary language, John Wideman writes that in most black fiction, dialect is contained within the linguistic hierarchy implied by a standard English narrative frame. According to Wideman, Jones's novels mark a significant development in the use of black dialect, for they provide

> no privileged position from which to view [the] fictional world, no terms into which it asks to be translated. . . . A Black woman's voice creates the only valid terms . . . ; the authority of her language is not subordinated to other codes; the frame has disappeared.[39]

It is true that the dialect in *Eva's Man*, used without a legitimizing frame, constitutes a literary language in its own right. But it is not so easy to agree with Wideman's assertion that the novel grants full authority to the black woman's voice, for Eva does not fully possess or exercise control over the language she uses. If anything, she seems imprisoned in the dialect, which, as it is presented in the novel, is emphatically not a black woman's language. Melvin Dixon argues that Eva is unable to achieve salvation because she is alienated from the regenerative possibilities of the black speech community.[40] In *Eva's Man*, however, the dialect is not invested with any regenerative possibilities for black women.[41] Throughout the novel, black dialect constructs black women as obscene sexual objects, as whores and bitches. In this dialect, with its profusion of derogatory terms for black women, black men possess the sole right to name women. Eva's rare attempt to usurp this masculine prerogative is promptly corrected by Tyrone: "Don't you call me evil, you little evil devil bitch" (p. 35). For the most part, Eva helplessly reproduces the dialect that she recognizes is not her own language: "I didn't give a shit what his name was, I was thinking in the kind of language Alfonso would use" (p. 97). Eva's entrapment in the dialect is accentuated by the novel's repetitive play with the dialect. Gayl Jones has drawn attention to her use of ritualized as opposed to naturalistic dialogue.[42] In *Eva's Man*, stylized repetition of dialogue fragments creates a ritual effect that denaturalizes black dialect, and forces a recognition of its non-dialogic construction of black women. The very fact that, so often in *Eva's Man*, dialogues are not even attributed to particular characters emphasizes the sameness of these dialogues. One dialogue after another defines and traps Eva in the same narrow terminology of bitch and whore.

On the level of narrative voice, then, *Eva's Man* upsets all the formal priorities of Black Aesthetic theory—the authority of realism, the immediate relationship between narrator and audience, and the use of black dialect to free a unique literary voice. Eva's first-person narration partly succeeds in containing the novel's treatment of lesbianism and castration, the two thematic elements that absolutely negate the heterosexual emphasis of black nationalist ideology. However, if the first-person narrator works as a device of thematic containment, it produces fresh contradictions at a formal level. The self-enclosure of the novel's first-person voice, and its resistance to interpretation, controvert both the collective and the didactic bent of Black Aesthetic discourse. Moreover, while using the dialect that would ostensibly liberate a new, distinctly black voice, *Eva's Man* filters the dialect through a feminine narrator (or, more accurately, filters a feminine narrator through the dialect), thus exposing the restricted liberatory possibilities of this language. Unlike *Corregidora*'s use of the blues, *Eva's Man* does not explore any alternative means of representing the black feminine difference from the Black Aesthetic. The novel does, however, graphically display the difficulty of reading or writing black femininity according to the codes of Black Aesthetic ideology.

VI

"TO SURVIVE WHOLE"
THE INTEGRATIVE AIMS OF WOMANISM IN
THE THIRD LIFE OF GRANGE COPELAND

In an interview with Charles Rowell, Gayl Jones praised Alice Walker's fiction for refusing "easy 'rightnesses,'" for admitting "ambivalences and contradictions . . . without making easy judgements."[1] Jones's comment is partly confirmed by Walker's own description of her intentions. Just as Jones claimed that an artist must be "wrong" in order to enter certain imaginative territories, so Alice Walker celebrated, in her essays, poems, short stories, and novels, the "incorrect" black women "who will not cram themselves into any ideological or racial mold."[2] Walker disavowed the didacticism of the militant black literature of the 1960s "because it requires only that the reader be a lazy reader and a prejudiced one."[3] Like Gayl Jones, Walker occasionally placed art beyond politics, as, for example, in her statement that her work develops "an awareness of and openness to mystery, which . . . is deeper than any politics."[4]

While sharing Gayl Jones's suspicion of the "easy rightnesses" of Black Aesthetic ideology, Alice Walker differs from Jones in her conception of art as necessarily functional. Walker's use of quilting as a metaphor for black women's artistry retains the functional emphasis of Black Aesthetic ideology. In her essay, "In Search of Our Mothers' Gardens," Walker describes quilting as an art form constructed from the "bits and pieces" of everyday life (*Search*, p. 239), a form that acquires its value only in the process of "everyday use."[5] Walker's quilting metaphor, however, points the function of art to feminine ends, significantly modifying the definition of artistic function in Black Aesthetic ideology. The purpose of Walker's art is to reclaim the suppressed creativity of her actual mother, as well as of all the unnamed black women who were constrained to channel their creative energies into traditionally accepted feminine activities such as quilting and gardening.

Unlike Gayl Jones, whose fiction is not implicated in any clear or acknowledged ideological enterprise, Walker's fiction explicitly declares its commitment to the ideology of "womanism" (*Search*, p. xi).

106

The term *womanism,* coined by Walker, may be interpreted as an attempt to integrate black nationalism into feminism, to articulate a distinctively black feminism that shares some of the objectives of black nationalist ideology. Taking the term *womanist* from a black folk expression, Walker distinguishes her ideology from white feminism; the womanist is "committed to [the] survival and wholeness of [the] entire people, male *and* female" (*Search,* p. xi). While the liberation of the entire black community is also the ostensible goal of black nationalism, Walker's fiction exposes the ways in which the nationalist conception of community implicitly marginalizes the concerns of black women.

Walker's first novel, *The Third Life of Grange Copeland* (1970), was highly controversial when it was first published, precisely because it unveiled the brutal sexual oppression of black women by black men that obstructed the "survival and wholeness" of the entire black community. In *The Third Life,* the very physical survival of black women is in jeopardy, as two of the novel's central women characters, Margaret and Mem, are directly or indirectly killed by their husbands. With the exception of Ruth, all the black women in the novel are subjected to violence and to sexual and economic exploitation by black men. Walker was undoubtedly aware that the novel's disclosure of sexism in the black community controverted the ideological agenda of the Black Aesthetic. In an afterword to the novel, Walker confessed that *The Third Life* was "an incredibly difficult novel to write" because it highlighted "violence among Black people" at a time when "all Black people . . . were enduring massive psychological and physical violence from white supremacists."[6] Walker's afterword justifies the novel's divergence from Black Aesthetic ideology in terms that substantially reinstate the Black Aesthetic conception of literature.

First, Walker defends the novel's presentation of domestic violence among black people on the grounds of its realism; as we have already seen in the chapter on *Eva's Man,* Black Aesthetic theorists like Addison Gayle invoked the authority of realism, asserting that black art should reflect the actual experience of blacks.[7] Walker states, in her afterword, that the novel's most controversial incident, Brownfield's murder of Mem, is "based on a real case" (p. 342), and that Mem's sexual victimization is a legitimate fictional subject because it is typical of black women's experience (p. 344). Unlike Gayl Jones, who sought to neutralize the controversial sexual violence in *Eva's Man* by claiming that Eva stands only for herself and not for black women generally,[8] Walker emphasized that Mem's name, based on "the French 'la même,' meaning 'the same,'" indicates that Mem is "symbolic of all women" (p. 344). Walker's defense of *The Third Life* also appeals to the Black Aesthetic dictate that black artists should portray and affirm a strong black community: "How can a family, a community, a race, a nation, a world, be healthy and strong, if one half dominates the other?" (p. 344). The novel's exposure of black women's sexual oppression thus serves an urgent political and communal function: the novel forces the recognition that because black women constitute one-half of the black community, their liberation is essential to the "survival and wholeness of [the] entire people, male *and* female" (p. xi).

When *The Third Life of Grange Copeland* was first published, few black critics recognized or applauded Walker's functional intentions. In a rare favorable contemporary review of the novel in *Black Books Bulletin*, Falvia Plumpp wrote that *The Third Life* is valuable for the black community because it "lays out a mental roadmap for us to follow."[9] In another telling recovery of the novel into the reading norms of Black Aesthetic ideology, Loyle Hairston argued that *The Third Life* "shows us how the pernicious effects imposed by the racial caste system corrode the sensibilities of *men*."[10] Alice Walker has remarked that Hairston was the only black male critic to give *The Third Life* a favorable review,[11] but Hairston forced the novel into the ideological format of the Black Aesthetic by centering it around the racial subjection of black men, and remaining conspicuously silent about the novel's treatment of black women's sexual oppression. Those black male critics who did notice the novel's focus on sexual oppression predictably censured its unsympathetic portrayal of black men. For example, Addison Gayle's disapproval of the novel hinged on Walker's alleged "inability to create complex male characters."[12]

The conflict between Hairston's and Gayle's readings is instructive, for it clarifies the novel's double focus, its intricate configuration of racial and sexual oppression. To an extent, *The Third Life* does substantiate Hairston's Black Aesthetic reading in that, through much of the novel, the black man's subjugation forms the main thematic concern. Grange and Brownfield occupy the center of the novel's plot, and their sexual and economic exploitation of black women is relentlessly traced back to their own oppression at the hands of white men. The novel graphically delineates the ways in which racial oppression denies the status of full subjects to black men. In particular, animal imagery figures the black man as a "deformed and grotesque" victim of racism (p. 57). The comparison of Brownfield to a hog, a rat, a toad, a lizard, and a jackass insistently conveys the dehumanization resulting from his experience of racial oppression. Moreover, silence and absence typically mark the helpless submission of the black man to his seemingly omnipotent white male oppressor. The "vacancy" (p. 17) and inauthenticity of black masculine identity under racism are powerfully communicated in Grange's encounter with his boss, Shipley, whose physical presence freezes Grange's face into a silent, "rigid," "unnaturally bland mask" (p. 9) that is "devoid of any emotion" (p. 17). Similarly, Brownfield becomes "hollow" (p. 32) and "speechless" (p. 113) in the presence of Shipley, and of his second white boss, Captain Davis.

This account of the novel's figuration of black masculine identity as absent and deficient is, however, not entirely complete or accurate. The novel's presentation of black masculine identity as an absence that enables the presence of the white masculine subject is accompanied by an equally unflinching focus on the absence of the black feminine subject, an absence produced by her subjection to black men. If animal imagery, for example, underlines the deformation of black masculine identity under racism, it also renders the dehumanizing effects of black women's victimization: Mem is likened to a cow, a pig, a gorilla, and a hound, and Josie to a cat, a snake, and a she-goat. Mem's story most clearly demonstrates how sexual oppression reduces the black woman to a condition of silence, absence, and grotesque subhumanity. In Brownfield's presence, Mem is usually "so silent it was as if she were not breathing or thinking or even being" (p. 130). After she dies, Brownfield cannot call her image to mind because "there had never been a self to her" (p. 228). Mem's absence directly stems from her husband's violent and abusive treatment of her: it is Brownfield's frequent beating of her that "reduce[s] her to nothing" (p. 131). Mem's grotesque lack and ugliness, as signified by her falling hair and skeletal frame, are also ultimately traced back to Brownfield. As Mem tells him in a rare moment of self-possession, "you *beat* the ugly into me" (p. 136).

The novel leaves no doubt that Brownfield's sexual victimization of Mem is a displaced effect of his own racial victimization. As a sharecropper for a white landowner who treats him and his family like workhorses, Brownfield suffers from a sense of economic impotence that motivates his violent treatment of black women. Like Cholly in *The Bluest Eye*, Brownfield beats his wife in order to certify his manhood, to prove that he is "still the man that wears the pants in this outfit" (p. 123). Like Cholly, who holds the black woman responsible for his disempowerment, Brownfield displaces his rage onto Mem: "his rage could and did blame everything, *everything* on her" (p. 79).

While pinpointing racism as the root cause of black women's predicament, *The Third Life* does not quite displace black men's responsibility for their exploitation of black women onto white men. In the novel's afterword, Walker argued that one form of oppression cannot condone another: "The white man's oppression of me will never excuse my oppression of you, whether you are man, woman, child, animal or tree" (p. 345). Loyle Hairston contended that Brownfield and Grange are "more victims than villains,"[13] but *The Third Life*, like *Sula*, refuses the image of black men as victims who cannot help but transfer to black women the effects of their own brutalization. Just as Sula demystifies Jude's narrative of himself as a helpless victim of racism, so Mem rejects Brownfield's "whiney tale"[14] about "how hard it is to be a black man down here" (p. 136). If Brownfield, and Grange in his first life, fail to attain a sense of manhood, it is not so much because they are emasculated by racism as because they are complicit in their own op-pression as well as in the oppression of black women. It is not difficult to see why a nationalist critic like Addison Gayle denounced Walker's depiction of black men in *The Third Life*. Even the novel's most sympa-thetically presented black male character, Grange, makes himself into a man in his second and third lives by means of violence and economic exploitation of women. In his second life in the North, Grange is politi-cally and psychologically "liberated" by his murder of a pregnant white woman, a murder that he views as "the necessary act that Black men must commit to regain, or manufacture their manhood" (p. 218). Grange's economic liberation in his third life is also achieved at the expense of a woman: Josie renounces her own economic self-sufficiency and sells her nightclub to finance Grange's independent farmstead.

Apparently concerned with Grange and Brownfield, *The Third Life* persistently traces the ramifications of their racial oppression for black women. Walker remarked, in an interview with John O'Brien, that the novel "is committed to exploring the oppressions, the insanities, the loyalties and triumphs of Black women. In *The Third Life of Grange Copeland*, ostensibly about a man and his son, it is the women and how they are treated that colors everything."[15] It is this focus that reveals the inadequacy of Hairston's nationalist reading of the novel, and that explains the feminist appropriation of the novel in the late 1970s and early 1980s. In 1979, for example, Mary Helen Washington described Walker as an "apologist and spokeswoman for Black women," and in an essay published in 1984, Bettye Parker-Smith argued that Walker's "cause is the liberation of Black womanhood."[16]

The Third Life is most amenable to the strand of black feminist criti-cism that is concerned with literary images of black women. Most black feminist readings of *The Third Life* revolve around the question of whether the novel presents full, positive, and realistic characteriza-tions, as opposed to negative stereotypes, of black women. Barbara Christian and Karen Gaston, for example, have argued that the novel discards stereotypes in favor of "graphic pictures of real women."[17] *The Third Life* alone, of all the novels considered here, firmly installs the model of a whole, authentic identity that is posited by images-of-black-women criticism. While several black feminine characters in the novel initially recall well-worn stereotypes, these stereotypes are invariably superseded by full psychological characterizations. Mem, for example, in her passive submission to her husband, evokes the stereotype of the black woman as a mule of the world, but the extensive psychological analysis of how Mem feels as a mule of the world exceeds the one-dimensional flatness of the stereotype. In chapter 25, Mem breaks out of the stereotype as, shotgun in hand, she reclaims the integrity of her proper name, denying Brownfield's stereotypical naming of her as a "Black ugly nigger bitch" (p. 139). Josie's characterization effects a similar realistic revision of a stereotype: she is introduced through Brownfield's stereotype of the loose black woman, but the following chapters, switching to Josie's point of view, add a psychological dimension that humanizes the stereotype. This corrective use of stereotypes distinguishes *The Third Life* from *The Bluest Eye* and *Eva's Man*, which confine their characters to the narrow fixity of the stereotype and offer no authentic psychological selfhood that precedes or resists the stereotype.

While *The Third Life* shares with *The Bluest Eye* and *Eva's Man* an exposure of the dominant construction of the black subject, whether masculine or feminine, as "an object, a cipher" (p. 9), it ultimately departs from these novels in its restoration of a full black identity. This restoration is executed through the character of Ruth, who is schooled by her grandfather to "survive *whole*" (p. 298), and whose possession of a whole self compensates for the absent, deformed identities of her mother, father, and grandmother. Ruth is remarkable as the only character in the novel who consistently defamiliarizes any stereotypical perception of race or gender, as, for example, when she confounds Grange's nationalist stereotyping of whites as "blue-eyed devils" (p. 198) with her own denaturalized view of them as "not exactly white, but a combination of gray and yellow and pink" (p. 254). Ruth's propensity to look "underneath revealed truth" (p. 255) compels a comparison with Sula: both characters herald a new black feminine identity that decisively breaks away from earlier literary and cultural stereotypes of black women.

However, a comparison of Sula's and Ruth's difference from the stereotypical identities imposed upon black women can only be sustained at a thematic level. While Ruth's character thematically inaugurates a new and, in Mary Helen Washington's term, "emergent" black feminine identity,[18] Sula's characterization formally as well as thematically surpasses the conventional fictional depiction of black women. The grotesque mode signifies Sula's identity as discontinuous, endlessly processual, and fissured by gaps and absences, thus rendering her character unreadable according to a realist grammar of psychological selfhood. Ruth's characterization, in contrast, is conducted securely within the realist mode of whole, psychologically coherent individuality. Ruth is described as a "womanish gal" (p. 251); Walker's derivation of the term *womanist* from the black folk word "womanish" (*Search*, p. xi) offers an important clue to the construction of black feminine identity in *The Third Life*. In an essay that outlines the principal features of a "Black womanist aesthetic," Chikwenye Okonjo Ogunyemi argues that *The Third Life* exemplifies the commitment of womanist fiction to the "dynamism of wholeness," and to an identity conceived in terms of "authenticity and transcendence."[19] Ogunyemi's definition of womanist selfhood is supported by Alice Walker's own statement that the womanist is committed to "wholeness" (*Search*, p. xi), and by the end of *The Third Life*, which affirms the plenitude of Ruth's completed self-development.

The novel's investment in the model of a whole identity does not, in itself, operate as an ideological constraint or determine the formal conventionality of its characterization of Ruth. In fact, the womanist's quest for a whole self assumes a strong oppositional value, given the novel's disclosure of the absent, deficient subject status imposed upon blacks in the United States. Moreover, as Molefi Asante has argued, the ideal of a "wholistic personality" can be traced back to West African culture, opening a rhetorical Afrocentric space that lies outside the terms of the contemporary Euro-American theorizing on the subject.[20] The concept of a whole, communally oriented black identity may thus be situated against both the stable individual self of bourgeois humanist ideology and the mobile, splintered subject of post-structuralist discourse. If the whole self developed in *The Third Life* does not fully attain its oppositional potential, this is not because of any intrinsic ideological defect of vision, but because the novel's heavy reliance on psychological realism collapses its alternative notion of a whole identity into the humanist model of full individuality. As we shall see later, its strict adherence to the formal elements of realism obstructs the novel's ideological aim of liberating a radically new vision of community and political change, as well as of black identity.

The realist characterization of Ruth's identity preserves intact the bildungsroman pattern of continuous development concluding with the protagonist's possession of a whole and stable self. Ruth's growth into womanhood is explicitly charted according to the structural coordinates of the bildungsroman. Unlike *The Bluest Eye, Sula, Corregidora,* and *Eva's Man*, all of which summon, only for parodic purposes, a bildungsroman structuring of the development of black feminine sexuality, *The Third Life* unquestioningly employs the bildungsroman to map Ruth's movement toward maturity, a linear process that culminates in Ruth's enlistment into the regimes of heterosexuality and reproduction. In *The Bluest Eye, Sula, Corregidora,* and *Eva's Man*, a young black girl's sexual initiation inevitably inserts her into a cycle of sexual violence. In *The Third Life*, the repetitive cycle of domestic violence that characterized the lives of Ruth's mother and grandmother is finally ruptured and transcended by Ruth. Ruth's nascent sexuality is first aroused when she meets the Civil Rights worker, Quincy, whose relationship with his pregnant wife, Helen, offers Ruth a brief glimpse of heterosexuality as a harmonious partnership between equals. This affirmative vision of heterosexuality fulfills a central function of womanist fiction, which, according to Ogunyemi, "ends in integrative images of the male and female worlds."[21]

Ruth's acceptance of Helen and Quincy as role models for her sexual development signals her adjustment to heterosexuality, marriage, and reproduction, the typical ends of the feminine bildungsroman. Of these, Ruth's reconciliation with the reproductive potentiality of her adolescent body is the most difficult. Ruth feels "defenseless" and afraid when her first menstrual period alerts her to the procreative possibilities of her body (p. 271). Her fear is confirmed by the novel's presentation of motherhood as a debilitating burden for several of its women characters, including Margaret, Josie, and the nameless white woman murdered by Grange. Mem's life provides the most striking instance of reproduction as an oppressive cycle that defeats a woman's quest for self-determination. Pregnancy is described as Mem's "weakness" (p. 143); her one moment of control over her life is dissipated by the "return" of her reproductive "cycle" (p. 143). The two pregnancies that follow are not only unproductive, they destroy her health and render her unfit for work and thus entirely dependent on her husband. Of all the pregnant women featured in the novel, Helen is the only one whose pregnancy appears to be a source of pride, pleasure, and hope in the future.

Except for this single positive image, *The Third Life*, like *The Bluest Eye*, *Sula*, and *Corregidora*, foregrounds the mutually antagonistic relationships between parents and children, and the crippling consequences of pregnancy for black women. However, like *Eva's Man*, *The Third Life* is haunted by a sense that only the reproductive cycle contains the buried seeds of a new future. The ancestors' bracelets in *Eva's Man* inchoately suggest the regenerative potential of the reproductive and generational cycles, a potential more fully developed in the relationship between Ruth and her grandfather, Grange. This relationship salvages the generational cycle of the Copeland family, and bears the burden of resolving the novel's fraught treatment of past and future, history and change.

Alice Walker's essays often stress the importance of ancestral heritage in bridging the past, present, and future, and in sustaining the development of a whole, temporally unified self. In a passage that strongly echoes Toni Morrison's comments on the ancestral past in "Rootedness: The Ancestor as Foundation," Walker writes: "If we kill off the sound of our ancestors, the major portion of us, all that is past, all that is history, that is human being is lost, and we become historically and spiritually thin, a mere shadow of who we were."[22] Many of the essays collected in her book *In Search of Our Mothers' Gardens*, and especially the title essay, underscore the special significance of the maternal ancestor for black women: "How simple a thing it seems to me that to know ourselves as we are, we must know our mothers' names" (*Search*, p. 276). Walker's essays repeatedly deploy maternal metaphors to authorize a new black feminine paradigm of cultural transmission, yet, as Dianne Sadoff has pointed out, Walker's metaphorical recovery of the mother in her essays clashes with the ambivalent portrayal of the mother in her fiction.[23]

This disparity between Walker's essays and her fiction is greatly revealing of the ways in which ideological pressures shape narrative choices. The black nationalist and the womanist ideologies, with their different conceptions of the mother, vie with each other in Walker's fiction. Walker's celebration of the mother in her essay "In Search of Our Mothers' Gardens" initiated the black feminist appropriation of the mother as a means of legitimizing a feminine revision of history and cultural tradition. *The Third Life*, published four years before this essay, anticipates Walker's later recovery of the mother in suggesting that the reproductive cycle carries the germinating possibilities of a new history. Yet this womanist insight seems blocked in *The Third Life*, perhaps due to the metaphorical alignment of the mother, in contemporary nationalist discourse, with the forces of political conservatism. In partial compliance with this ideological construction of the mother as "the undisputed enemy of all revolutionary ideas,"[24] *The Third Life* displaces the politically transformative potential of the mother-daughter relationship (which is severely strained in the novel) to the relationship between a girl and her grandfather. That Grange, in his third life, represents a displaced mother has been noted by several critics,[25] and is clearly signaled by his entry into Ruth's life at the exact moment that her mother dies. Grange's figurative alignment with the maternal rather than the paternal principle becomes even more apparent when he instigates Ruth's rejection of her father, and encourages her retrospective identification with her mother.

The novel thus performs its womanist task of reclaiming the mother in an oblique and displaced fashion. Significantly, the maternal principle is displaced onto the one character in the novel, Grange, who personifies black nationalist manhood. Grange's second life, in particular, evokes the celebrated rebirth of the new black man. Several black nationalist men predicated their achievement of manhood upon rape or murder of the white woman, the protection of whose chastity had historically required the symbolic and actual emasculation of black men.[26] Grange, too, firmly grasps his masculinity only after he murders a white woman. His political rhetoric, propounding violence and hatred of whites, unmistakably echoes the black nationalist impatience with the Civil Rights creed of love and nonviolence. Grange's skepticism about the means and ends of the Civil Rights movement is often couched in explicitly black nationalist terms: "The gun is important. For I don't know that love works on everybody" (p. 275). He can imagine racial solidarity among blacks only if it is cemented by an absolute, "necessary hate" for whites (p. 204).

If Grange's character embodies the black male nationalist, this, taken with his role as a displaced mother, produces a curious ideological hybrid. The novel's grafting of the mother onto the male nationalist serves two important ideological functions. Most obviously, in combining the mother and the male nationalist, Grange's characterization neutralizes the novel's womanist recovery of the mother. But the amalgamation, in Grange's character, of the opposed ideological semes of nationalism and womanism may also be read as an attempt to integrate the womanist power of the mother with the masculine power of the nationalist, and thus to resolve the central disagreement, concerning the mother, between the two ideologies.

The final section of the novel, dealing with Grange's third life, tries to integrate the nationalist and womanist ideologies at several different levels. If the second life of Grange Copeland enacts the birth of the black male nationalist, Grange's third life, centering around his relationship with Ruth, undertakes a womanist revision that preserves even as it surpasses the collective ideology of black nationalism. Employing Ruth's point of view, the end of the novel supplements Grange's conception of a nationalist community joined by hatred ("Hatred for them will someday unite us" [p. 220]) with a womanist vision of community inspired by love and forgiveness. Grange fails to instill his necessary hate into Ruth because of her strong belief in the power of forgiveness. Love and forgiveness are qualities invested not only in Ruth but in all the major black women characters in the novel. Margaret "could love all sorts of folks she didn't have any business" (p. 275); Josie "could love in spite of all that had gone wrong in her life" (p. 222); and Mem, despite her brutalization, could continue to believe that "forgiveness" and "kindness . . . can convert the enemy" (p. 228). The novel's affirmation of this womanly capacity to love and forgive is not as simple a repudiation of black nationalist ideology as it may initially seem. Ruth's forgiveness is tested in chapter 46, when she spurns her father's tentative offer of reconciliation. This scene concedes the limited validity of Grange's creed: Ruth "hated and liked herself for this lack of charity. She glimpsed for the first time what Grange had known, the nature of unforgiveness and the finality of a misdeed done" (p. 303). The novel's resolution of the contradiction between the nationalist and womanist notions of community is not easy or reductive; the womanist's creed of love can be installed as an unsentimental, viable value only after it is tempered by the "necessary hate" of the black nationalist.

The Third Life locates its vision of community in the explicitly political contexts of black nationalism, in Grange's case, and of the Civil Rights movement in the case of Ruth. However, the novel's emphasis on collective political action is crossed by the individualistic rhetoric that describes the political initiation of Grange and Ruth. Grange, for example, is converted to black nationalism in the urban North. His exposure to racism in the Northern ghettos convinces him that economic advancement for black Americans can be won only by means of militant political struggle. While Grange's experience of the North typifies the collective disappointment of Southern blacks with the Northern dream, his conversion to the Northern black nationalist movement is acclaimed as the psychological transformation of a unique individual. Grange undergoes a series of transformations that make him, by the end of his second life, "a reborn man" (p. 223). Grange's rebirth abruptly shifts the question of historical change from a political and collective to a psychological and personal register.

Ruth's story effects a similar displacement of political change from a collective to an individual level. Her womanist credo of love, charity, and forgiveness invokes the Christian rhetoric of the Civil Rights movement in the South. The novel overtly draws this connection between womanism and the Civil Rights movement in the last few chapters, as Ruth's growing political awareness leads to her eager acceptance of the goals and methods of the Civil Rights movement.[27] However, the Civil Rights movement is presented not so much as a political movement directed against institutionalized racism, but as an effort to "change those crackers' hearts" (p. 320). Ruth's commitment to this collective political movement uneasily coexists with the novel's celebration of Ruth's political awareness as a distinctive individual gift. Her readiness for political action is exceptional and does not seem to entail a corresponding political consciousness in her community. Ruth can count "on three fingers" the number of black people who would be willing to rise up in political protest (p. 276). She declares that she would be "bored stiff waiting for Black folks to rise so I could join them. Since I'm already ready to rise up and they ain't, it seems to me I should rise up first and let them follow me" (pp. 275–76). The novel does not question the efficacy of this kind of individual activism, nor does it clarify how Ruth's leadership might galvanize her community into political action. The Third Life seems unable to imagine change except at a psychological level and then, too, only for unique individuals like Ruth and Grange.

This affirmation of individual, psychological changes appears especially inadequate because it follows a thorough diagnosis of the structural causes of racial and sexual oppression. Except for the final section dealing with Ruth and Grange, the novel insistently poses the question of change at a systemic level, discrediting the liberal notion of change as originating in the free choice and action of an individual. But the third section, taking recourse to the realist rhetoric of psychological awakening, inadvertently reinscribes the liberal conception of political change as a matter of individual changes of heart. Its formal reliance on psychological realism thus nudges the novel in unintended ideological directions and, again, as with its treatment of black identity, inhibits its attempted thematic articulation of a radically new vision of collective political transformation.

The Third Life thematically elaborates the question of historical change through an interplay between cyclic and linear conceptions of time. The narratives of Grange's and Brownfield's lives inexorably enact the cyclic repetition of the past in the present. Grange and Brownfield are the representative Southern black sharecroppers who try unsuccessfully to escape the material and ideological conditions of slavery that persist in the modern South. Each of the plot movements dealing with these characters' lives arouses expectations of linear change that are frustrated as each projected change lapses into the sameness of the past cycle. For example, Grange's life follows a "kind of cycle" (p. 14) in which past, present, and future coalesce into meaningless stasis; as he later describes it, "my days done all run together. There wa'n't no beginning nor no end" (p. 101). Grange can envisage a release from the monotonous repetition of his life only in terms of a linear break, a geographical movement from South to North. However, in the North, Grange realizes that white people "ruled New York as they did Georgia" (p. 201); his disenchantment with the North reflects the collective experience of Southern blacks whose exposure to Northern ghettoes effectively banished any vision of the North as the site of a new phase of black history. The migration of blacks from the South to the North, a presumably progressive movement in black history, is represented in *The Third Life* as a failed linear quest. Grange's Northern journey ultimately ends with his circular return to the South of his birth.

The plot line dealing with Brownfield is characterized by a similar tension between anticipated linear progress and actual cyclic regression. Brownfield, like Grange, goes North in search of economic advancement, but his linear journey is truncated at the most literal level as Brownfield relinquishes all hopes of ever arriving North, and arbitrarily settles down at whichever spot he finds himself. His marriage with Mem constitutes the next seeming forward drive of the plot, as Mem rekindles his desire to escape the suffocating conditions of his life in the South. A mere seven pages later comes Brownfield's "year of awakening" (p. 78), an ironic awakening not to newness or change but to the interminably repetitive quality of his life: "That was the year he first saw how his own life was becoming a repetition of his father's. He could not save his children from slavery" (p. 78). Far from marking linear progress, Brownfield's year of awakening resigns him to the knowledge that the historical past of slavery, supposedly obliterated by the Emancipation Proclamation, continues to linger in the twentieth-century South.

This conflict between linear progress and cyclic repetition is thematically resolved in the final section of the novel, which projects a synthetic vision of time in which "each day must be the past, present and future" (p. 298). In his third life, Grange wishes to prepare Ruth for a new future free of the oppressive past, a future that can be realized only through a break with the familial past of the Copelands, which has been marred by hatred, violence, and murder. Through Ruth's agency, Grange does succeed in forgetting his own past: "quickly he rolled up his past and lay back on it, obliterating the keen spots, completely erasing the edges" (p. 251). The novel's resolution, however, cannot completely erase the edges; some destructive remnants of the past, embodied in Brownfield, cannot be transcended or redeemed. Brownfield has to be expelled from the plot before the novel can resolve itself because he represents that residue of the Copelands' familial past that absolutely resists transformation. Brownfield "could never renew or change himself" (p. 315), unlike Grange, the sum of whose wisdom amounts to a realization "that people change" (p. 274). Grange's commitment to Ruth's future requires an act that simultaneously kills and repeats the past. Grange's killing of his son repeats the Copelands' familial history of kin-killing, but it also ensures Ruth's entry into a new future free of familial violence.

The resolution of Ruth's own plot involves a similar subtle balancing of past and future, cyclic continuity and linear rupture. Ruth's achievement of a new identity free of her sordid familial history constitutes a decisive linear departure from the past. But Ruth's progressive self-discovery is located within a generational frame that organizes time as a continuum of past, present, and future. Generational continuity is valued in *The Third Life* because, as in *Corregidora*, it provides the most effective means of perpetuating cultural heritage. Like the Corregidora matriarchs who transmit their unofficial version of slave history down to each new generation, Grange teaches Ruth the "untaught history" (p. 190) of black people. Through Grange's oral performances, Ruth reclaims a rich cultural legacy originating in Africa. Grange instills in Ruth a pride in black cultural history that surely fuels her desire to work for a new political future for black people in the United States. At the end of the novel, Ruth stands poised for a linear change that is sustained by her understanding of her own familial history as well as of the cultural history of her race. The conclusion of *The Third Life* thus reaches for a unified, whole temporal vision that can resolve the novel's earlier tension between past and present, cyclic and linear time.

This integrative temporal vision is, however, elaborated only at a thematic level and, in fact, remains entirely inaccessible at the level of narrative structure. While thematically affirming an interplay between cyclic and linear time, the novel itself is structured by an exclusively and relentlessly linear logic. The novel's plot moves in a strictly chronological direction, and is never derailed by the abrupt cuts and returns that characterize the plots of all the other novels considered here. This disjunction between its thematic and structural articulations of time, like all the other disjunctions between the novel's thematic and formal levels, derives from its dependence on the realist mode. Alice Walker herself has acknowledged the formal constraints imposed by the "rigorous realism" of *The Third Life*. Walker described *The Third Life* as a "very realistic" novel that is "chronological in structure,"[28] implying rather than explicitly drawing the connection between the novel's linearity and its realism. The bildungsroman structuring of Ruth's development secures the realist model of time as a linear medium of change and progress, a model that restricts and even contradicts the novel's attempted thematic presentation of a unified temporal continuum.

An interplay between cyclic and linear temporal models is crucial to the novel's integrative project: only a representation of change as both linear rupture and cyclic continuity can enable a synthesis of the nationalist and womanist ideologies, integrating the womanist's attachment to the cultural past with the nationalist's commitment to a radically new future. Grange's character provides the fictional site of this particular mediation, as of all the novel's other mediations between the nationalist and womanist ideologies. Grange is the nationalist who liberates a new future by violently destroying the past (as embodied in Brownfield). Yet the man who kills his own son is also the figurative mother who performs the crucial womanist task of preserving and transmitting the black cultural past to succeeding generations. Through the figure of Grange, the novel establishes black nationalism as the precondition of its own womanist redefinition of historical change. Susan Willis has argued that the end of *The Third Life* achieves a decisive "rupture from the past" in its "transition from the male to the female principle";[29] the novel's conclusion transfers power and centrality from the black man (Grange) to the black woman (Ruth). However, this centering of Ruth as "the new defining figure of history"[30] accomplishes a womanist reconstruction of history that fully grants the political value of black nationalism. Grange's economic and psychological empowerment, and his discovery of his manhood, make possible the full development of Ruth's womanhood. The novel's refocusing of history around the black woman, therefore, subsumes rather than negates the historical vision of black nationalism.[31]

The novel inscribes its new version of history in a narrative and linguistic mode that is, again, determined by its impulse to reconcile the nationalist and womanist ideologies. *The Third Life* presents two alternative and contrasting ways of narrating history: the history textbook that Ruth reads in school, and the oral folk history she learns from Grange. The novel's suspicion of printed, official history is forcefully communicated in chapter 42. That Ruth learns a white U.S. version of history is evident in the fact that her all-black school has no history textbook of its own, and must depend on a book sent over from a neighboring white school. Ruth soon uncovers the racial hierarchy that subtends the dominant version of U.S. history. The cover of Ruth's history textbook, like the Dick and Jane primer in *The Bluest Eye*, establishes a white, blond child as the normative center of its narrative. Ruth's position as a subject and a reader of history is further displaced as she finds the signature of a white girl, Jacqueline Paine, on the inside cover of the book. Under this signature is a drawing entitled "The Tree of the Family of Man," which graphically depicts the naturalized racial hierarchy of white people at the top, followed by the "yellow" and "red" races, and finally, at the very bottom, "a nigger" (pp. 260–61). This nigger is pictured in terms of the crudest racist stereotype of blacks as primitive savages; he has "a bone sticking through his nose" and is "wearing a grass skirt" (p. 261).

Ruth rebels against this institutionalized stereotype of blacks by hurling her "huge stock of Grange-inherited words" at her history teacher: "You goddam mean evil *stupid* motherfucker" (p. 262). That Ruth draws on Grange's black dialect to contest the printed history textbook is not surprising, for Grange's oral narration of black history is the source of Ruth's pride in the rich cultural and historical legacy of blacks. As Trudier Harris has remarked, Grange's oral history revises black folklore in the interests of political liberation,[32] shaping folk material to suit the ideological agenda of black nationalism. Grange's imaginative recreation of black folklore challenges the assumption of official American history that blacks were entirely overwhelmed and dehumanized by slavery.[33] Grange counters the distortion of black folklore in Joel Chandler Harris's Uncle Remus tales with his own stories about a slave named John who becomes Ruth's hero because of his inventive verbal ability to manipulate his white masters. Grange's tales of conjurers and two-heads commemorate a similar imaginative and resourceful mode of cultural opposition. Sister Madelaine, who becomes a conjure woman to escape being a domestic servant, exemplifies Alice Walker's conviction that the black folk practice of conjuring often functioned as "a weapon against oppression."[34] Grange's hilarious and irreverent tale about his absurd conversion to Christianity also serves a corrective function: Ruth becomes aware of the historical use of Christianity, by white slavemasters, to resign slaves to their oppression. Grange's story of his blasphemous trickster bargain with god provides a folk account of Christianity that helps Ruth discount the textbook version, in which the unenlightened, heathen nigger looks "as if he expected, at any moment, a visiting missionary" (p. 261).

While celebrating the liberatory possibilities of Grange's folk history, *The Third Life* does not fully endorse the black nationalist perception of folklore as a vehicle of political liberation. A programmatic political appropriation of black folk culture would have to efface the duplicities and contradictions embedded in this culture. Alice Walker recognized the frequent recalcitrance of folklore to the nationalist affirmation of black pride: "There's a lot of self-criticism in the folklore, . . . and things that are really, sometimes, unsettling."[35] *The Third Life* employs black folklore in a manner that foregrounds its ambivalence, its resistance to a univocal ideological interpretation. For example, as Gayl Jones has demonstrated, the third part of the novel echoes the redemptive tones of the spiritual, with its celebration of the resilience that helped black Americans to transcend their dehumanizing predicament.[36] But if the folk form of the spiritual enables the novel to assert the "survival whole" of its characters and thus offers an unmistakably positive response to oppression, another folk creation evoked in the novel, the legend of the bad nigger, is not so readily affirmed. The characters of Brownfield and the early Grange are modeled on this folk figure who confronts his oppression through selfish and destructive acts of violence that are often directed at his family and his community.[37] As Keith Byerman points out, "Walker demystifies the legend [of the bad nigger] by showing its roots in self-hatred and its impact upon female characters. By such a process, she calls into question the cultural function of such images."[38]

In addition to questioning the political efficacy of black folk images, *The Third Life* also reveals the limited power of folk speech to authorize a new black literary language. The very beginning of the novel poses the question of black language as an urgent necessity, in its persistent attention to the silencing of the black voice under racial oppression. The resounding silence of the Copeland family in the first few chapters of the novel reflects their absolute incapacity not only to alter but even to name their condition in their own terms. Throughout the novel, the linguistic competence of characters indicates the extent of their control over their situation. For example, Brownfield is unable to resist his white boss because fear ties his tongue, and, at the lowest point in Mem's life, when she completely yields to Brownfield's violence, she lapses into the incoherent dialect spoken by Brownfield, which is characterized by the narrator as "a tongue broken and trying to mend itself in desperation" (p. 82).

This characterization of dialect as a broken tongue obviously counters the nationalist celebration of the dialect as a powerful, new, self-determined tongue. Like *Eva's Man*, *The Third Life* exposes the ways in which the dialect often works as a tool of linguistic domination over black women. Just as the dialect in *Eva's Man* repeatedly names the black woman a bitch and a whore, so in *The Third Life* the dialect monologically constructs the black woman as a "Black ugly nigger bitch" (p. 139). The dialect constitutes an important terrain of Mem and Brownfield's marital conflict. Brownfield considers his speech a badge of his economic and cultural dispossession, and he first feels drawn to Mem because her literacy and her fluency in standard English attest to her escape from "the culture of poverty" (p. 81). Brownfield tries to learn how to read and write from Mem, in the hope that literacy can show him a way out of his situation. But when, later in their marriage, Brownfield abandons all hope of bettering his condition, he resents Mem's linguistic superiority over "the rest of us poor niggers" (p. 81). He forces Mem to revert from standard English to black dialect because the dialect identifies her as a degraded victim, thus feeding his desperate desire for masculine power; he wants her "to talk like what she was, a hopeless nigger woman who got her ass beat every Saturday night" (p. 81).

If the dialect signifies Mem's inability to determine her life, it equally reveals Brownfield's own lack of self-determination. Brownfield's dialect is a mark of his exclusion from literate culture. Precisely because of the racist representation of blacks in the dominant literate culture (such as the stereotype of the nigger in the history textbook), the novel promotes literacy as an important tool of political and cultural advancement for black Americans. Only through literacy can blacks challenge their absolute cultural marginalization, and correct the racist imbalances of dominant cultural texts. In a marvelous passage in chapter 39, Brownfield, while in prison, meditates on his powerlessness to resist the authority of printed texts:

> "I feel just like these words here in the newspaper must feel, all printed up. The line already decided. No moving to the left or right. . . . Just think how this word here'd feel if it could move right out of this line and set itself down over here!" [Brownfield] pondered the power of the mobile, self-determined word. (p. 234)

Several canonized moments in the history of black American narrative converge in this remarkably resonant passage: Frederick Douglass writing his pass to freedom, invoking the "power of the mobile, self-determined word" to contest the bill of sale that defines him as property; Richard Wright's Bigger Thomas in prison, attempting to redefine himself against the stereotypical representation of the black man as a primitive savage in the white newspapers; Toni Morrison's Pecola, whose madness derives from her inability to read critically and to demystify the normative Dick and Jane reader that signifies the black girl as an absence. In his influential book *From Behind the Veil*, Robert Stepto has described the quest for literacy as a constitutive feature of the black American narrative tradition.[39] *The Third Life* resumes this tradition, presenting literacy as a necessary route to black cultural self-determination. Brownfield's exclusion from literate culture bolsters his fatalistic vision of himself as a helpless victim of racism. Significantly, his one attempt at self-definition is also the only time in the novel that Brownfield tries to write: "Leaning heavily on his pencil Brownfield wrote m-e-n, then waited glumly for the word to rise and beat its chest" (p. 235).

Laying bare the racist premises of dominant literate culture, the novel draws on the robust energy of black dialect to defy the authoritative finality of printed texts such as history books and newspapers. Yet the dialect is not unreservedly affirmed in *The Third Life*, for it reinforces the cultural marginalization of blacks, and carries the traces of racial and sexual oppression. The linguistic mode advanced at the end of the novel fuses dialect and standard English, oral and literate culture. In the scene involving the history textbook, Ruth uses her grandfather's dialect to correct the racial biases embedded in literate culture, but she also often uses standard English to correct Grange's speech and to display the advantages of her literate education. In an unusual move, the novel aligns the father with orality and the mother with literacy; as Harold Hellenbrand has observed, Ruth's book learning and her standard English are maternal legacies, while the black dialect is transmitted to her by her father and grandfather.[40] As we have already seen, the verbal skirmishes between Ruth's mother and father reveal language to be a charged field of struggle between black men and women. Through Ruth's mode of speech, the novel preserves the black nationalist use of the dialect to proclaim cultural pride, but criticizes the dialect for its monologic, derogatory construction of black women. Ruth's speech, combining dialect and standard English, effectively decenters the masculine emphasis, but maintains the racial centering, of the black nationalist position on the dialect.

However, at the level of narrative voice, *The Third Life* fails to achieve the integrated linguistic mode represented by Ruth's speech. The figurative energy of black folk speech occasionally animates the narrator's language, in such vivid phrases as "he asked hoarsely, his mouth tasting like somebody'd died up in it" (p. 133). On the whole, however, the narrator's entirely literate and literary standard English is clearly demarcated from the dialect spoken by some of the novel's characters. Standard English frequently widens the gap between the narrator and the black "folk" community portrayed in the novel: "To most of the people at the funeral Shipley's presence was a status symbol and an insult, though they were not used to thinking in those terms and would not have expressed such a mixed feeling" (p. 31). The narrator's standard English is valorized in this passage as a linguistic mode enabling a complex expression that is inaccessible to the black folk speech community.

While refusing to privilege the oral voice as the source of a new black literary authority, *The Third Life* does not supply any alternative means of authorizing a distinctly black voice in fiction. In fact, *The Third Life* is the only one of all the novels discussed here that retains intact the conventional authority of the omniscient narrator's discourse in classic realist fiction. The first-person narration of both of Gayl Jones's novels evokes the "subjective testimony" mode of black oral forms.[41] Let alone omniscience, Jones's narrators do not even claim the authority of realism, as reality and fantasy inseparably merge in the narrative discourse of both *Corregidora* and *Eva's Man*. Toni Morrison's novels do utilize third-person narrators but in neither novel is this narrator invested with omniscient powers. In *The Bluest Eye*, the dialogic interplay between the first- and third-person narrations, as well as the unusual framing of the third-person narration within the first, decenters the authority of the novel's third-person narrator. The third-person narrator of *Sula* disclaims omniscience by leaving gaps and absences of meaning in the text that can only be filled by the competing interpretations of the narrator, characters, and reader.

In marked contrast to these novels, *The Third Life* employs a third-person narrator who assumes the absolute ontologizing and explanatory power of the omniscient narrator of classic realist fiction.[42] We are never in any doubt about the reality or authenticity of the novel's discourse. Further, the highly directive omniscient narrator of *The Third Life* leaves little room for conflicting interpretations of the novel's characters and events. Unlike Morrison's and Jones's novels, in which the reader's active collaboration is a necessary component of the texts' production of meaning, *The Third Life* enacts a one-way transmission of meaning from the narrator to the reader, thus confirming the narrator's all-knowing authority, and delegating the reader a fairly uncomplicated function in the production of narrative meaning.

Paradoxically, then, we find that a text that sets out to subvert the "easy rightnesses" of Black Aesthetic reading modes actually ends up assigning its hypothetical reader the undemanding role of a passive receptor of narrative meaning. The omniscient narrator's uncontested authority represents only one instance of the way in which the novel's indebtedness to realist conventions restricts the full elaboration of its womanist project. We have already seen how, at a thematic level, *The Third Life* executes its ideological purpose by heralding, through the character of Ruth, an emergent black femininity that forms the center of a new womanist vision of community, time, and language. However, the novel's confinement within the realist mode (particularly conspicuous in a period of immense formal experimentation in black women's fiction) seriously curtails its ideological reach. The "rigorous realism"[43] of *The Third Life* not only secures the most conventional contract between narrator and reader, but also foregrounds the psychological changes of unique individuals, changes that disrupt the collective tradition. Walker's womanist project, on the contrary, is to integrate the past and the present, the individual and the community, personal and political change, into a unified whole. In *The Third Life*, a realist narrative focus on individual, psychological conversions eclipses the womanist concern with the political transformation of the "entire people" (*Search*, p. xi).[44] Showing realism to be an ineffective formal vehicle for Walker's womanist project, *The Third Life* clarifies, by default, the importance of a symbiotic connection between formal innovation and ideological opposition in Walker's subsequent fiction. The oppositional scope of Walker's project may be truly measured only in Walker's second novel, *Meridian*, which strives to expand the formal as well as the ideological domain of black women's fiction.

VII

"A CRAZY QUILT"
THE MULTIVALENT PATTERN OF *MERIDIAN*

Alice Walker used the phrase "crazy quilt" to describe the form of her second novel, *Meridian* (1976). Walker characterized the crazy quilt as an innovative fictional form that eschewed the "rigorous realism" of her first novel.[1] A capacious, highly flexible form, the crazy quilt offers Walker a womanist medium that thoroughly scrambles the reading codes of Black Aesthetic ideology. The quilting metaphor secures the functional intent of *Meridian*, but as a "crazy" quilt, the novel exhibits a formal irregularity and an ideological multivalence that resist any reduction to the "easy rightnesses" of the Black Aesthetic.[2] While *The Third Life of Grange Copeland* attempts an integration of black nationalism and womanism, *Meridian* admits no compromise with black nationalist ideology. Disclosing the inability of black nationalism to accommodate the ideological intentions of womanism, *Meridian* appropriates the feminine folk form of quilting to refract Walker's womanist ideology.

Of all the novels examined here, *Meridian* is the most topical and overtly political, in its direct thematic engagement with the black nationalist and Civil Rights movements. *Meridian* has often been labeled "a Civil Rights novel";[3] Walker herself remarked that the novel is "about the Civil Rights movement" and about "feminism."[4] In fact, the novel's rather nostalgic recovery of the Southern Civil Rights movement supports its sustained feminist critique of the nationalist movements of the North.[5] In her collection of poems, *Revolutionary Petunias*, Walker commemorates those "crazy," politically incorrect black women who "hated judgements / (black and otherwise) / and wove a life / of stunning contradiction." Like the women in *Revolutionary Petunias*, who "love the questions themselves,"[6] Meridian, too, views revolution as a matter of asking questions rather than "a handing down of answers."[7] As we saw in chapter 1, black feminist writers of the 1970s such as Ntozake Shange and Audre Lorde refused the rigid, absolutist stance of black nationalism in favor of a politics that could admit and encourage questions, differences, and contradictions. In keeping with this black feminist spirit, *Meridian* celebrates a revolutionary who is "exemplary" precisely because she is "flawed."[8] The "stubborn ambivalence" of Meridian's nature (p. 188) guarantees her exclusion from a nationalist movement that projects itself as an imposing political monolith.

More specifically, Meridian is a political outcast because she questions, among other things, the definition of black femininity in nationalist discourse. The novel's central black male nationalist, a character with the telling name Truman, idealizes, in his paintings and sculptures, an abstract African woman who is a repository of superhuman strength. Meridian corrects this perception, admitting, "I *am* strong, actually," but "I'm just not superwoman" (p. 32). For Truman, the black woman's strength is admirable only as long as it gratifies "his own sense of masculinity" (p. 113); Meridian initially appeals to him because of "her brown strength that he imagined would not mind being a resource for someone else" (p. 141). In actuality, however, Meridian challenges, in the most dramatically visible terms, Truman's conception of the black woman as a nurturer of the black nationalist's newfound sense of manhood. Her closely cropped hair, railroad cap, and dungarees signal her refusal of the conventional physical signs of femininity. Truman's nationalist art portrays black women as "fat," "voluptuous," "magnificent giants" with "monstrous" flanks and "breasts like melons" (p. 168). Meridian's skeletal frame is her most conspicuous bodily mark of difference from this ideal black woman conceived as sheer bodily abundance.

Meridian's body, as the symbolic site of a radical redefinition of black womanhood, contests not only Truman's nationalist fantasy of the black woman as an Amazonic bodily plenitude, but also the black middle-class ideal of "processed" femininity (p. 39). Saxon College, a black middle-class institution dedicated to suppressing funk and producing ladies, attempts to squeeze the black woman's body into the straitjacket of conventional white femininity.[9] Meridian's bodily revolt against the repressive Saxon regime takes the form of severe stuttering, headaches, and, most theatrically, a physical paralysis that parodies an objectified conception of femininity. In the first chapter of the novel, for instance, Meridian wills her body into a catatonic trance that mimics the paralysis of Marilene O'Shay, the white mummy woman whose body is exploited by her husband as a profitable commercial spectacle. Marilene O'Shay is billed as an "Obedient Daughter," a "Devoted Wife," and an "Adoring Mother" (p. 19). A fourth sign, "Gone Wrong," perhaps most accurately captures Meridian's deviance from these traditional feminine roles: Meridian leaves her husband and proves to be a disobedient daughter as well as an errant mother when she gives away her child.

Meridian resists these prescribed feminine identities only by means of a complete desexualization of her body. Her asceticism is an inevitable consequence of her suspicion of heterosexual pleasure. Heterosexuality, as it is presented in the novel, is never fulfilling for women because it requires passive submission to masculine pleasure. Meridian's body "never had any intention of giving in" (p. 67), and thus she "had not once been completely fulfilled by sex" (p. 115). Not only Meridian's, but all the heterosexual relationships in the novel remain caught in a set of fixed, constricting definitions of sexual and racial identity. Truman, for example, frequently lapses into a racist, stereotypical perception of his wife, Lynne, as a "white bitch" (p. 132), just as Lynne often reduces him to the racist stereotype of the "nigger" (p. 148). For Lynne, interracial sex leads to a rape that she does not report because she wants to escape the stereotype of the white woman whose cry of rape historically instigated the indiscriminate lynching of black men. The stereotypical nature of the rape scene is conveyed by Lynne's impression that she is passively enacting a heavily predetermined heterosexual encounter. Lynne imagines herself at the center of a racist *Esquire* painting that depicts a nude white woman being raped by a gang of black men. Despite her best intentions, Lynne assumes the painting's racist angle of vision, seeing her black rapist, Tommy Odds, and his friends as "savages" with "sharp, pointed," "gleaming teeth" (p. 161).

The novel can find no way of retrieving a natural heterosexuality that precedes or exceeds this socially overdetermined racist and sexist structuring. Its representation of heterosexuality would seem to set *Meridian* apart not only from Black Aesthetic fiction, but even from the typical womanist novel, which, as Ogunyemi has argued, always ends with integrative images of the black male and female spheres.[10] In a conciliatory statement that betrays her discomfort with *Meridian*'s treatment of heterosexuality, Walker insisted: "No matter in what anger I have written about the Black man, I have never once let go of his hand."[11] And indeed, despite its thematic critique of heterosexuality, *Meridian* does accomplish a structural integration of the black masculine and feminine principles. The novel's structure, consisting of three parts titled "Meridian," "Truman," and "Ending," seems to support a heterosexual division of masculinity and femininity that is resolved in the synthesis of the final section.

Like *Sula*, however, *Meridian* evokes a binary heterosexual structure only in order to redefine and to divest the terms *masculine* and *feminine* of their traditional connotations. Just as the Nel-Sula pair both retains and displaces the gender dualism of heterosexuality, so Meridian and Truman are opposed and finally fused in a structural dialectic that does not quite endorse the rigid gender opposition that undergirds both black nationalist and white American middle-class ideologies. As Marie Buncombe has argued, *Meridian* affirms an androgynous vision that destabilizes any absolute polarization of masculinity and femininity.[12] Meridian's character combines masculine and feminine elements throughout the novel, and she is reconciled to Truman only after his feminization.[13] At the end of the novel, Meridian is able to love Truman, but this ending can scarcely be read as an affirmation of heterosexual love, for Meridian's love is "not sexual," and is, in fact, a love that is "totally free" of the possession and exchange ethic of heterosexuality (p. 173). Truman's "intensely maternal" love for Meridian at the end of the novel (p. 213) illustrates a similar subversion of heterosexual gendering. The final union of Meridian and Truman thus presents a womanist reconfiguration of sexuality that exceeds the heterosexual vision of black nationalist ideology. Seemingly obeying the nationalist dictate that black literature should celebrate the complementarity of black men and women, *Meridian* challenges a heterosexual structuring of masculinity and femininity as stable, essential attributes.

That Truman feels "intensely maternal" toward Meridian at the end of the novel is significant, for it exemplifies the novel's revision not only of the heterosexual but also of the reproductive definition of femininity in black nationalist discourse. Earlier in the novel, Truman's conception of the black woman displays all the repressed contradictions of the nationalist celebration of black motherhood. Like Eldridge Cleaver's and Robert Staples's encomiums to the black woman's procreative contribution to the revolution,[14] Truman's art celebrates a mythicized black mother "breeding forth the warriors of the new universe" (p. 168). Truman entreats Meridian to "*have* his beautiful Black babies" (p. 16), but he turns away in shame and disgust when he learns that Meridian actually has a child. Truman's ambivalence mirrors the contradictory attitude to reproduction in black nationalist discourse, which devalued actual mothers as reactionary obstacles to revolution while celebrating the abstraction of mythical black motherhood.

Throughout the novel, Meridian attempts to bridge the gap between this mythicized black mother and her own experience of motherhood as an oppressive burden. Like Ursa Corregidora, Meridian feels racked by guilt and inadequacy because she cannot live up to the maternal history of her ancestors. While Ursa feels unworthy because her hysterectomy disables her from fulfilling the reproductive goal of her maternal ancestors' history, Meridian disqualifies herself from the historical tradition of black motherhood by giving away her child. Meridian is aware, like Ursa, of the oppositional political value of reproduction for black slave women:

> Enslaved women had thought their greatest blessing from "Freedom" was that it meant they could keep their own children. And what had Meridian Hill done with *her* precious child? She had given him away. She thought of her mother as being worthy of this maternal history, and of herself as belonging to an unworthy minority, for which there was no precedent and of which she was, as far as she knew, the only member. (p. 91)

Like Ursa and Sula, Meridian achieves a new and free black feminine identity by denying the reproductive imperative of her maternal ancestors. However, unlike Sula, Meridian mourns her inability to "live up to the standard of motherhood that had gone before" (p. 91).

Meridian is intimidated by this standard because she shares, to a great extent, the black nationalist idealization of the black mother, even viewing her own mother as "Black motherhood personified" (p. 96). *Meridian*, like *The Bluest Eye*, *Sula*, and *Corregidora*, militates against this kind of mythicized perception of reproduction in its presentation of several specific maternal narratives that deviate from the exacting standard of ideal black motherhood. Even Mrs. Hill, who embodies, for Meridian, the glorious institution of black motherhood, is shown, from the narrator's point of view, to be an ordinary woman who reluctantly meets the staggering obligations of black motherhood. Mrs. Hill's first pregnancy marks the end of her personal life, and distracts her from "who she was" (p. 50). Her children are "burdens to her always" because they steal her "emerging self" (p. 51). It is precisely this contradiction between self-development and nurturance of children that motivates Meridian's rejection of her own child, recalling the logic of Sula's often-quoted refusal of motherhood: "I don't want to make somebody else. I want to make myself."[15] Viewing childrearing as a kind of "slavery," Meridian demystifies the traditional image of "The Happy Mother" (p. 69), just as Mrs. Hill learns to distrust the "secret joy" that mothers are expected to feel (p. 51). Meridian's and her mother's perceptions of motherhood as an oppressive condition are corroborated by the narratives of many of the novel's minor characters, such as Nelda, whose pregnancy is described as "her fall" (88), and Nelda's mother, whose loss of hair with each pregnancy signals her successive loss of herself in her children.

Meridian is able to tolerate and survive her brief experience of motherhood only by taking recourse to guilt-ridden fantasies of suicide and infanticide, again recalling *Sula*, in which Eva Peace finally frees herself from motherhood by burning her own son. Meridian's experience of motherhood is presented as typical of the experience of black women, for suicide and infanticide are the twin motifs that are woven through most of the novel's narratives about pregnant women. For example, the nameless girl in prison kills her own child, and Wile Chile kills herself and her unborn baby by running under a car. In addition to these characters, who inhabit the narrative present of the novel, *Meridian* also presents several instances of black women in the past who committed infanticide. The slave woman Louvinie, for example, violates the mammy's role thrust on her by her slavemaster by indirectly killing his child. In a later phase of black women's history, the legendary Fast Mary of the Tower kills her newborn child and subsequently commits suicide.

These stories of several black women for whom reproduction entails suicide and/or murder serve the function of demythicizing the tradition of ideal black motherhood. The novel's treatment of reproduction is, however, far more complicated and contradictory than a simple realistic demystification of the myth of black motherhood. The image of the Sojourner tree offers one possible route toward understanding the novel's difficult representation of reproduction. Louvinie's murder of the white child in her charge is an act of political resistance against the enforced duty of black motherhood. The fact that Louvinie kills the child through her storytelling establishes the novel's disconcerting connection between infanticide and the expression of black women's verbal creativity. Louvinie's act is, however, punished by her symbolic and literal loss of speech: her white slavemaster cuts off her tongue, which Louvinie buries in the ground, and which nourishes the flourishing growth of the magnolia tree.[16] For succeeding generations of black women, this tree becomes the site of a nonreproductive black feminine community. Decades after Louvinie's death, the girls at Saxon College hold a "commemoration" around the magnolia tree, to which "any girl who had ever prayed for her period to come was welcome" (p. 45). This ceremony, which commemorates the death of Fast Mary, another black woman who challenged the reproductive obligation, is the only occasion when all the women at Saxon College are joined into a cohesive collective unit: "It was the only time in all the many social activities at Saxon that every girl was considered equal. On that day, they held each others' hands tightly" (p. 45).

In the next phase of the history of the magnolia tree, the girls at Saxon College unite to demonstrate because the authorities refuse to bury Wile Chile within the college grounds. This contestatory act is, like Louvinie's, a protest against the societal construction of black motherhood, for Wile Chile's illegitimate pregnancy reinforces her marginal social status and ultimately leads to her suicide. However, in the course of their demonstration, the Saxon students chop down the Sojourner tree, thus destroying the symbolic source of their own collectivity as well as the (literally) buried possibility of their political voice. In cutting down the magnolia tree, the Saxon women only succeed in rupturing the continuity between themselves and preceding generations of black women, a generational continuity paradoxically predicated on their rejection of reproduction.

The Sojourner tree, then, is the contradictory symbolic locus where the novel's exposure of motherhood as a kind of "slavery" (p. 69) uneasily coexists with its metaphorical celebration of the mother as the source of a liberatory black feminine history. Several critics have observed that the Sojourner tree symbolizes the buried possibilities of an alternative maternal history.[17] The very name of the tree recalls a historical figure, Sojourner Truth, who is often celebrated as the originator, or "mother," of black women's political resistance in the United States. Imagery further identifies the Sojourner tree with a specifically black maternal tradition: the leaves of the tree are "like the inverted peaks of a mother's half-straightened kinky hair" (p. 48).

However, sharply contradicting the novel's metaphorical recovery of an oppositional maternal tradition, the novel's actual mothers invariably represent obstacles to political resistance and change. Meridian's mother, for example, uses her Christian faith to bolster her political conservatism (p. 78), and is "infuriate[d]" by Meridian's involvement in the Civil Rights movement (p. 85). This characterization of the mother as the prime barrier to revolutionary change recalls the black nationalist alignment of the mother with the "Old Spirituality."[18] To an extent, then, the novel's womanist exploration of an oppositional maternal history is blocked by the contemporary ideological portrayal of the mother as a reactionary force allied with the oppressive past. This blockage is apparent in the tension between the novel's mythical and realistic registers; the novel's realistic demystification of motherhood vies with its celebration of a maternal tradition that frequently takes on mythical and legendary proportions, especially in the treatment of the Sojourner tree, Louvinie, and Fast Mary.

Despite this ambivalence toward the mother, which the novel shares with *The Third Life*, *Meridian* more fully and overtly develops the emancipatory possibilities of maternal history than does *The Third Life*. The novel's womanist revision of history, authorized by the maternal metaphor, may be better appreciated with reference to Dianne Sadoff's essay "Black Matrilineage: The Case of Alice Walker and Zora Neale Hurston," which compares three different models of literary history. In Harold Bloom's oedipal model, the white masculine writer can clear his own place in the tradition only by means of a symbolic murder of cultural ancestors. Virginia Woolf, and Sandra Gilbert and Susan Gubar, proffer an alternative model of cultural tradition for white women authors, which, according to Sadoff, "alters Bloom's 'anxiety of influence' to 'matrilineal anxiety.'" This anxiety is produced by the white woman writer's discovery of "signs of inferiorization, self-hatred and suppressed rebellion" in the texts of her maternal precursors.[19] The black woman writer, in contrast, disguises her anxiety about the double sources of her cultural disinheritance by means of an idealized celebration of matrilineage and of the cultural past.[20] It is her unequivocal commitment to the ancestral past and to cultural continuity that differentiates the black woman writer's relation to the prior tradition from the anxiety-ridden relation of white men and women writers to their cultural past.

Unfortunately, Sadoff does not offer a model of cultural influence for the black masculine writer, for such a model would help to distinguish even more sharply the unique dynamics of a black feminine cultural

tradition. Most black male writers have predictably denied the presence of white cultural ancestors in their works, but perhaps not as easy
to understand is their equally vehement disavowal of the black cultural
past. Canonized writers such as Richard Wright, James Baldwin, and
Ralph Ellison have all pitted their work against that of their predecessors, lamenting the absence of a usable black literary tradition.[21] Later,
in the 1960s, the title of Baraka's essay "The Myth of a 'Negro Literature'" bespeaks Baraka's reluctance to concede the very existence of a
black literary tradition. Baraka's sense of the "almost agonizing medi-
ocrity" of his literary precursors leads to his dismissal of the prior
black literary tradition as a mere "myth."[22] Like Baraka, many Black
Aesthetic theorists expressed their rejection of the cultural past in absolute, hyperbolic terms. In his essay "The Function of Black Literature at
the Present Time," Addison Gayle denounced the entire black fictional
tradition, from William Wells Brown to James Baldwin and Ralph Ellison, for its tendency toward cultural assimilationism. Relegating his
literary ancestors to an obsolete past,[23] the male Black Aesthetic writer
affirmed his own commitment, in Hoyt Fuller's words, to "new forms,
new limits, new shapes."[24] As we saw in chapter 1, this emphatic denial
of cultural ancestry produced its own contradictions; the Black Aestheticians' search for new cultural forms reverted to a search for origins,
inadvertently staging the return of their repressed past.

In exact opposition to the black masculine writer, the black woman
writer eagerly embraces her cultural predecessors in an attempt to
contextualize her own work within an enduring historical tradition.
Sadoff's essay probes some of the fears and anxieties that motivate the
black woman writer's recovery of her matrilineal heritage. As Sadoff
argues, the black woman writer tends to mask her fear of cultural disinheritance in a frequently idealized affirmation of her cultural fore-
bears.[25] Many of Alice Walker's essays on the achievements of earlier
black women writers amply illustrate Sadoff's argument. Where the
Black Aesthetic critic would censure the assimilationist impulses of
early writers such as Phyllis Wheatley, Alice Walker acknowledges the
ideological ambivalence of Wheatley's work, but finally makes her
peace with this most-maligned foremother of the black women's literary tradition:

> At last, Phyllis, we understand. No more snickering when your stiff,
> struggling, ambivalent lines are forced on us. We know now that you
> were not an idiot or a traitor; only . . . a woman who still struggled to
> sing the song that was your gift, although in a land of barbarians who
> praised your bewildered tongue. It is not so much what you sang, as
> that you kept alive, in so many of our ancestors, *the notion of song.*
> (*Search,* p. 237)

In another essay with the telling title "Saving the Life That Is Your

Own: The Importance of Models in the Artist's Life," Walker recounts the cautionary tale of her discovery of Zora Neale Hurston as a literary model, arguing that the contemporary black woman writer can fend off her sense of cultural dispossession only through a conscientious reclamation of the lost maternal tradition (*Search*, pp. 3–14).

Meridian undertakes this womanist project of excavating the submerged layers of black maternal history. What justifies the term *maternal history* is the novel's commitment to the past and to generational continuity as the necessary grounds for future development. The novel explicitly contrasts its womanist paradigm of historical transformation to the model posited in black nationalist discourse. A typical black male nationalist, Truman overstates his own radical difference from the past: "unlike any other Black man," Truman is "courageous and new" (p. 100). Sharing the nationalist vision of change as an abrupt break from the past, Truman is shocked by the persistence of racial segregation in Chicokema, for it belies his expectation that "the Civil Rights movement changed all that!" (p. 19). At the beginning of the novel, before his nationalist notion of time is revised under Meridian's influence, Truman imagines political revolution as a linear movement with a definite beginning and end (p. 27).

Given the novel's scathing critique of this naive conception of change, it is hardly surprising that nationalist critics were dismayed by Walker's representation of history in *Meridian*. Addison Gayle, for example, remarked that "if Alice Walker is writing a good historical novel, then we're in trouble."[26] Walker's womanist version of history is most incompatible with black nationalist discourse in its redirection of the focus of history toward the past rather than the future. Meridian is debarred from the nationalist group at Saxon College because she is "held by something in the past" (p. 27), held even by the "decidedly unrevolutionary" elements of the past (p. 30). As a casualty of the brave new world of the revolutionaries, Meridian fears that she will be left behind, "listening to the old music, beside the highway" (p. 201). Even when Meridian's true revolutionary stature is established at the end of the novel, her rebirth into a revolutionary cannot be read in black nationalist terms. Unlike the birth of the new black male nationalist, Meridian's rebirth does not require an abrupt, decisive rupture from the past: "something in her was exactly the same as she had always been. . . . The new part had grown out of the old" (p. 219).

Paralleling Meridian's personal transformation, the novel envisions political change as a continuous process assisted rather than impeded by the past. Alice Walker repeatedly expresses, in her essays, her conviction that "there are always people in history (or herstory) who help us."[27] Refusing the nationalist view of the past as entirely dispensable, *Meridian* reclaims the liberatory possibilities of unofficial history, possibilities that have been effaced by dominant, official versions of history. In one of the most suggestive essays published on *Meridian*, Alan Nadel writes that the novel treats "narrative as archeology," unearthing and reconstructing the buried layers of the history of marginal cultural groups in the United States.[28] One such layer, as we have already seen, is uncovered in the novel's gradual revelation of the unwritten history of black mothers in the United States, a history that symbolically converges around the Sojourner tree. Another such layer is the unofficial history of Native Indians, which has been overlaid and disguised by official American history. Walter Longknife, for example, struggles to preserve his "historical vision" of himself and his people (p. 55), but the geographical site of his vision, the burial mound of the Sacred Serpent, is appropriated and violated by the county officials who turn the mound into a public amusement park.

Meridian, however, is able to retrieve the historical significance of the Sacred Serpent through her recursion into her own ancestral history. As elsewhere in the novel, it is the feminine ancestors who preserve the transformative possibilities of unofficial history. Meridian's great-grandmother, Feather Mae, prevents her husband from erecting his farm over the burial mound. Sharing the Native Indian vision of life and death as a unified continuum, Feather Mae is "renewed" by her communion with the spirits of the dead buried in the Sacred Serpent (p. 57). Taking after her great-grandmother, Meridian respects the value invested in the ancestral dead in Native Indian culture. At the burial mound, Meridian rejoices over "so tangible a connection to the past" (p. 59). Her experience of ecstasy at the Sacred Serpent subtends the political activism of her later life, as she draws the strength to fight for change from her own ancestral past: "She could summon whatever energy a task that had to be performed required, and . . . this ability seemed to her something her ancestors had passed on from the days of slavery" (p. 145).

The novel's tribute to the sustaining power of the ancestral past is itself a gesture of cultural renovation, restoring the belief system of Native Indian culture, a system that, with the construction of the amusement park, seems to be "already and forever lost" (p. 59). Walker's epigraph to *Meridian*, a passage taken from *Black Elk Speaks*, mourns the massacre at Wounded Knee: "A people's dream died there. It was a beautiful dream. . . . [T]he nation's hoop is broken and scattered. There is no center any longer, and the sacred tree is dead" (p. 11). Black Elk's elegy reverberates throughout *Meridian*, as the novel attempts an imaginary recuperation of each of the values lost at Wounded Knee. The dream of the Native Indian people, historically put to death at Wounded Knee, is imaginatively recaptured in Feather Mae's dream of ancestral spirits at the Indian burial mound (p. 57). If Black Elk laments the loss of a centered vision, Meridian's experience at the Sacred Serpent replaces this center, reassembling what has been historically scattered: "The outward flow, the rush of images, returned to the center of the pit where she stood, and what had left her at its going was returned" (p. 58). The novel symbolically compensates for the death of the "sacred tree" through its celebration of the Sojourner tree, "that mighty, ancient, sheltering" tree (p. 48) that seemingly dies early in the novel only to be resurrected at the end.

The one image from the Black Elk passage that resonates most powerfully throughout the novel is the image of the broken hoop, a circular image that authorizes the title, structure, and temporal vision of *Meridian*. One of the definitions of "meridian" that Walker provides at the beginning of the novel is the astronomical sense of the word as "an imaginary great circle" (p. 13). Walker's use of the circle image in one of her essays amplifies its meaning in *Meridian*. In an essay partially titled "Welcoming the Old, Funny-Talking Ancient Ones into the Warm Room of Present Consciousness," Walker writes that "the love one feels for them [the ancestors] keeps the circle unbroken."[29] The circle here describes a temporal wholeness, a unification of past and present that depends on ancestral continuity. *Meridian* attempts to reconstitute the broken hoop through a circular structure that smoothly mediates between different temporal moments. Walker has described the structure of *Meridian* as a "crazy quilt," a pattern that "can jump back and forth in time."[30] Eschewing chronology, the circular structure of *Meridian* shifts rapidly back and forth in time, focusing similar experiences and issues through different temporal lenses. In the narrative time of the novel, the historical past of slavery (represented in the story of Louvinie), Meridian's ancestral past (the story of Feather Mae), and the narrative present of Meridian's life are quilted into a multilayered vision of time as a synthesis of past and present. Interweaving the narratives of the dead and the living, and cataloging the casualties of "a decade marked by death" (such as Medgar Evers, Malcolm X, and Martin Luther King, Jr.), the novel strives to counterbalance the loss of "shared rituals for the dead" in contemporary U.S. society (p. 33). The circular structure of *Meridian* in a sense compensates for the temporal chaos and fragmentation that result when the "hoop is broken and scattered," and when the past is devalued in a society that depends on television as its only "repository of memory" (p. 33).

In addition to this compensatory function, the novel also takes on the more difficult task of symbolically enacting the very process of revolutionary transformation.[31] The circular structure of *Meridian* is radically dissimilar to the cyclic structure of novels such as *The Bluest Eye* or *Eva's Man*, which stage a bleak drama of history as overdetermined repetition. *Meridian* is also designed on the principle of repetition, but each of the novel's repetitive returns executes a variation on the preceding turn of the cycle, thus leaving open the possibility of transformation. In this respect, the novel's use of a repetition-with-variation structure resembles the spiral structure of *Sula* and the blues form of *Corregidora*, all of which depart from the historical vision of black nationalism in their figuration of change as a processual development of the past cycle.

It is not accidental that *Meridian*, like *Sula* and *Corregidora*, utilizes the temporal structure of black oral forms to elaborate its vision of historical change as a continuous process. Sherley Anne Williams argues that black oral forms constitute "a ritualized way of talking about ourselves and passing it on," and thus provide "a basis of historical continuity for Black people."[32] *Meridian* establishes a sense of historical continuity by means of its structural reliance on the circular method of black storytelling. The novel's frequent and flexible movement across different historical periods exemplifies a central structural feature of oral storytelling, which, as Gayl Jones describes it, is marked by "rapid transitions between one period and the next."[33] The novel's circular, incremental structure almost exactly replicates the nonlinear structure of black folk tales. Roger Abrahams has characterized the black folk tale as an achronological presentation of "repeated and over-repeated action" that is episodic, improvisatory, and "open to interruption and digression."[34] Exhibiting each of these structural elements, *Meridian* consists of short episodic anecdotes that are connected to each other not by a linear logic but by a technique of improvisatory repetition with variation. Several short chapters in *Meridian*, such as "Gold," appear to be pointless interruptions and digressions that do not further the linear progress of the plot or directly contribute to the revelation of theme. The "'to-be-continued' feeling at the conclusion" of black folk tales[35] also hangs over the end of *Meridian*, which, instead of completing the novel's action, passes it on to Truman, who is to resume Meridian's endless quest. A self-reflexive passage in *Meridian* explicitly rejects the linear closure of conventional fictional plots: Meridian dreams "she was a character in a novel and that her existence presented an insoluble problem, one that would be solved only by her death at the end" (p. 117). But Meridian does not die at the end of the novel; she simply goes away, resisting the death-like finality and the problem-solving impetus of typical linear plots. In this respect, again, the novel fits Abrahams's description of the black folk tale as "a story that has no end," a processual unraveling of a problem that has no final solution.[36]

In addition to its structural dependence on storytelling, *Meridian* thematically treats other oral and folk forms as the most effective vehicles of lasting political transformation. Any political change that does not build on the centuries-old folk tradition is shown to be self-destructive, as, for example, in the scene in which the Saxon students cut down the Sojourner tree in the course of their political protest. Unlike the Saxon students, who misdirect their anger against their own folk tradition, Meridian can proclaim her full commitment to revolutionary politics only in a folk context. The church scene in the chapter titled "Camara" most explicitly develops the oppositional potential of black oral culture. Unlike the church of Meridian's mother, which is a bulwark of political conservatism, the church in "Camara" is a black folk institution that has adapted itself to contemporary political needs, becoming an instrument of militant black power. Instead of the "traditional pale Christ" (p. 198), this church flaunts a photograph of a slain Civil Rights martyr. The preacher shocks Meridian out of her preconception of the "Black church as mainly a reactionary power" (p. 199) through his spirited political sermon, which satirizes Richard Nixon and echoes the voice of Martin Luther King, Jr. What most surprises Meridian is that the congregation has replaced the traditional church music with a "quite martial melody" (p. 195). A picture titled "B. B., With Sword" (p. 199), with its obvious allusion to the famous blues musician B. B. King, further confirms the new militant spirit of black oral forms.

In her essays, Walker often presents black music as a cultural paradigm for black Americans: "I am trying to arrive at that place where Black music already is, to arrive at that unselfconscious sense of collective oneness."[37] In the church scene, music is the force that binds the congregation into "One Life": "It is the song of the people, transformed by the experiences of each new generation, that holds them together" (p. 201). The black musical tradition is the source of a new, politicized black collectivity that is empowered rather than constrained by its long history: "the music, the form of worship that has always sustained us, the kind of ritual you share with us, these are the ways to transformation that we know" (p. 200). The necessary alignment of the terms *collectivity* and *temporal continuity* in the novel's treatment of the oral tradition indirectly clarifies the incoherent articulation of these terms in black nationalist discourse. Like *Sula*, *Meridian* obliquely reveals the nationalist notion of collectivity to be untenable because it so absolutely disavows the past cultural tradition.

In *Meridian*, Walker tries to activate the collective dynamics of black oral forms, an attempt that only partially succeeds for, as we shall see later, the narrative voice of *Meridian* does not quite reproduce the collective voice of black oral forms. However, at the level of narrative structure, the novel successfully models itself on black musical forms, soliciting a collective approach to thematic problems through its use of the call-and-response pattern of black music. To give an example, the various narrative pieces dealing with Louvinie, Fast Mary, Wile Chile, Meridian's mother, Nelda, and Miss Treasure all develop the common theme of reproduction. The meaning of reproduction in the novel can be understood only through a call-and-response interplay between these various episodes that inserts each woman's experience of reproduction into a collective history.

However, the communal narrative frame established by the novel's call-and-response method does not quite approximate the cohesive community posited in black nationalist discourse. As we have already seen, Black Aesthetic theorists invested oral forms with the special power to authorize a pure and untroubled collective voice in black literature. *Meridian* repeatedly tests its own communal vision, guarding against any easy assumption of a collective voice. The novel's diverse short narratives about women do not, through a simple process of accretion, amount to a unified representation of black feminine collectivity. In fact, several characters, such as Wile Chile, Anne, and the nameless girl in prison, are included in the novel primarily because they stretch and finally escape the feminine collectivity that the novel, as well as Meridian, seeks to establish. The narrative of Wile Chile most dramatically illustrates the novel's refusal of a totalized collective vision. Wile Chile personifies the absolutely marginal other who cannot be contained by any collective construct. The word *capture* insistently recurs in the chapter describing Meridian's attempt to induct Wile Chile into the black feminine community at Saxon College. In a scene that disturbingly recalls the archetypal conquest of the primitive other, Meridian lures Wile Chile into the cultured world of Saxon College "with bits of cake and colored beads and unblemished cigarettes" (p. 36). Dragged onto the campus "with a catgut string around her arm" (p. 36), Wile Chile is forced into a community she does not wish to join. Meridian's ugly, coercive capture of Wile Chile ends, appropriately, with Wile Chile's death in the process of escape. The chapter ironically evokes the vocabulary of call and response to signal the failure of community in this scene; when confronted by Wile Chile, Meridian falls into a comatose trance in which "she did not respond to anything; not the call to lunch, not the phone, nothing" (p. 36). The Wile Chile chapter acknowledges what eludes the novel's representation of black feminine community, thus counteracting the somewhat facile conversion of black folk such as Mabel Turner and Margaret Treasure to Meridian's politicized black feminine community. Clarifying the limits of a monolithic vision of community, the novel offers, instead, a tentative collective vision enriched by its failures, differences, and contradictions.

However, the novel's vision of community seems strained rather than enriched at the level of narrative voice. Alice Walker believed that the artist should be "the voice of the people" (*Search*, p. 138), but the narrative voice of *Meridian* is quite distinct from the "voice of the people." In fact, the troublesome use of the generalized term "the people" betrays the novel's difficulty in assuming a collective voice. After rejecting the absolutist nationalist community at Saxon College, Meridian decides to go South in search of "the people" (p. 31). The symbolic equation of South and community is typical of Walker's fiction, exemplifying her belief that "what the Southern writer inherits as a natural right is a sense of community" (*Search*, p. 17). However, this "natural" sense of community is tested at a linguistic level in the chapters dealing with "the people" in the South. The standard English of Meridian and the narrator sets them apart from "the people," who usually speak a form of Southern black dialect. Moreover, the narrator frequently assumes the stance of an ethnographic interpreter rather than a representative of the black community. This ethnographic posture is most intrusive in the narrator's generalized reference to the black community as "these people":

> "But that's nothing," these people said, who had done nothing before beyond complaining among themselves and continually weeping. "People will laugh at us because that is not radical," they said, choosing to believe radicalism would grow over their souls like a bright armor overnight. (p. 191)

The political naivete of "these people" is rather condescendingly treated by the narrator, who seems to be implicitly addressing a readership that is, like the narrator, more politically canny than the represented black community.

The narrator's distance from "the voice of the people" is most conspicuously apparent in the chapter dealing with the unnamed girl in prison who kills her own child. Not only does this girl spurn Meridian's attempt to politicize her, but she also eludes the narrator's attempted linguistic appropriation of her. Describing how this girl felt when she killed her child, the narrative discourse switches back and forth between the past and the present tenses, and between "I" and "she," in an unsuccessful effort to claim an experience out of its own linguistic reach. The free indirect discourse in this passage strains awkwardly toward a fusion of the narrator's and character's voices, betraying the narrator's inability to represent the "voice of the people."

This inability to assume the untroubled collective voice of black oral forms would undoubtedly constitute a failure in Black Aesthetic terms. Meridian's divergence from the black oral paradigm, however, can be viewed more positively as an attempt to open a new formal space in black women's fiction that does not fully overlap with oral forms. Walker's metaphor of the crazy quilt describes a folk feminine form that is distinctly visual, and that should caution us against conflating the novel with the oral tradition. The crazy quilt is a formal melange constructed out of different fragments that do not necessarily cohere to produce a unified construct. The formal indeterminacy of the crazy quilt has generated a great deal of critical disagreement and confusion. While some critics, such as Susan Willis, have read the novel entirely as a fictional adaptation of the oral storytelling tradition, others, such as John Callahan, argue that the novel is not modeled on the oral tradition but instead takes its form "from the labyrinth of Meridian's mind."[38] Meridian provides ample support for each of these readings, stitching together oral as well as novelistic elements into a hybrid form that produces a highly complex and self-contradictory vision of black feminine identity.

We have already seen how the novel's intermeshing of oral and fictional modes produces a vision of collectivity that is greatly indebted to the call-and-response structure of oral storytelling, but that ultimately refuses the unified collective voice invested in oral forms by Black Aesthetic ideologues. The quilting metaphor most appropriately captures the novel's conception of collectivity as a composite of diverse, disparate elements. The novel's representation of the black feminine subject achieves a similar quilted effect, as several types of narrative rhetoric (oral storytelling, grotesque, mystical, and psychological) intersect to displace but not quite discard the category of the individual subject. The call-and-response structure of oral storytelling locates Meridian's character within a constantly shifting communal context that prohibits any extended narrative focus on a single individual. Moreover, the fragmentary, nonlinear structure typical of oral storytelling renders the development of Meridian's character as a discontinuous process. It is difficult to sustain a psychologically coherent image of Meridian's character, as her story is so often interrupted by abrupt temporal cuts and returns, and is interpenetrated by the stories of numerous other characters.

In its subversion of the realist category of self-sufficient, self-consistent individuality, the storytelling model is aided by the grotesque mode, which, as in *Sula*, signifies black feminine identity as unfinished and heterogeneous. The scene in which we are first introduced to Meridian calls attention to an absence in her character ("she ain't all there" [p. 22]), an impression later confirmed by Meridian's own feeling that "something's missing" in her (p. 27). It is in the grotesque representation of Meridian's body that the novel most seriously challenges the realist notion of self-sufficient individuality. Meridian's body is marked by grotesque lack and disability; she has "practically no hair" (p. 24), and she suffers from severe headaches, inexplicable fits of stuttering, blurred vision, and catatonic absences from herself. Meridian's incomplete body gives her a freedom unavailable to Toni Morrison's Pecola and Pauline, whose grotesque deficiency signifies their helpless entrapment in the distorted white cultural representation of the black feminine body. Affiliated to *Sula* rather than *The Bluest Eye*, *Meridian* explores the creative energies of a black feminine body conceived as grotesquely lacking and unstable.

Meridian goes even further than *Sula* in its deployment of the grotesque mode against the realist category of the individual subject. Alan Nadel has remarked on the connection the novel draws "between Meridian's body and the body politic," as it repeatedly enacts social and political conflicts upon the body of Meridian.[39] Two obvious instances

are Meridian's comatose trances during her first encounter with Wile
Chile and during a particularly violent Civil Rights demonstration. In
both situations, Meridian performatively transfers upon her own body
the social signs of sexual and racial disorder, as represented in the
pregnant body of Wile Chile, and in the surreal violence inflicted by
the police upon the Civil Rights demonstrators. Both incidents blur
the boundary between Meridian's body and the bodies of others, and
between the individual and the body politic. The black feminine subject
takes shape in these scenes not as an autonomous, self-contained individual, but as an open, intersubjective space crisscrossed and literally,
bodily, invaded by others. This representation of Meridian's body is
congruent with Bakhtin's celebratory description of the grotesque
body, as opposed to the unified, self-enclosed body of classic realism:
"the confines dividing it [the grotesque body] from the world are obscured, . . . and the exchange between the body and the world is constantly emphasized."[40]

However, whereas the grotesque body, as defined by Bakhtin, is thoroughly material and political, Meridian's body often fades off into a
mystical haze that blurs the novel's political focus. Meridian invites
moments of mystical ecstasy that transcend the material plane, and she
ultimately denies her body altogether in her commitment to asceticism.
Meridian's asceticism can be partly understood as a political gesture
of protest against the limited and constraining sexual roles allotted to
black women in a racist and sexist society. The political dimension of
Meridian's asceticism is, however, frequently overwritten by a Christian rhetoric of sainthood and martyrdom.[41] After one of her catatonic
spells, Meridian's head glows with a halo-like "full soft light" that reminds her friend, Anne-Marion, of Jesus Christ (p. 120), and at the end
of the novel, Meridian's "return to the world cleansed of sickness" is
likened to the resurrection of Lazarus (p. 219). The narrative line elevat-
ing Meridian into a saint runs unevenly throughout the novel, often
deflecting the line that characterizes her as a political revolutionary.
Meridian's politics seem to amount, in Dianne Sadoff's phrase, to nothing but the "powerless volunteer suffering" of a martyr, leaving no dis-
cernible impact upon the material world.[42] The political and mystical
levels most curiously intersect in the scene in which Meridian is beaten
by the police during a Civil Rights demonstration:

> Only once was she beaten into unconsciousness, and it was not the dam-
> age done to her body that she remembered when she woke up, but her
> feeling of yearning, of heartsick longing for forgiveness, as she saw the
> bright lights explode behind the red blood that curtained her face, and
> her feeling of hope as the harsh light of consciousness began to fade.
> (p. 97)

In this passage, the disturbing political implications of the police brutality inflicted on black demonstrators are entirely obfuscated by Meridian's mystical perception of violence as a means of bodily transcendence. Meridian's presence at the Civil Rights demonstration seems motivated not by a political impulse to protest the racist balance of power, but by a desire to scourge her body of some vague, unspecified sense of personal guilt. The novel's mystical rhetoric moves toward a transcendence of the body and of personal consciousness, conflicting with the grotesque mode, which seeks not to transcend the body but rather to mobilize and merge the individual body into a collective body politic.

The formal and ideological contradictions in the novel's characterization of Meridian are exacerbated by the presence of a fourth narrative mode, psychological realism, which activates a rhetoric of individualism that undermines the trans-individual focus of the storytelling, the grotesque, and the mystical modes. Despite its refusal of a linear structure, *Meridian* invokes the main thematic concerns of the bildungsroman to authorize the development of Meridian's unique self. In a thoughtful analysis of the tension between the novel's individual and collective emphases, Deborah McDowell demonstrates that *Meridian* contains all the principal thematic elements of the bildungsroman, such as: childhood, the conflict of generations, provinciality, self-education, alienation from society, ordeal by love, sexual initiation, and the search for a vocation and a working philosophy. McDowell concludes that these bildungsroman elements constitute Meridian's character as "a prototype for psychic wholeness and individual autonomy."[43] The novel's psychological delineation of full, self-sufficient individuality is distinctly at odds with the incomplete subject figured by the grotesque mode, and with the communal intersubjectivity implicit in both the grotesque and the storytelling modes.

The action in a bildungsroman novel is generated by a tacit faith in individual, psychological changes that do not necessarily accompany changes in the social and political system represented in the novel. Despite its self-avowed political focus, *Meridian* often tends to slide from the political to the individual register in its depiction of unique psychological changes that transcend the novel's given sociopolitical context. For example, when Lynne casts doubt on Meridian's political intentions, asking, "What are you looking for? These people will always be the same. You can't change them. Nothing will," Meridian replies, "But I can change. . . . I hope I will" (p. 152). Meridian's hope is fulfilled at the novel's conclusion, which abruptly shifts the earlier grotesque figuration of Meridian's body into a psychological frame; with "her newly grown hair," and "cleansed of sickness" (p. 219), Meridian is reborn into a whole individual. This psychological transformation is the only kind of change affirmed at the end of the novel, as we are given no reason to believe that Meridian's change has catalyzed, or been enabled by, a corresponding transformation of her social and political context.[44]

These various contradictions between the novel's oral, grotesque, mystical, and psychological modes defy any final resolution or synthesis, as *Meridian* provides us no basis for privileging one of these modes over the others. The coexistence of these disparate modes of characterization produces a highly fraught, indeterminate vision of black feminine identity. Resisting any clear formal or ideological characterization, the black feminine subject figured in *Meridian* confounds the functional expectations of the typical Black Aesthetic reader. The multiform representation of black feminine identity in *Meridian* is patterned on the crazy quilts produced by Walker's maternal ancestors. While serving the function of channeling black feminine creativity into useful, everyday practice, the crazy quilt eschews the simple functionality of black nationalist art. *Meridian* quilts together fragments of different, often incongruous materials and colors without subduing them to an overarching pattern. This refusal to conform to any aesthetic or ideological mastercode is frequently celebrated as a peculiarly feminine form of madness in Walker's work, especially in *Revolutionary Petunias*, in the short stories of *In Love and Trouble*, and in *Meridian*: hence her use of the term *crazy quilt*.[45]

While Meridian's character appears to be incoherent when subjected to a Black Aesthetic reading, the ideological frame of Walker's womanism is meant to reformat this incoherence into a creative multivalence. However, it is difficult to say precisely how the multivalence of *Meridian* offers a viable alternative to Black Aesthetic reading norms, except in the most obvious sense that any refusal of coherence constitutes a challenge to Black Aesthetic ideology. The novel's conflicting modes of characterization seem to overload Meridian's character with an abundance of meanings that it sometimes cannot carry. Meridian is simultaneously a saint, a revolutionary, an exceptional individual, and a representative member of her community. The novel plays with a profusion of formal possibilities that do not necessarily add up to produce a creative plenitude of meaning. *Meridian*'s boundless formal play certainly opens a new characterization of the black feminine subject, but it is difficult to grasp the newness of this subject with any exactitude or clarity. In its attempt to exceed the limits of Black Aesthetic ideology, *Meridian* over-signifies black feminine identity to an extreme where multivalence risks sliding into a limitless dispersal of meaning.

CONCLUSION
BLACK WOMEN'S FICTION IN THE 1970S

The multivalence of *Meridian*, bordering on incoherence, offers an extreme instance of the difficult negotiation with contemporary conditions of readability that characterizes all the novels discussed here. The hypothetical reader of Toni Morrison's, Gayl Jones's, and Alice Walker's fiction in the 1970s was a Black Aesthetic reader who expected to find clear, functional meanings in fiction. Even a cursory glance at these novelists' comments on their fiction, in interviews, essays, and prefaces, reveals their concern with this implied Black Aesthetic reader's expectations. Toni Morrison, in "Rootedness: The Ancestor as Foundation," declares that "the work must be political," but it cannot be "a case study" or "a recipe."[1] Gayl Jones, in an interview, defends her refusal to include "direct political statements" in her fiction.[2] Alice Walker berates the "lazy" Black Aesthetic reader, yet tries to placate this reader in her afterword to *The Third Life of Grange Copeland*.[3] These and other assertions, apologies, and justifications are clearly attempts to address the Black Aesthetic belief that only an ideologically unambiguous fiction can serve a useful political function for the black community. While assuming the presence of a Black Aesthetic reader, Morrison, Jones, and Walker seriously jeopardize this reader's interpretive function in their novels; indeed, these novelists' efforts to negotiate Black Aesthetic reading norms often culminate in a profound questioning of the very activities of reading and writing, compelling attention to what cannot be written or read about black femininity in the 1970s.

In *The Bluest Eye*, black femininity initially appears to be quite easily readable according to the popular black sociological and psychological discourses of the period. Pecola's pathology derives from her (and her society's) uncritical acceptance of the white middle-class norm, and her inability to see her own difference from this norm as anything but grotesque lack. The novel's use of the grotesque mode for the purposes of social satire is, of course, perfectly comprehensible in Black Aesthetic terms. It was precisely the seeming universality of white middle-class cultural norms that the Black Aestheticians wished to challenge through the use of grotesque caricature. However, *The Bluest Eye* also deploys the grotesque mode to other ends that are not quite commensurate with Black Aesthetic intentions. Through its entanglement of racial and sexual perspectives, the grotesque mode makes it impossible for us to resolve the novel's contradictory representation of black femininity.

145

While its grotesque parody of the Dick and Jane primer assists the novel's critique of the ways in which dominant cultural texts construct the black woman as a sign of lack or invisibility, *The Bluest Eye* does not advance any other adequate means of writing or reading black femininity. The novel's narrators disclaim the power to read or to write Pecola's subjectivity definitively, emphasizing instead the inappropriable residue that escapes the processes of narration and interpretation. The reader is left discomfited, at the end of the novel, by the narrators' sense that the acts of reading and writing have been "too late";[4] we are left with only the awareness that we cannot know, and that the text cannot represent, the full nature of Pecola's subjectivity.

If Pecola's subjectivity is shrouded from the reader's gaze, Sula's poses a different but equally challenging problem for the reader. While Pecola's character is delineated according to the victim stereotype of the protest tradition, *Sula* achieves a radical departure from prior fictional characterizations of black women. Sula's thematic newness is accompanied and enhanced by the novel's refusal of the modes of characterization conventionally used to depict the black woman in fiction. Specifically, Sula's character is unreadable according to the codes of psychological realism. The novel defies the reader's impulse to gather the discontinuous fragments of Sula's character into a unified psychological whole. Aside from its refusal of realism (the fictional mode privileged by Black Aesthetic critics), *Sula* would undoubtedly baffle the Black Aesthetic reader looking for univocal ideological messages. *Sula* plays havoc with the fixed polarities of black nationalist discourse: if read in Black Aesthetic terms, Sula's character incongruously combines the ideologically valorized term "newness" with the negative values of "absence" and "individuality." Displacing the binary structuring of meaning in Black Aesthetic ideology, *Sula* celebrates instead the heterogeneity of black feminine identity and its resistance to any single or stable meaning. Sula's birthmark, variously interpreted as a copperhead, a rose, and a tadpole, bodily figures the creative multivalence of the new black feminine subject. This multivalence, however, is not as unreservedly affirmed in *Sula* as it is in *Meridian*, for it tends to scatter itself into mere meaninglessness. As Sula herself acknowledges, at the end of the novel, "I didn't mean anything. I never meant anything."[5] While the multivalence of Sula's character confounds the functional reading norms of the Black Aesthetic, the novel, unlike *Meridian*, self-reflexively clarifies the problems with instituting sheer multivalence as the basis of a new and alternative representation of black femininity. Sula's newness ultimately turns back upon itself and leads to a denial of the very possibility that black feminine identity can be rendered in radically new forms: "There aren't any more new songs and I have sung all the ones there are" (p. 137).

Two years after the publication of *Sula*, as Ursa Corregidora searches for "a new world song,"⁶ it becomes clear that black women's fiction has not yet exhausted all the possible means of constructing a new and emergent black feminine identity. Like *The Bluest Eye*, *Corregidora* expresses a deep distrust of the written narrative texts of the dominant culture, because these texts (specifically, the official historical narratives of slavery) exclude black perceptions of experience. It is precisely this absence of the black perspective in white U.S. culture that the Black Aesthetic sought to fill. *Corregidora* contains a displaced and heavily disguised Black Aesthetic text: the oral, didactic, functional, and collective narrative of the Corregidora women. However, even this oppositional black text cannot adequately express Ursa's femininity, for its didactic political intention dictates its suppression of the ambivalent nature of black feminine sexuality. The novel ultimately affirms the blues mode as the most suitable means of figuring black femininity because of its capacity to contain contradictions in a state of taut disequilibrium. Moreover, the blues mode intimates a black feminine identity that cannot be explicitly or authoritatively written or read. Again, as with *The Bluest Eye* and *Sula*, the essential meaning of black feminine subjectivity remains contradictory and even inaccessible; the blues help Ursa "to explain what [she] can't explain" (p. 56), and this explanation remains concealed "somewhere behind the words" (p. 66). The blues mode enables the novel to suggest the "more," the surplus that cannot be represented in language. In *Sula*, this "more" produces a bewildering diffusion of meaning because Sula lacks a form in which to bind her creative newness. As though cognizant of *Sula*'s critique of formless, unprecedented newness, *Corregidora* grounds the newness of Ursa's identity within the tightly structured form of the blues. Rendering Ursa's newness in this oldest of black cultural forms, *Corregidora* transforms the blues into a distinctly feminine form that can convey the linguistically unrepresentable elements of black feminine identity.

While *The Bluest Eye*, *Sula*, and *Corregidora* attempt, in various ways, to mediate and to communicate the unreadable nature of black feminine identity, *Eva's Man* vehemently denies the very possibility of narrative communication. Of all the novels discussed here, *Eva's Man* arouses the keenest sense of discomfort and frustration in the reader, as the narrator perversely seals off all possible means by which the reader might enter the text. Through the use of reader surrogates, *Eva's Man* anticipates only to mock and to discredit several different readings of Eva's story. Gayl Jones remarked that the novel's refusal to present Eva's story coherently constitutes a means of preserving the narrator's "autonomy."⁷ That a text should seek to protect its integrity and its privacy from the reader obviously forces the question of why such a text should be written or read at all. *Eva's Man* characteristically refuses to answer this question, as well as several other questions that it raises about the value of reading and writing. The opacity and self-containment of Eva's fictional discourse prevent the reader from distilling any kind of meaning from the text. *Eva's Man* not only subverts the functional reading norms of Black Aesthetic ideology, but it also refuses to entertain the possibility that *any* reading can do justice to Eva's story. Eva's insistent pleas that the reader refrain from explanation effectively jam the reader's interpretive gears, while the incoherence of her narration compels us to confront the unreadability of black feminine subjectivity. *Sula* and *Corregidora* are haunted by a sense that black femininity cannot be fully rendered within the contemporary conditions of readability. The "more," the unreadable excess that is evoked in these two novels is taken to its logical extreme in *Eva's Man*, so that the novel offers us only that which we cannot read, and which the text cannot or will not explain.

If *Eva's Man* takes the three earlier novels' exploration of unreadability to an absolute impasse of narration and interpretation, Alice Walker's novels suggest one possible avenue out of this impasse. Walker's fiction stridently declares her conviction that the "easy rightnesses"[8] of Black Aesthetic ideology preclude a full rendering of black femininity. But unlike Morrison and Jones, Walker does not rest with an evocation of all that is unrepresentable and unreadable about black femininity in the 1970s. Walker proposes an alternative ideological frame—womanism—that can incorporate and transform the radical elements of black nationalism, as well as enable a fictional creation of a new black femininity that exceeds the bounds of Black Aesthetic ideology. With its emphasis on wholeness, Walker's womanism attempts to fill in the gaps and absences, and to render completely the "more" of Morrison's and Jones's fiction. *The Third Life of Grange Copeland* takes on this womanist enterprise, clarifying the oppositional intention that motivates Walker's affirmation not only of a whole black subjectivity, but also of the ability to read and to write this subjectivity fully and coherently. The novel constructs itself against the racist texts of the dominant culture (as exemplified in Ruth's history textbook), which represent black Americans as the absent objects rather than as the subjects of narration. In seeking to remedy the exclusion of black Americans from dominant cultural texts, *The Third Life* invests the acts of reading and writing with immense political power; black Americans must be able to read, critically, the master-texts of American culture, as well as to write themselves as the subjects of cultural discourse. In its attempt to project this new black subject in all its plenitude and clarity, *The Third Life* is the most coherent and easily readable of all the novels considered here and, not surprisingly, this very readability operates as the novel's greatest constraint. While, in Morrison's and Jones's fiction, grotesque modes serve to sabotage the conventional reader's presuppositions, the straightforward realist representation of

Ruth's identity in *The Third Life* ensures a smooth reading and fails to redefine conventional reading norms in any significant sense. The novel's adherence to psychological realism inevitably carries its own ideological weight: the presumably new black feminine subject of *The Third Life* cannot but reinscribe the traditional humanist notion of full, coherent individuality that inheres in the realist mode. The novel's formal conventionality thus saps the oppositional ideological value of its conception of a whole black identity.

Walker's commitment to wholeness produces a different and, in fact, exactly contrary set of problems in *Meridian*. As opposed to the formal conventionality of *The Third Life*, *Meridian* flirts with a number of innovative formal possibilities in its attempt to render the plenitude of black feminine identity. Like *The Bluest Eye*, *Corregidora*, and *The Third Life*, *Meridian* constructs itself in opposition to the master-texts of white American culture. In *Meridian*, this master-text takes the form of "The True Story of Marilene O'Shay," a conventional narrative about a white middle-class woman that is written by her husband and then commercialized as a profitable object of consumption. *Meridian*'s newness resides primarily in her ability to resist the literal and symbolic mummification of Marilene O'Shay into the prescribed feminine identities of "Obedient Daughter," "Devoted Wife," and "Adoring Mother."[9] *Meridian* elaborates a new black feminine identity that contests the objectified representation of femininity in conventional narratives such as "The True Story of Marilene O'Shay." The novel's use of several mutually incommensurate modes of characterization discourages any essential or fixed definition of black femininity. The formal and ideological incoherence of *Meridian* is unreadable according to Black Aesthetic codes, but when placed within the frame of Walker's womanism, this incoherence is meant to translate into a creative fullness of meaning. While assailing, like the novels of Morrison and Jones, the easy functionality of Black Aesthetic readings, *Meridian* does not seem to share the other two novelists' suspicion of the very processes of fictional signification. Through its formal experimentation, *Meridian* gropes for alternative modes of figuring black femininity as a creative plenitude. Our discussion of *Sula* has already indicated some of the problems of this affirmative rendering of the black feminine subject as sheer possibility and multivalence. While Walker's womanist project subverts itself in *The Third Life* because of its formal conventionality, it overwrites itself in *Meridian* ironically because it recognizes no formal limits. If the formal conventionality of *The Third Life* secures a too-easy readability, the formal experimentation of *Meridian* verges on incoherence. Its incoherence allows *Meridian* to elude the easy meanings of Black Aesthetic ideology, but the novel also comes precariously close to escaping meaning altogether.

A consideration of the variable readability of these six novels offers several interpretive lessons about how new fictional meanings may be engendered and new forms rendered readable within a specific set of ideological conditions. With the exception of *The Third Life*, all the novels examined above construct themselves as unreadable to different degrees and ends. *The Bluest Eye* and *Eva's Man* produce a new, defamiliarized perception of prior fictional modes of characterizing black women by obsessively recycling these old forms and imprisoning their protagonists as well as the reader in the narrow enclosure of these forms. Both novels provoke an acute sense of discomfort in the reader by presenting black femininity as an inauthentic lack that cannot be written or read within the given cultural context. In *Sula* and *Corregidora*, this unreadability is celebrated as a surplus rather than a lack of meaning; black femininity is figured in these novels as the excess that destabilizes, while remaining structured by, the contradictory terms of black nationalist discourse. *Meridian* attempts to appropriate, authenticate, and fill this lack with an unbounded wholeness of meaning that, in its absolute negation of contemporary reading conditions, risks incoherence. The exceptional coherence of *The Third Life* obliquely clarifies the creative function of unreadability in the other five novels, for the text that constitutes itself as fully readable also proves to be the only text that opens no new formal possibilities for contemporary black women's fiction.

As a critical convenience, the term *readability* helps to organize and distribute some of the lines of similarity and difference that run through the six novels; it cannot, however, be inflated into an all-inclusive critical device, a means of imposing an overarching principle of unity, or disunity, upon the six novels. A consideration of the varying readability of these novels does not enable any definitive formulation of what is typical of the 1970s black woman novelist's negotiation with contemporary reading norms. The most the term allows is a tentative tracing of the several different methods of executing a common project: to dislocate the functional expectations of Black Aesthetic readers, and to evoke that about black femininity which cannot be written or read within the parameters of Black Aesthetic ideology. We have already seen how, given this shared concern, the six novels address and exploit their contemporary conditions of readability in a number of different ways.

In moving this discussion toward a conclusion, it may help to bear in mind Toni Cade Bambara's expressive description of the appearance of ideological messages in her work: "lessons come in sprawled-out ways."[10] Ideological lessons appear in especially sprawled-out ways in Morrison's and Jones's fiction, which provides an important corrective to the critical impulse to chart literary periods in terms of their representative unities. The fiction of Morrison and Jones is unique, and even atypical, in its refusal to engage contemporary ideological material as theme. Alice Walker's fiction more directly addresses topical political issues and, quite unlike the fiction of Morrison and Jones, overtly declares its ideological intentions. Like Walker, most black women novelists of the late 1960s and early 1970s explicitly treat, as central themes, the ideological issues raised in black nationalist discourse. For example, Mary Vroman's *Harlem Summer* (1967) and Carlene Polite's *The Flagellants* (1967) consider the contemporary political debate between integration and separatism, nonviolent resistance and violent revolt, that polarized the differences between the Civil Rights movement and black nationalism. Louise Meriwether's *Daddy Was a Number Runner* (1970), Alice Childress's *A Hero Ain't Nothin' but a Sandwich* (1973), and Alexis DeVeaux's *Spirits in the Street* (1973) all thematically regard black nationalism as a possible means of transforming the oppressive cycle of life in the Harlem ghettos. Carlene Polite's *Sister X and the Victims of Foul Play* (1975) advances the most explicit and unqualified vindication of the sexual, temporal, and communal vision of black nationalist ideology. A brief and selective survey of some of these novels may help to situate the works of Toni Morrison, Gayl Jones, and Alice Walker within a wider context of diverse but interrelated fictional and ideological strategies. More importantly, it might help to sprawl out our sense of the 1970s and to guard against a closed construction of this "period" as a unified moment in the history of black women's fiction.

Two novels that bring into sharp focus the limits within which black femininity was rendered readable during the 1970s are Ann Allen Shockley's *Loving Her* (1974) and Carlene Polite's *The Flagellants*. Contemporary ideological material blatantly jumps out of the fictional discourse of these two novels. Both novels insistently attempt to come to terms with the black nationalist discourse on castrating matriarchs and emasculated black men. While many of the black women's novels published in this period, such as *The Bluest Eye, Sula, Corregidora, Daddy Was a Number Runner, A Hero Ain't Nothin' but a Sandwich, The Third Life of Grange Copeland,* and *Journey All Alone* (1971), present fictional situations involving matriarchs and emasculated black men, *Loving Her* and *The Flagellants* extensively and directly incorporate the ideological discourse on matriarchy into their fictional language. *Loving Her* reproduces this discourse in a particularly undigested manner. Statements such as "Black women had been made masculine all their lives by forced matriarchy"[11] and "The Black man was the superstud" (p. 44) appear in free indirect discourse that voices the protagonist's and the narrator's ideology. Nowhere in the novel are such reductive generalizations fictionally tested; the novel remains trapped in an unmediated reflection of ideological stereotypes that are disquieting because they are presented not as stereotypes but as accurate reflections of reality. Polite's *The Flagellants* also obsessively recycles the stereotypes of the matriarch and the emasculated black man, but this novel formally prefigures *The Bluest Eye* and *Eva's Man* in a number of ways. Unlike the passive mirroring of ideological stereotypes in *Loving Her*, the use of structural overdetermination and repetition in *The Bluest Eye*, *Eva's Man*, and *The Flagellants* renders intolerable the grotesquerie and the suffocating sameness of the stereotype. The extremely stylized narrative voice of *The Flagellants* prohibits a smooth reading and, compulsively drawing attention to the constructedness of its fictional language, succeeds in derealizing the seeming transparency of ideological discourse.

Although *Loving Her* does not exhibit the complex fictional reworking of ideological material evident in *The Bluest Eye*, *Eva's Man*, and *The Flagellants*, it cannot be written off as poor or insignificant fiction. *Loving Her* is nonrepresentative but highly significant as the only novel published by a black woman in the 1970s that follows its critique of heterosexuality to an unapologetic affirmation of lesbianism. The novel's critique of heterosexuality is not in itself unique; most of the black women's fiction published in this period, with the singular exception of Carlene Polite's *Sister X and the Victims of Foul Play*,[12] challenges the heterosexual emphasis of black nationalist ideology. Novels such as *Daddy Was a Number Runner*, *Journey All Alone*, *Loving Her*, and *The Flagellants* share with the novels of Morrison, Jones, and Walker an association of heterosexuality with loss and violence, and often with rape and death. All these novels, however, except for *Eva's Man* and *Loving Her*, conclude with a strained adjustment to the heterosexual parameters of black nationalist ideology. *Eva's Man* refuses this adjustment, but withdraws meaning from its lesbian conclusion, recalling the awkward containment of lesbian material in *Corregidora*, *Sula*, and Rosa Guy's *Ruby*.[13] *Loving Her* stands virtually alone, then, in unequivocally celebrating lesbianism as "what comes naturally" (p. 104).

As we have seen in our discussion of *Sula*, *Corregidora*, and *Eva's Man*, lesbianism was strictly debarred from any fictional representation of "the black experience" as constituted by Black Aesthetic ideology. *Loving Her* castigates this contemporary ideological equation of lesbianism and non-blackness, but the novel itself seems unable to connect the terms *lesbian* and *black* in a way that surpasses this equation. The identification of lesbianism with non-blackness is even endorsed in such statements as "There is no Black lesbian world" (p. 97). Lesbianism in *Loving Her* entails alienation from the black community and integration with a liberal community of white homosexual men and women. All traces of Renay's black past, including her husband, her black female friends, her hometown community, her love of soul food, and most disconcertingly, her daughter, have to be expelled from her life before her lesbian relationship with a white woman can be established and affirmed. Along with this thematic alignment of lesbianism and whiteness, the novel invests its white characters with individuality and psychological depth, while rendering black characters in reductive, generalized terms. The novel's formal repudiation of blackness is also apparent in its use of black dialect in quotation marks, solely for the purposes of mockery and stereotyping. In order to construct itself as a lesbian novel, then, *Loving Her* forfeits any claims to being a black novel, thus ensuring its own exclusion from most critical attempts to map the black fiction of this period. The terms *black* and *lesbian* remain incompatible in black women's fiction until the publication of Alice Walker's *The Color Purple*, Gloria Naylor's *The Women of Brewster Place*, and Audre Lorde's *Zami*,[14] in 1982, when lesbianism could be written in a black literary language, and posed as an urgent concern for the black community.

Instead of dismissing *Loving Her* for its difference from most black women's fiction of the 1970s, it may be more illuminating to view this difference as an extreme narrative choice that sharply highlights the ideological limits that determine what is readable at a given literary and historical conjuncture. *Loving Her* throws into stark relief the ideological terms within which "blackness" could be written and read in the 1970s, and enables a clearer appreciation of the difficult relation between difference and representative blackness in the black women's fiction published in this period. While *Loving Her* disavows blackness in order to express its own radical difference, most other contemporary black women's novels seek to expand the prevalent ideological construction of literary blackness. *Loving Her* demarcates the boundary of this expansion, for lesbianism is the one difference that remains outside all fictional explorations of blackness in the 1970s. *Eva's Man*, the only other contemporary novel that offers lesbianism as its point of resolution, also delimits its own reach by presenting itself as the unreliable discourse of a nonrepresentative protagonist.

Unlike *Loving Her* and *Eva's Man*, most of the other black women's novels published in this period are able to balance a critique of the contemporary ideological celebration of a unified black community with an alternative fictional elaboration of community as a productive interplay of differences. *The Bluest Eye*, *Sula*, and *Corregidora* interrogate a cohesive black community that cannot accommodate the differences represented by Pecola's ugliness, Sula's evil singularity, and Ursa's lack of a womb. Similarly, *The Third Life of Grange Copeland* and *Meridian* question the black nationalist ideal of a community cemented by its hatred and exclusion of white people, and by its unqualified commitment to violence. Rosa Guy's *The Friends* (1973) delineates the differences—between poor and middle-class blacks, and between West Indians and African-Americans—that obstruct the development of a unified black community. Toni Cade Bambara's "My Man Bovanne," from her collection of short stories *Gorilla, My Love*, and Alice Childress's *A Hero Ain't Nothin' but a Sandwich* celebrate the "stubborn ambivalence"[15] of the unrevolutionary "folk" who escape the black nationalist conception of collectivity. Benjie, the protagonist of Childress's *A Hero*, thus voices his suspicion of the black nationalist discourse on community: "they be sighin' and shakin' heads while they eyes sayin', 'My people, my people, yall some bad-luck, sad-ass niggas.'"[16] Benjie's words recall Zora Neale Hurston's ironic use of the phrase "My people! My people!" as the title of a chapter in her autobiography which sketches the various divisions that impede the construction of a unified black collectivity.[17]

While Hurston's exploration of these differences led her to the conclusion that there are only black individuals, and that "there is no such thing as Race Solidarity,"[18] black women novelists of the 1970s insist upon a communal perspective that seriously unsettles the category of the individual subject. Like *The Bluest Eye*, *Sula*, and *Meridian*, novels such as Childress's *A Hero*, DeVeaux's *Spirits in the Street*, and Polite's *Sister X* are composed of short narrative units that recall the black oral storytelling tradition and establish a communal frame through their constant and rapid shifts between different characters and points of view. In addition to the nonlinear structure of storytelling, these novels evoke a variety of black oral forms, predominantly music, in order to affirm a collective vision. Margaret and Melvin Wade have correctly argued that the Black Aesthetic influenced the use of formal models derived from black music in the post-1960s black novel.[19] The blues mode in *Corregidora*, jazz in *Spirits in the Street* and in Toni Cade Bambara's fiction, and rap in *Sister X* all attempt to recreate the communal call-and-response structure of black musical forms.

A full appreciation of the fictional strategies of black women novelists of the 1970s cannot rest with an identification of the oral modes adapted in their fiction. What is, in a sense, most exciting about this fiction is its ideologically charged and playful recasting of the generic boundaries of the novel. Instead of being passively inducted into the novel, oral modes dialogically redefine the conventional horizons of the fictional form, even as they are themselves transformed in the process of fictional appropriation. Black women's fiction of the 1970s constructs itself as a processual, open-ended form that can challenge the authoritative finality of newspapers, sociological and historical documents, and other dominant cultural texts that define the black subject in monological terms. Oral modes are crucial to this oppositional enterprise, for they foreground the fluid, improvisatory uses of language and succeed in subverting the static closure of the printed text. Novels such as *The Bluest Eye*, *Spirits in the Street*, *Sister X*, and *A Hero Ain't Nothin' but a Sandwich* convey the competition between dominant and marginal social and literary languages by means of ironic juxtapositions of oral and printed devices. In all these novels, a definitive, nonfictional printed text (newspapers in *A Hero* and *Spirits in the Street*, the Dick and Jane primer in *The Bluest Eye*, and a toothpaste advertisement in *Sister X*) is not only orally tested against the "heard" quality of the surrounding black dialect, but is also visually destabilized by means of typographical play.[20]

Toni Morrison thus described the intention that motivates the presence of oral materials in her fiction: "I have to rewrite, discard, and remove the print-quality of the language to put back the oral quality, where intonation, volume and gesture are all there."[21] In actual practice, oral modes do evoke a "heard" immediacy that disrupts the finality of printed language, but this oral quality is itself dialogized by the gaps and silences that reinscribe the "print-quality" of the fictional text. In *Sula*, for example, the reader inhabits the absences of meaning, the silent holes in the text; this fictional positioning of the reader is vastly different from the immediate, vocal presence of the listener in the call-and-response framework of black oral forms. Alexis DeVeaux's *Spirits in the Street* employs the call-and-response structure of jazz, but the novel is visibly marked by half-empty pages that summon the "silence [that] is the third part of every dialogue."[22] DeVeaux's narrator assumes a collective voice authorized by oral modes of narration, but this voice is troubled by the narrator's sense that writers are "spies," "outsiders" (p. 21) who cannot easily speak for the "collective spirit" of the street (p. 11). Like DeVeaux's narrator, the reader in Gayl Jones's *Corregidora* is uncomfortably situated as an outsider spying upon Ursa's deeply private psychological spaces; the novel's reliance on the call-and-response structure of the blues cannot reproduce the immediate presence or the collective unity of characters, author, and reader. *Meridian* utilizes the call-and-response pattern of oral storytelling and of black musical forms in an attempt to establish a communal perspective, but the narrator's sharp linguistic difference from the black folk community prevents the novel from representing the "voice of the people."[23] The interchange between oral and fictional modes thus generates a complex vision of identity and of community; in these novels, black feminine identity is constructed at the crossing point of the two modes, between the stable individual subject of the novel and the shifting communal intersubjectivity of black oral modes.

Black women's fiction of the 1970s does not uncritically posit either a self-sufficient individuality or a unified communal sensibility. The notion of an integral self is most effectively displaced by the nonrealist strategies of characterization employed in the fiction of Toni Morrison and Gayl Jones. *The Bluest Eye* represents black feminine identity as a distorted, grotesque reflection in a white cultural mirror. The grotesque mode in *Sula* figures black feminine subjectivity as a creative absence and heterogeneity that subvert the conventional realist representation of a fixed, self-present individual. The expressionistic dream sequences of *Corregidora* render Ursa's self as a dispersed space invaded by the presence of absent others. *Eva's Man* draws heavily upon stereotypes and uncanny repetition to signify identity as an infinitely deferred process with no "real" end or origin. A similar sense of the fundamental absence and inauthenticity of the black feminine subject is evident in some of the other black women's fiction published at this time. In Ann Petry's "The Mirror," from *Miss Muriel and Other Stories* (1971), the mirror functions as a metaphor for the hollow, reflective nature of black identity. Carlene Polite's *The Flagellants* denaturalizes black identity through the use of repetitive stereotypes, ritualized dialogue sequences, and mask and mirror imagery.

These works are, however, unique in their unqualified refusal of the authentic, knowable subject of realist fiction. Most of the novels published by black women in this period vacillate impossibly between two contradictory representations of black feminine identity. Carlene Polite's suggestively named protagonist, Sister X, for example, runs through a series of "fast changes" (p. 88) of costume and name (such as Lilly La Belle, Glory Maria, Our Lady Anita of Cabrera, and so on) that communicate the indeterminate and mobile status of her identity. However, the representation of Sister X's identity as an ad hoc, performative construct coexists with the narrator's strong investment in whole, natural selfhood. This contradiction is acknowledged and explained in the novel: the "dead world" of American capitalism produces "displaced likenesses" and alienates individuals from their natural, "original selves" (p. 72).

Other contemporary black women's novels do not always manipulate this contradiction between absent and present identity as self-consciously as does *Sister X*. In *Meridian*, for example, a powerful figuration of black feminine identity as absence is crossed by the presence of realist modes that conventionally inscribe an essential individuality. At one level, *Meridian*'s characterization assaults the notion of an autonomous, integral individual; Meridian's "self" is an open, intersubjective area of overlap between fragments of different characters. Meridian's lacking and grotesque body figures a new freedom and power similar to Sula's and Ursa's, but unlike *Sula* and *Corregidora*, *Meridian* employs modes of psychological realism that reinstate the humanist model of the full, integral self. The extensive realist analysis of Meridian's psychological motivation, the representation of her epiphanic moments of awakening, and her final rebirth as a whole person, all place Meridian's character within a bildungsroman rhetoric that discloses the self as a continuous, coherent development.

Once again, the fiction of Toni Morrison and Gayl Jones is atypical in this respect. *The Bluest Eye*, *Sula*, *Corregidora*, and *Eva's Man* all evoke, only in order to parody, the bildungsroman representation of the self as a unified, continuous movement into the future. In all four of these novels, nonrealist modes of characterization and cyclic, repetitive structures subvert both the model of the psychologically unified self and the developmental linear structure that characterize the bildungsroman. Unlike Toni Morrison and Gayl Jones, most black women novelists of this period retain the unified character model, but refuse the linear directions of the bildungsroman form, in a complicated formal maneuver that is greatly revealing of these novels' visions of personal and political change.

None of the novels published by black women in the 1970s is able to envisage history or political change in linear terms. In fact, the two presumably progressive developments in black American history, the emancipation of blacks from slavery and their migration from the rural South to the urban North, are repeatedly figured in these novels as failed linear movements. The ideological and even material conditions of slavery persist into the narrative present of many of these novels: Sister X's very name reflects her "slave nature" (p. 60); Ursa's relationship with her husband repeats her maternal ancestors' relationship with their slavemaster; the Bottom community in *Sula* lives by the survival strategies of their slave ancestors; Grange and Brownfield, in *The Third Life of Grange Copeland*, are sharecroppers on "some white man's property like in slavery times" (p. 118); Francie, in *Daddy Was a Number Runner*, learns that her experience of sexual exploitation by white men is a historical legacy originating in slavery; and Ideal and Jimson in *The Flagellants* remain trapped in a "slavery-time credo"[24] that debars them from living in "nineteen hundred and now" (p. 190).

If the emancipation of slaves is not represented as a real historical rupture in these novels, neither is the urban migration of black Americans from the South to the North. *The Third Life* conducts a sustained analysis of the economic and ideological conditions in the South that ensure the cyclic repetition of the historical past. All the characters in the novel view the Northern migration as a means of escaping this oppressive cycle; Grange's Northern journey, however, results not in linear progress but in a circular return to the South. Novels set in the North, such as *Daddy Was a Number Runner, A Hero Ain't Nothin' but a Sandwich, Journey All Alone*, and *Spirits in the Street*, emphasize the cyclic sameness of time in the urban ghettos, exposing the Northern migration to be a failed linear quest. The use of cyclic structures in these and other novels produces a vision of history as overdetermined repetition, allowing little possibility of change or transformation.

Black women's fiction of the 1970s approaches the question of historical change in a number of different ways. Novels such as *The Bluest Eye, Eva's Man*, and *Daddy Was a Number Runner* trap the reader in the claustrophobic enclosure of their repetitive cyclical structures, posing the problem of historical change as an urgent but unresolved question. Unlike the protagonists of *The Bluest Eye* and *Eva's Man*, Francie, the heroine of *Daddy Was a Number Runner*, is affirmed for her psychological capacity to withstand the dehumanizing effects of the oppressive cycle.

The celebration of Francie's individual spirit does not resolve or obviate the question of structural oppression in *Daddy Was a Number Runner*, but this is precisely what occurs in novels such as *The Friends*, *Journey All Alone*, *Loving Her*, and *The Third Life of Grange Copeland*. All these novels retreat from a thorough diagnosis of the structural determinants of oppression to a celebration of the individual's power to resist or transcend her oppressive conditions. Transferring the problem of historical change from a social to an individual level, these novels take recourse to a liberal humanist vision of political change as originating in the free choice of an individual subject. In *Loving Her*, *Journey All Alone*, *The Friends*, and *The Third Life*, traces of a bildungsroman model strain to preserve a free individual space that can escape the historical structures of oppression. All these novels depend on moments of psychological awakening and self-discovery characteristic of the bildungsroman, and resolve the problem of historical change by means of affirming individual changes of heart. *The Third Life* is the only one of these novels that situates its protagonist's change of heart in a larger political context, but this context—the Civil Rights movement—is itself defined as an effort to "change those crackers' hearts" (p. 320). The conclusion of *The Third Life* shifts the question of change from a socio-political to an individual register, and thus leaves intact the novel's powerful diagnosis of the structural causes of oppression.

The difficulty of fictionally imagining a satisfactory resolution to the cyclic problem of oppression differently marks the temporal vision of another set of novels, such as *The Flagellants*, *A Hero Ain't Nothin' but a Sandwich*, and *Spirits in the Street*, which offer two contradictory visions of time as the medium of both cyclic repetition and miraculous change. *The Flagellants*, for example, presents Ideal "going mad awaiting rebirth" (p. 28), awaiting the word or deed that will release her from the cyclic sameness of time and catapult her into a different future. The entire novel is a frenzied meditation on the urgent necessity of a change that remains inaccessible except at the level of miracle. Abruptly displacing the problem of change from a political to a mystical level, the novel can offer only the blind hope that, "assuming the role of faith healer, time would excise our ill-founded pathology, leaving us ethereal creatures transfused with a changed fate" (p. 96).

A Hero Ain't Nothin' but a Sandwich and *Spirits in the Street* seek resolutions at a political level, grasping at black nationalism as the means of "forcing the miraculous change."[25] After a detailed disclosure of the multiple, cyclic nature of oppression in the ghetto, *A Hero* ends with the proclamation, "It's nation time!" (p. 126). This phrase, earlier attributed to the novel's only black nationalist character, Nigeria Greene, cannot be read as anything but wishful declaration, for

Greene's black nationalist rhetoric has been exposed throughout the novel as mere rhetoric that cannot transform the material conditions of ghetto existence. The novel itself, however, does not finally offer a resolution so much as a rhetorical affirmation of a new, changed present. The end of *Spirits in the Street*, too, invokes black nationalism to authorize an abrupt break from the oppressive cycle, and a new vision of "politics" as "a word spelled N-O-W" (p. 125). However, the narrator's final assertion that "this is the future. it [*sic*] is now and tomorrow on my block" (p. 192), does not quite overwrite the conviction of the novel's characters that "our future is we already trapped" (p. 183). *Spirits in the Street* wavers irresolutely between two representations of time as both cyclic sameness and linear rupture.

Of all the novels published by black women in the 1970s, *Sister X and the Victims of Foul Play* offers the most unqualified justification of the black nationalist conception of change as an abrupt linear rupture. The novel provides a concise statement of the temporal project of black nationalist ideology: "We are trapped, seemingly forever, in that vicious circle, trying our best to escape or to build that New World" (pp. 75–76). This "New World" can be constructed only through a ruthless destruction of the past ("kill a past and then turn around and shoot it") and a commitment to the "Right Here and Right Now" (p. 36). However, the novel's own reiterated intention of moving "Straight Ahead" (pp. 9, 53, 87) is undermined by numerous circular detours, speculations, and digressions, and most effectively by the fact that the entire narrative is a process of "remembering when" (p. 35), of recalling the past of the dead Sister X. This contradiction between linear progress and circular return at the level of plot betrays the incoherence of the novel's temporal and political vision: "We are getting back to the Nation which will be our brand-new world, our original world. That means that we are going straight ahead, stone right on!" (p. 105). Such statements abound in *Sister X*, directly reflecting the unresolved contradiction between origin and end, circular return and linear progress, in black nationalist discourse.

It is no accident that the only black women's novels of the 1970s that are able to synthesize past and future, cyclic and linear time, are also the novels that most forcefully question the temporal scheme of black nationalist ideology. *Meridian, Sula*, and *Corregidora* are all exactly opposed to *Sister X* in their commitment to the past as the necessary ground of change. Meridian's rebirth as a revolutionary is facilitated by her appreciation of her own ancestral past as well as the historical past of black women, just as Ursa's achievement of a new identity is sustained by the heritage of her maternal ancestors, and Sula's radical difference proves ineffective because she does not respect the value of the "ancestor as foundation."[26] None of these novels endorses the black nationalist conception of change as a complete break from the past.

Toni Morrison goes so far as to characterize the nationalist equation of change and discontinuity as "masculine": "You don't have to change everything. . . . Under the guise of change . . . , you destroy all sorts of things. . . . That kind of change is masculine."[27]

Sula, Corregidora, and *Meridian* feminize the question of historical change in more ways than one, not only by refusing the "masculine" affirmation of absolute change, but also by posing the question of change in terms of the reproductive and generational cycles. Reproduction in these novels functions as a privileged site for mediating the contradictions between past and future, continuity and change, cyclic and linear time. The reproductive cycle is ambivalently presented in these novels as a means of perpetuating the oppressive cycle of the past, as well as of preserving the continuity of the black historical and cultural heritage. Ursa, Sula, and Meridian all distance themselves from their mothers' reproductive ideologies in order to liberate a new black feminine identity free of the oppressive cycle of the past. However, the newness of these protagonists is always situated within a historical frame that reasserts the political significance of reproduction for black women. For example, Ursa's awareness of the oppressive consequences of reproduction for many black women is counterbalanced by her historical understanding of the womb as an important means of political resistance for her maternal slave ancestors. Similarly, when Meridian decides to give away her child in order to free herself, she is disturbed by her difference from her enslaved ancestors, whose conception of "'Freedom' was that it meant they could keep their own children" (p. 91). This kind of appraisal of the historical importance of reproduction for slave women does not discredit Ursa's, Sula's, or Meridian's search for a new, nonreproductive femininity, but it does firmly locate the questions of change and newness within a continuous history. These novels, then, figure political change not as a sudden, linear rupture, but as a development that preserves the transformative possibilities of past history. These transformative possibilities are embodied in the cyclical narrative structures of *Sula, Corregidora,* and *Meridian.* The spiral form of *Sula,* the blues form of *Corregidora,* and the circular storytelling form of *Meridian* all depend on a structure of repetition with variation that resolves, at a formal level, the nationalist opposition between past and future, change and continuity.

In their reclamation of the historical past as the foundation of change, *Sula, Corregidora,* and *Meridian* represent an emergent strain[28] in black women's fiction of the 1970s that not only counters the contemporary nationalist repression of the past, but also anticipates the directions taken by later black women's fiction. *Sula, Corregidora,* and *Meridian* initiate a fictional recovery of past history and a transformation of the cyclic form that is fully developed in later novels. While the depiction of slavery in *Sula* and *Corregidora* is fraught with ambivalence, black women's novels of the 1980s, such as Sherley Anne Williams's *Dessa Rose* (1986), Toni Morrison's *Beloved* (1987), and Gloria Naylor's *Mama Day* (1988) are able to reclaim the historical past of slavery with a clear-eyed acceptance of its contradictory, double legacy.[29] These novels foreground not only the continuity of contemporary black Americans with "the slaves who were ourselves,"[30] but also the value of the generational cycle that helps sustain, through oral transmission, the black cultural heritage. An emphasis on generational continuity is, as we have already seen, an emergent impulse visible in *Corregidora* and *Meridian*,[31] but the redemptive possibilities of the generational cycle are fully realized only in later novels, such as Paule Marshall's *Praisesong for the Widow* (1982) and Gloria Naylor's *Mama Day*. All of the 1980s novels mentioned above use cyclical structures to enact an imaginative recovery of the historical past, of the black oral heritage, and of the lost value of cultural community.

The treatment of each of these three terms—the past, the oral heritage, and community—is deeply contradictory in the black women's fiction of the 1970s, which, while challenging the contemporary ideological construction of these terms, also tends to block or cancel its own fictional reworking of these terms. Perhaps the freer exploration of these blocked trends in 1980s black women's fiction is facilitated by the changed cultural context and, in particular, by the diffusion, in the 1980s, of the black nationalist emphasis on community and on the political urgency of the immediate present. These factors, as well as the increasing commercial and academic appropriation of black women's fiction, may partly explain its oppositional and compensatory use of oral material as a means of regaining a uniquely black cultural community situated in the past. It would, of course, be absurdly simplistic and inaccurate to argue that 1980s black women's fiction is entirely motivated by an impulse to recover and to compensate, at an imaginary level, for the dispersion of the cohesive sense of cultural community created by black nationalism in the 1960s and early 1970s. Black women's fiction in the 1980s is engaged in salvaging the values of community, of the oral heritage, and of the historical past in ways that redefine the black nationalist construction of these terms. Fictionally positing the Dessa Roses, the Sethes, and the Mama Days as the "mothers" of black political and cultural resistance,[32] these novels are refiguring not only black history but also black nationalism from a feminine perspective. This revisionist endeavor is surely enabled by the tense dialogue between black nationalist discourse and black women's fiction in the 1970s.

NOTES

Introduction

1. Throughout this book, I use the term *Black Aesthetic* in a very specific sense to refer to the aesthetic program advocated by black cultural nationalists of the 1960s and 1970s. Addison Gayle, Jr., describes the Black Aesthetic as "nothing more than the cultural arm of black nationalism," in "Addison Gayle Interviewed by Saundra Towns," *The Black Position* 2 (1972): 12. Although formulated by several different artists and critics, Black Aesthetic ideology is remarkably homogeneous in its conception of the function of black art. Addison Gayle's anthology *The Black Aesthetic* (New York: Doubleday, 1972) offers a representative sampling of Black Aesthetic theory.

2. Black feminist literary criticism may be dated from the publication of Barbara Smith's "Toward a Black Feminist Criticism," in *Conditions: Two* 1, no. 2 (October 1977): 25–32.

3. I am quoting from Audre Lorde's call for a recognition of the "creative function of difference" in black feminist theory, *Sister Outsider* (New York: Crossing Press, 1984), p. 111.

4. For example, see Pauli Murray, "The Liberation of Black Women," in *Voices of the New Feminism*, ed. Mary Lou Thompson (Boston: Beacon, 1970), pp. 87–102; Toni Cade, ed., *The Black Woman* (New York: NAL, 1970); Mary Ellen Weathers, "An Argument for Black Women's Liberation as a Revolutionary Force," in *Voices from Women's Liberation*, ed. Leslie B. Tanner (New York: NAL, 1971), pp. 303–306; Inez Smith Reid, *"Together" Black Women* (New York: Emerson, 1972); Combahee River Collective, "A Black Feminist Statement," 1977, rptd. in *This Bridge Called My Back: Writings by Radical Women of Color*, ed. Gloria Anzaldúa and Cherríe Moraga (Watertown, Mass.: Persephone Press, 1981), pp. 210–18; and Jeanne Noble, *Beautiful, also, Are the Souls of My Black Sisters* (Englewood Cliffs: Prentice-Hall, 1978).

5. Barbara Christian, *Black Women Novelists: The Development of a Tradition* (Westport, Conn.: Greenwood Press, 1980), p. 73.

6. Ibid., p. 34. Also see Faith Pullin's essay "Landscapes of Reality: The Fiction of Contemporary Afro-American Women," in *Black Fiction*, ed. Robert Lee (London: Vision Press, 1980), pp. 173–203, which affirms the fact that black women writers of the 1970s "are beginning to provide their audience with the truth about themselves" (p. 183).

7. Mary Helen Washington, "Teaching Black-Eyed Susans: An Approach to the Study of Black Women Writers," 1977, rptd. in *All the Women Are White, All the Blacks Are Men, but Some of Us Are Brave*, ed. Gloria Hull, Patricia Bell Scott, and Barbara Smith (New York: Feminist Press, 1982), pp. 216, 214.

8. Addison Gayle, Jr., "Cultural Strangulation: Black Literature and the White Aesthetic," in *The Black Aesthetic*, pp. 38–45; Carolyn F. Gerald, "The Black Writer and His Role," in *The Black Aesthetic*, pp. 349–56.

9. Carolyn F. Gerald, p. 352.

10. Deborah McDowell, "Boundaries: Or Distant Relations and Close Kin," in *Afro-American Literary Study in the 1990s*, ed. Houston A. Baker, Jr., and Patricia Redmond (Chicago: University of Chicago Press, 1989), p. 57.

11. Ibid., p. 58.

12. Hortense Spillers, "Response" to Deborah McDowell's "Boundaries," in *Afro-American Literary Study in the 1990s*, pp. 71, 72.

13. Karla Holloway, *Moorings and Metaphors: Figures of Culture and Gender in Black Women's Literature* (New Brunswick, N.J.: Rutgers University Press, 1992), pp. 117, 133.

14. Deborah McDowell, "Boundaries," p. 53.

15. Such a double gesture is effectively enacted in Mae Gwendolyn Henderson's discussion of black women's fiction as "an expressive site for a dialectics/dialogics of identity and difference." See "Speaking in Tongues: Dialogics, Dialectics, and the Black Woman Writer's Literary Tradition," in *Changing Our Own Words*, ed. Cheryl Wall (New Brunswick, N.J.: Rutgers University Press, 1989), p. 37.

16. Ibid., p. 34.

17. For example, Mary Helen Washington, in "Teaching Black-Eyed Susans," extensively quotes from Alice Walker to substantiate her claim that black women's fiction is presenting increasingly full characterizations of black women.

18. For a rigorous analysis of the character model of realist fiction, see Thomas Docherty, *Reading (Absent) Character: Towards a Theory of Characterization in Fiction* (Oxford: Clarendon Press, 1983).

19. Karla Holloway, *Moorings and Metaphors*, p. 33. In his caustic critique of Deborah McDowell's "poststructuralist privileging of 'otherness' and self-difference," Michael Awkward argues that the model of the whole black self cannot be equated with "static essence" but must instead be understood as an "exploration of the possibilities of black unity in a historically divisive and racist setting." "Response" to Deborah McDowell, "Boundaries," in *Afro-American Literary Study in the 1990s*, pp. 73–75.

20. Marjorie Pryse and Hortense Spillers, eds., *Conjuring: Black Women, Fiction and Literary Tradition* (Bloomington: Indiana University Press, 1985); Susan Willis, *Specifying: Black Women Writing the American Experience* (Madison: University of Wisconsin Press, 1987); Elsa Barkley Brown, "African-American Women's Quilting," in *Black Women in America*, ed. Micheline R. Malson et al. (Chicago: University of Chicago Press, 1990), pp. 9–18; and Joanne V. Gabbin, "A Laying On of Hands: Black Women Writers Exploring the Roots of Their Folk and Cultural Tradition," in *Wild Women in the Whirlwind: Afra-American Culture and the Contemporary Literary Renaissance*, ed. Joanne M. Braxton and Andrée Nicola McLaughlin (New Brunswick, N.J.: Rutgers University Press, 1990), pp. 246–63.

21. For example, see Joanne V. Gabbin, "A Laying On of Hands," pp. 247–48; Marjorie Pryse, "Zora Neale Hurston, Alice Walker, and the 'Ancient Power' of Black Women," in *Conjuring*, pp. 1–24; and Lorraine Bethel, "'This Infinity of Conscious Pain': Zora Neale Hurston and the Black Female Literary Tradition," in *But Some of Us Are Brave*, pp. 177–80.

22. Susan Willis, *Specifying*, p. 16.

23. Ibid., pp. 14–21.

24. Zora Neale Hurston emphasized the highly metaphorical nature of black folk speech in "Characteristics of Negro Expression," 1934, rptd. in Zora Neale Hurston, *The Sanctified Church* (Berkeley: Turtle Island Press, 1983), pp. 49–51.

25. Several folkloric and ethnographic studies have drawn attention to the oblique, double uses of language in black oral culture. Especially interesting are Roger Abrahams's and Claudia Mitchell-Kernan's discussions of the black verbal ritual of signifying. Abrahams examines signifying in early Southern folk tales, while Mitchell-Kernan focuses on signifying in the Northern urban

black community, but both writers stress the "slippage between words and meaning" that characterizes signifying, whether in a rural Southern or an urban Northern context. See Roger D. Abrahams, "Introduction" to *Afro-American Folktales* (New York: Pantheon, 1985), p. 6; and Claudia Mitchell-Kernan, "Signifying, Loud-Talking and Marking," in *Rappin' and Stylin' Out: Communication in Urban Black America*, ed. Thomas Kochman (Urbana: University of Illinois Press, 1972), p. 317. Also see Henry Louis Gates, Jr., *The Signifying Monkey* (New York: Oxford University Press, 1988), pp. 74–88, whose extended discussion of the double-voiced nature of signifying expands upon the insights of Abrahams and Mitchell-Kernan.

26. See Frederick Douglass, *Narrative of the Life of Frederick Douglass, an American Slave* (1845; New York: Viking, 1982), p. 58; and Linda Brent, *Incidents in the Life of a Slave Girl* (1861; New York: Harcourt, 1973), p. 73.

27. Hazel Carby, *Reconstructing Womanhood: The Emergence of the Afro-American Woman Novelist* (New York: Oxford University Press, 1987), p. 166.

28. Keith Byerman, *Fingering the Jagged Grain* (Athens, Ga.: Georgia University Press, 1985), p. 7; and Michael Awkward, *Inspiriting Influences: Tradition, Revision, and Afro-American Women's Novels* (New York: Columbia University Press, 1989), pp. 49–56.

29. Gloria Wade-Gayles, *No Crystal Stair: Visions of Race and Sex in Black Women's Fiction* (New York: Pilgrim Press, 1984), argues that "fiction is often a mirror of reality," and that black women novelists create "an imaginary world that is strikingly similar to the real world" (p. 56). Also see Carol McAlpine Watson's *Prologue: The Novels of Black American Women: 1891–1965* (Westport, Conn.: Greenwood Press, 1985) and Melissa Walker's more recent book, *Down from the Mountaintop: Black Women's Novels in the Wake of the Civil Rights Movement, 1966–1989* (New Haven: Yale University Press, 1991), both of which are thematic studies that treat black women's novels as valuable sources of information about black history and political thought.

30. Etienne Balibar and Pierre Macherey, "On Literature as an Ideological Form," in *Untying the Text*, ed. Robert Young (London: Routledge, 1987), p. 87.

31. As Lillian Robinson points out in "Feminist Criticism: How Do We Know We've Won?" *Feminist Issues in Literary Scholarship*, ed. Shari Benstock (Bloomington: Indiana University Press, 1987), pp. 141–49, even in (white) feminist literary criticism, "a curious double standard is in effect whereby only the women's literature produced by middle-class white women is subjected to the full range of critical apparatus. . . . Literature by women of color and, perhaps, even by working-class women, . . . is almost never read according to the modish new ways of reading" (p. 147).

32. Cheryl A. Wall, "Introduction: Taking Positions and Changing Words," in *Changing Our Own Words*, p. 9.

33. For critiques of the aesthetic standard of universality that has been historically applied against black literary texts, see Frances and Val Gray Ward, "The Black Artist—His Role in the Struggle," *The Black Scholar* 2, no. 5 (1971): 27–28; and Adam David Miller, "Some Observations on the Black Aesthetic," in *The Black Aesthetic*, pp. 374–80. Despite their overt rejection of "universal" aesthetic values, their very naming of their movement as the "Black Aesthetic" betrays these writers' strong and often-unacknowledged investment in the category of the aesthetic. Rather than operating as a constraint, this contradictory impulse—to retain the term *aesthetic* even while placing it under erasure—precisely constitutes the critical edge of Black Aesthetic theory.

34. See Hoyt W. Fuller, "Towards a Black Aesthetic," in *The Black Aesthetic*, pp. 8–9, for a discussion of the reflective function of black art.

35. "Addison Gayle Interviewed by Saundra Towns," *The Black Position* 2 (1972): 17.

36. Hazel Carby, *Reconstructing Womanhood*, pp. 9, 16; Karla Holloway, *Moorings and Metaphors*, pp. 4–5; Valerie Smith, *Self-Discovery and Authority in Afro-American Narrative* (Cambridge, Mass.: Harvard University Press, 1989), pp. 6–7; and Susan Willis, *Specifying*, pp. 13–15.

37. Mikhail Bakhtin, *The Dialogic Imagination*, trans. Caryl Emerson and Michael Holquist (Austin: University of Texas Press, 1981), p. 259. All subsequent references to this work are cited in the text.

38. See David Carroll, "The Alterity of Discourse: Form, History, and the Question of the Political," *Diacritics* 3, no. 2 (1983): 65–83, for a cogent discussion of the ways in which Bakhtin's work overcomes the limitations of both formalist and Marxist criticism.

39. For an outstanding Bakhtinian study of the dialogic development of black narrative, see William L. Andrews, *To Tell a Free Story* (Urbana: University of Illinois Press, 1986). Some recent black feminist writings that apply Bakhtin's insights to black women's novels are Mae Gwendolyn Henderson, "Speaking in Tongues: Dialogics, Dialectics and the Black Woman Writer's Literary Tradition," pp. 17–20; Karla Holloway, *Moorings and Metaphors*, pp. 11, 53, 195; and Mary O'Connor, "Subject, Voice, and Women in Some Contemporary Black American Women's Writing," in *Feminism, Bakhtin, and the Dialogic*, ed. Dale M. Bauer and S. Jaret McKinstry (Albany: SUNY Press, 1991), pp. 199–217.

40. For discussions of the many and often mutually contradictory connotations of the term *dialogic*, see Ken Hirschkop, "Introduction: Bakhtin and Cultural Theory," in *Bakhtin and Cultural Theory*, ed. Ken Hirschkop (Manchester: Manchester University Press, 1989), pp. 1–38; and Paul de Man, "Dialogue and Dialogism," *Poetics Today* 4, no. 1 (1983): 99–107.

41. In the early sections of "Discourse in the Novel," Bakhtin often refers to "the primordial dialogism of discourse" (p. 275), or to dialogism as "the natural orientation" of all discourse (p. 279).

42. Allon White, "The Struggle Over Bakhtin: A Fraternal Reply to Robert Young," *Cultural Critique* 8 (Winter 1987–88): 229.

43. Louis Althusser, *Lenin and Philosophy and Other Essays*, trans. Ben Brewster (New York: Monthly Review Press, 1971), pp. 222, 223. Althusser's Bakhtinian formulation of the relation between fiction and ideology reappears in several ideological narrative studies. For example, Pierre Macherey, in *A Theory of Literary Production*, 1978, trans. Geoffrey Wall (London: Routledge, 1986), argues that the "finished" fictional text always "reveals the gaps in ideology" (p. 60); and Dominick LaCapra, in *History, Politics and the Novel* (Ithaca, N.Y.: Cornell University Press, 1987), suggests that "significant novels" make challenging contact with ideology by refusing "satisfying symbolic resolutions to the problems they disclose" (p. 213).

44. Althusser, *Lenin and Philosophy*, p. 221.

45. Ibid., p. 159.

46. Althusser uses the word *interpellate* to describe the process by which ideologies "hail" and enlist subjects, in *Lenin and Philosophy*, p. 173. Several feminist theorists have tried to interrelate the terms *race, class,* and *gender* in ways that interrogate Marxist theorizations of ideology. Some of the difficulties of transferring a theory of class ideologies to the domain of gender are outlined in Michèle Barrett, *Women's Oppression Today* (London: Verso, 1988) and Lise Vogel, *Marxism and the Oppression of Women* (New Brunswick, N.J.: Rutgers University Press, 1983). Gloria Hull, in "Notes on a Marxist Interpretation of Black American Literature," *Black American Literature Forum* 12 (1978): 148–53, has argued that the encounter between black cultural criticism and Marxist

theory is necessarily strained, for black critics assign priority and structural determination to race rather than class. Gloria Joseph, in "The Incompatible Menage à Trois: Marxism, Feminism, and Racism," *Women and Revolution*, ed. Lydia Sargent (Boston: South End, 1981), pp. 91–107, contends that the "categories of Marxism are sex-blind *and* race-blind" (p. 93).

47. Deborah H. King, in "Multiple Jeopardy, Multiple Consciousness: The Context of a Black Feminist Ideology," *Black Women in America*, pp. 265–95, persuasively argues against the additive model, advancing instead an analysis of the "multiplicative relationships" among "several, simultaneous oppressions" (p. 270). Hazel Carby attacks the analogical model in "White Woman Listen! Black Feminism and the Boundaries of Sisterhood," *The Empire Strikes Back*, Centre for Contemporary Cultural Studies (London: Hutchinson, 1982), pp. 212–35; and Evelyn Brooks Higginbotham critiques totalizing discourses on race in "African-American Women's History and the Metalanguage of Race," *Signs: Journal of Women in Culture and Society* 17, no. 2 (1992): 251–74.

1. "I Am New Man"

1. Alphonso Pinkney, *Red, Black and Green: Black Nationalism in the United States* (Cambridge: Cambridge University Press, 1976), p. 14. Also see John H. Bracey, Jr., August Meier, and Elliott Rudwick's "Introduction" to *Black Nationalism in America*, ed. Bracey, Meier, and Rudwick (New York: Bobbs-Merrill, 1970), which draws a similar distinction between cultural and revolutionary nationalism; and Bobby Seale's discussion of the Marxist basis of revolutionary nationalist ideology in *Seize the Time* (New York: Random House, 1970), p. 417.

2. Ron Karenga, in Floyd B. Barbour, ed., *The Black Power Revolt* (Boston: Porter Sargent, 1968), p. 165.

3. For the sake of brevity and convenience, I have used the term *black nationalism* throughout this book to refer to cultural, and not revolutionary, nationalism.

4. La Frances Rodgers-Rose, ed., *The Black Woman* (Beverly Hills: Sage, 1980), p. 241.

5. Ibid., p. 279.

6. Toni Morrison, "What the Black Woman Thinks about Women's Lib," *New York Times Magazine* (August 22, 1971): 15.

7. The lady/woman opposition also motivates Alice Walker's preference for the term *womanist* rather than *feminist*. See *In Search of Our Mothers' Gardens* (New York: Harcourt, 1984), p. xi.

8. See Inez Smith Reid, *"Together" Black Women* (New York: Emerson, 1972), p. 43.

9. See bell hooks, *Ain't I a Woman: Black Women and Feminism* (Boston: South End Press, 1981), p. 70.

10. Barbara Omolade, "Black Women and Feminism," in *The Future of Difference*, ed. Hester Eisenstein and Alice Jardine (New Brunswick, N.J.: Rutgers University Press, 1985), p. 256.

11. Combahee River Collective, "A Black Feminist Statement," 1977, rptd. in *This Bridge Called My Back: Writings by Radical Women of Color*, ed. Gloria Anzaldúa and Cherríe Moraga (Watertown, Mass.: Persephone Press, 1981), p. 211.

12. *All the Women Are White, All the Blacks Are Men, but Some of Us Are Brave*, ed. Gloria T. Hull, Patricia Bell Scott, and Barbara Smith (New York: Feminist Press, 1982).

13. Paula Giddings, *When and Where I Enter: The Impact of Black Women on Race and Sex in America* (New York: Bantam, 1985), p. 314.

14. Michele Wallace, *Black Macho and the Myth of the Superwoman* (New York: Warner, 1978), p. 95.

15. Alvin Poussaint, "White Manipulation and Black Oppression," *The Black Scholar* 10, nos. 8–9 (1979): 55. Also see "Addison Gayle Interviewed by Saundra Towns," *The Black Position* 2 (1972): 4–36. Gayle claims that black women have "had it easier because the entire paraphernalia of this country: its educational institutions, its courts, its political structures, have not been aimed at the black woman. It has been aimed at destroying black men as men" (p. 30).

16. Daniel Patrick Moynihan, *The Negro Family: The Case for National Action*, 1965, rptd. in *The Moynihan Report and the Politics of Controversy*, ed. Lee Rainwater and William L. Yancey (Cambridge, Mass.: MIT Press, 1967), p. 62. Subsequent references to this work are parenthetically cited in the text.

17. Pauli Murray has demonstrated that black women in fact constituted the lowest paid and the most highly unemployed group in the country. "The Liberation of Black Women," in *Voices of the New Feminism*, ed. Mary Lou Thompson (Boston: Beacon, 1970), p. 101.

18. For a discussion of Moynihan's failure to compute hidden factors such as the differential availability of contraception, abortion, and adoption facilities in black and white communities, see Rainwater and Yancey, *The Moynihan Report*, pp. 457–63.

19. Jacqueline Jones, in *Labor of Love, Labor of Sorrow* (New York: Vintage, 1986), has described the ambivalent response of black nationalists to the Moynihan Report: "Carmichael accused Moynihan of 'playing the dozens' with Black men; 'To set the record straight,' Carmichael wrote in 1966, 'the reason we're in the bag we're in isn't because of my mama, it's because of what they did to my mama.' Still, other outspoken Black men lent their street-wise support to Moynihan's analysis" (p. 313).

20. Nathan Hare, "Will the Real Black Man Please Stand Up?" *The Black Scholar* 2, no. 10 (1971): 32.

21. Eldridge Cleaver, *Soul on Ice* (New York: Dell, 1968), p. 162.

22. Ibid., p. 181.

23. Calvin Hernton, *Sex and Racism in America* (New York: Grove, 1965), p. 136.

24. Audre Lorde analyzes the ideological lure of masculinity in the home as a means of disguising the black man's economic oppression in "The Great American Disease," *The Black Scholar* 10, nos. 8–9 (1979): 18.

25. I use the heavily disputed term *patriarchy* in Michèle Barrett's restricted definition of the term as descriptive not of the general oppression of women by men, but of a structure of oppression based on legal paternal privilege. See Barrett, *Women's Oppression Today* (London: Verso, 1988), p. 16.

26. bell hooks, *Ain't I a Woman*, p. 79.

27. See Theodore Draper, *The Rediscovery of Black Nationalism* (New York: Viking, 1969), p. 138.

28. Amiri Baraka, cited in Paula Giddings, *When and Where I Enter*, p. 318.

29. Robert Staples, "The Myth of the Black Matriarchy," 1970, rptd. in *The Black Woman Cross-Culturally*, ed. Filomina Chioma Steady (Cambridge, Mass.: Schenkman, 1981), p. 345.

30. Robert Staples, "The Myth of Black Macho: A Response to Angry Black Feminists," *The Black Scholar* 10, nos. 6–7 (1979): 27.

31. Toni Cade, "On the Issue of Roles," in *The Black Woman*, ed. Toni Cade (New York: NAL, 1970), p. 107.

32. Eldridge Cleaver, *Soul on Ice*, p. 208.

33. Robert Staples, "The Myth of the Black Matriarchy," p. 346.

34. See Bonnie Thornton Dill, "The Dialectics of Black Womanhood," in *Feminism and Methodology*, ed. Sandra Harding (Bloomington: Indiana University Press, 1987), p. 99.

35. See Carol Stack, "Sex Roles and Survival Strategies in the Urban Black Community," in *The Black Woman Cross-Culturally*, p. 365.

36. These generalizations are informed by Marxist-feminist discussions of middle-class familial ideology, especially Michèle Barrett, *Women's Oppression Today*, pp. 152–86, and Joan Kelly, *Women, History, and Theory* (Chicago: University of Chicago Press, 1984), pp. 51–65, 110–52.

37. For black feminist analyses of this contradiction, see Mary Ellen Weathers, "An Argument for Black Women's Liberation as a Revolutionary Force," in *Voices from Women's Liberation*, ed. Leslie B. Tanner (New York: NAL, 1971), p. 303; Eleanor Holmes Norton, "For Sadie and Maude," in *Sisterhood Is Powerful*, ed. Robin Morgan (New York: Random House, 1970), p. 356; and Bettina Aptheker, *Woman's Legacy: Essays on Race, Sex and Class in American History* (Amherst: University of Massachusetts Press, 1982), pp. 132–33.

38. Florynce Kennedy, cited in Robert Staples, *The Black Woman in America* (Chicago: Nelson-Hall, 1973), p. 147.

39. For example, see Andrew Billingsley, *Black Families in White America* (Englewood Cliffs: Prentice-Hall, 1968), p. 72.

40. Margaret Walker, in Claudia Tate, *Black Women Writers at Work* (New York: Continuum, 1983), p. 203.

41. Cleaver, *Soul on Ice*, p. 160.

42. W. Keorapetse Kgositsile, "Towards Our Theater: A Definitive Act," in *Black Expression*, ed. Addison Gayle, Jr. (New York: Weybright, 1969), p. 147.

43. Larry Neal, "Some Reflections on the Black Aesthetic," in *The Black Aesthetic*, ed. Addison Gayle, Jr. (New York: Doubleday, 1972), p. 13.

44. Calvin Hernton, "The Sexual Mountain and Black Women Writers," *Black American Literature Forum* 18 (1984): 141. Two particularly pointed critiques of what Hernton calls the "male-centered aesthetic" of black nationalism (p. 143) are Deborah McDowell, "Reading Family Matters," in *Changing Our Own Words*, ed. Cheryl Wall (New Brunswick, N.J.: Rutgers University Press, 1989), pp. 75–87; and Valerie Smith, "Gender and Afro-Americanist Literary Theory and Criticism," in *Speaking of Gender*, ed. Elaine Showalter (New York: Routledge, 1989), p. 60.

45. See Ronald S. Copeland, "Community Origins of the Black Power Movement," in *Black Life and Culture in the United States*, ed. Rhoda L. Goldstein (New York: Crowell, 1971), pp. 234–42.

46. Stokely Carmichael, "Power and Racism," in *The Black Power Revolt*, ed. Floyd B. Barbour, p. 70.

47. Charles Hamilton, "An Advocate of Black Power Defines It," in *The Black Revolt and Democratic Politics*, ed. Sondra Silverman (Lexington, Mass.: Heath, 1970), p. 64.

48. A brochure published by Floyd B. McKissick Enterprises, Inc. explicitly announces its objective of providing "a means for Black people to become part of the American capitalist system." See *Black Nationalism in America*, ed. Bracey, Meier, and Rudwick, pp. 494–95.

49. Harold Cruse, *The Crisis of the Negro Intellectual* (New York: Morrow, 1967), p. 371. Also see Julius Hobson, "Black Power: Right or Left?," in *The Black Power Revolt*, ed. Floyd B. Barbour, pp. 199–203; and Arthur L. Smith, *Rhetoric of Black Revolution* (Boston: Allwyn, 1969), pp. 3–4. Robert Allen's entire book, *Black Awakening in Capitalist America* (New York: Anchor, 1970) is a detailed analysis of the capitalist goals of black nationalism.

50. Stokely Carmichael and Charles Hamilton, *Black Power: The Politics of Liberation in America* (New York: Random House, 1967), p. 39.

51. Etheridge Knight, cited in Larry Neal, "The Black Arts Movement," in *The Black Aesthetic*, ed. Addison Gayle, Jr., p. 259.

52. Ron Karenga, "Black Cultural Nationalism," in *The Black Aesthetic*, p. 33.

53. Kimberley Benston, "The Aesthetic of Modern Black Drama: From Mimesis to Methexis," in *The Theater of Black Americans*, ed. Errol Hill (Englewood Cliffs: Prentice-Hall, 1980), pp. 61–78.

54. Sonia Sanchez, *We a BadddDD People* (Detroit: Broadside, 1970), p. 15.

55. Audre Lorde, in Claudia Tate, *Black Women Writers at Work*, p. 101.

56. Nikki Giovanni, in *Black Women Writers at Work*, p. 63.

57. Alice Walker, *Revolutionary Petunias* (New York: Harcourt, 1973), pp. 47, 38.

58. Ntozake Shange, *nappy edges* (New York: St. Martin's, 1978), p. 2.

59. Jeanne Noble, *Beautiful, also, Are the Souls of My Black Sisters* (Englewood Cliffs: Prentice-Hall, 1978), p. 188.

60. Joe Weixlmann, "The Changing Shape(s) of the Contemporary Afro-American Novel," *Studies in Black American Literature* 1 (1983): 114.

61. Larry Neal, "And Shine Swam On," 1968, rptd. in Neal, *Visions of a Liberated Future* (New York: Thunder's Mouth Press, 1989), pp. 20–21; and Don L. Lee, "Toward a Definition: Black Poetry of the Sixties (After Leroi Jones)," in *The Black Aesthetic*, pp. 222–23.

62. See Stephen A. Henderson, "Blues, Soul, and Black Identity: The Forms of Things Unknown," *Black Books Bulletin* 1 (Fall 1971): 13; and Larry Neal, "The Ethos of the Blues," 1971, rptd. in *Visions of a Liberated Future*, p. 107. Askia Toure calls blues musicians the "PRIEST-PHILOSOPHERS" of the race, in "Keep On Pushin': Rhythm and Blues as a Weapon," 1965, rptd. in *Black Nationalism in America*, ed. Bracey, Meier, and Rudwick, p. 446.

63. Amiri Baraka/LeRoi Jones, "The Changing Same (R&B and New Black Music)," in *The Black Aesthetic*, p. 115; and Larry Neal, "Some Reflections on the Black Aesthetic," in *The Black Aesthetic*, p. 13.

64. Sonia Sanchez, *We a BadddDD People*, p. 54.

65. Sherley Anne Williams, in *Black Women Writers at Work*, p. 208.

66. Houston A. Baker, Jr., *The Journey Back* (Chicago: University of Chicago Press, 1980), p. 127. Also see David Lionel Smith, "The Black Arts Movement and Its Critics," *American Literary History* 3, no. 1 (Spring 1991): 93–110.

67. Amiri Baraka/LeRoi Jones, *Home: Social Essays* (New York: Morrow, 1966), p. 217.

68. Ibid., p. 247.

69. Julian Mayfield, "You Touch My Black Aesthetic and I'll Touch Yours," in *The Black Aesthetic*, p. 27.

70. Addison Gayle, Jr., *The Black Situation*, p. 218.

71. Ibid. Also see John Henrik Clarke, "The New Afro-American Nationalism," *Freedomways* 1, no. 3 (1961): 292.

72. Stephen Henderson, "Survival Motion: A Study of the Black Writer and the Black Revolution in America," in *The Militant Black Writer*, by Mercer Cook and Stephen Henderson (Madison: University of Wisconsin Press, 1969), pp. 63–129, discusses the ideological ambivalence, the fusion of "two contradictory attitudes toward one's blackness" in black oral culture (pp. 89–90). Eldridge Cleaver, "As Crinkly As Yours," 1962, rptd. in *Mother Wit from the Laughing Barrel*, ed. Alan Dundes (Englewood Cliffs: Prentice-Hall, 1973), pp. 9–21, counsels militant black writers to root out those elements of black folk culture that express feelings of racial shame and self-hatred.

73. Larry Neal, "The Black Arts Movement," p. 265.

74. Julian Mayfield, "You Touch My Black Aesthetic," p. 30.

75. The quoted phrase is from Bonnie Barthold, *Black Time: Fiction of Africa, the Caribbean, and the United States* (New Haven: Yale University Press, 1981), p. 37.

76. Stokely Carmichael and Charles Hamilton, *Black Power*, p. 156. Alvin F. Poussaint, "The Negro American: His Self-Image and Integration," in *The Black Power Revolt*, pp. 94–102, describes the oppressive past through the image of a "vicious circle," and welcomes the Civil Rights and black nationalist movements as disruptions of this cycle (pp. 97–98). Kenneth Clark, *Dark Ghetto* (New York: Harper and Row, 1965), after a detailed analysis of the "vicious circle" of oppression in the black ghettos, argues that the urban violence of the mid-1960s "suggests that the past cycle . . . is being supplanted" (p. 14).

77. Addison Gayle, Jr., *The Black Situation*, p. 61.

78. Ibid., p. 216.

79. Stokely Carmichael and Charles Hamilton, *Black Power*, p. 38. Houston Baker, Jr., in *The Journey Back*, remarks that the rebirth represented in Black Aesthetic discourse is "an exclusively lexical one" (p. 134).

80. John E. Johnson, "Super Black Man," in *The Black Power Revolt*, p. 225.

81. Stephen E. Henderson, "Survival Motion," p. 124. For an extended effort to define the quality of soul, see *Black Experience: Soul*, ed. Lee Rainwater (United States: Trans-action Books, 1970).

82. Stephen Henderson, "Survival Motion," p. 96.

83. Amiri Baraka/LeRoi Jones, *Home*, p. 221.

84. Eldridge Cleaver, *Soul on Ice*, p. 203.

85. John O'Neal, "Black Arts: Notebook," in *The Black Aesthetic*, p. 50.

86. See Amiri Baraka/LeRoi Jones, *Home*, p. 209; and William Grier and Price Cobbs, *Black Rage*, pp. 177–79.

87. The quoted phrase is from Stephen Henderson, "Survival Motion," p. 88. Also see Eldridge Cleaver, "As Crinkly As Yours"; and Addison Gayle, Jr., "Cultural Strangulation: Black Literature and the White Aesthetic," in *The Black Aesthetic*, pp. 38–45.

88. Carolyn F. Gerald, "The Black Writer and His Role," in *The Black Aesthetic*, p. 354.

89. Henry Louis Gates, Jr., "Preface to Blackness: Text and Pretext," in *Afro-American Literature: The Reconstruction of Instruction*, ed. Dexter Fisher and Robert Stepto (New York: MLA, 1978), p. 48.

90. Henry Louis Gates, Jr., *Figures in Black* (New York: Oxford University Press, 1987), p. 274.

91. Keith Byerman, "Remembering History in Contemporary Black Literature and Criticism," *American Literary History* 3, no. 4 (1991): 811. Also see David Lionel Smith, "The Black Arts Movement and Its Critics," who argues that "the concept of 'blackness' was—and is—inherently overburdened with essentialist, ahistorical entailments" (p. 95).

92. Chris Weedon, *Feminist Practice and Poststructuralist Theory* (New York: Blackwell, 1987), p. 32.

93. Ron Karenga, "Black Cultural Nationalism," p. 34. Also see Vincent Harding, "Black Reflections on the Cultural Ramifications of Identity," *Black Books Bulletin* 1 (Winter 1972): 4–10, for a discussion of the communal orientation of black identity as opposed to the "private" basis of Western conceptions of identity.

94. The quoted phrase is from Stephen Henderson, "Survival Motion," p. 126.

95. Henry Louis Gates, Jr., *Figures in Black*, p. 275.

96. Melissa Walker, "The Verbal Arsenal of Black Women Writers in

America," in *Confronting the Crisis*, ed. Francis Barker et al. (Essex: University of Essex Press, 1984), p. 120.

97. I am drawing upon Fredric Jameson's discussion of management devices as those formal means by which a text attempts to defuse or neutralize its troublesome political impulses, *The Political Unconscious: Narrative as a Socially Symbolic Act* (Ithaca, N.Y.: Cornell University Press, 1981), p. 266.

2. "What Did We Lack?"

1. Frances Foster, "Changing Concepts of Black Womanhood," *Journal of Black Studies* 3 (1973): 448–51.

2. Arthur Davis described *The Bluest Eye* as "a powerful protest novel," and Pecola as "the most tragic victim," in "Novels of the New Black Renaissance," *CLA Journal* 21 (1978): 475–76. Several critics have commented on the novel's stereotypical characterization. Chikwenye Okonjo Ogunyemi, for example, sees this as a defect in Morrison's writing: "Morrison's forte does not lie in characterization, since the main characters lack individuation and roundedness." "Order and Disorder in Toni Morrison's *The Bluest Eye*," *Critique* 19 (1977): 119.

3. Addison Gayle, Jr., "Blueprint for Black Criticism," *Black World* 1, no. 1 (1977): 43.

4. Addison Gayle, Jr., in Roseann Bell, "Judgement: Addison Gayle," in *Sturdy Black Bridges*, ed. Roseann Bell, Bettye J. Parker, and Beverly Guy-Sheftall (New York: Anchor, 1979), p. 213.

5. Ruby Dee, Review of *The Bluest Eye*, *Freedomways* 11, no. 3 (1971): 319.

6. Dellita Martin, "In Our Own Images: Afro-American Literature in the 1980s," *MELUS* 8, no. 2 (1981): 68.

7. Melissa Walker points out that *The Bluest Eye* evokes Kenneth Clark's study of "the damaging effects of the white aesthetic on black children." Clark's "doll test" revealed the ambivalent feelings of black schoolchildren, who preferred the white doll although they identified more with the black doll. *Down from the Mountaintop: Black Women's Novels in the Wake of the Civil Rights Movement, 1966–1989* (New Haven: Yale University Press, 1991), p. 56.

8. Toni Morrison, "Rootedness: The Ancestor as Foundation," in *Black Women Writers*, ed. Mari Evans (New York: Anchor, 1984), p. 341.

9. Ibid., p. 344.

10. Addison Gayle, Jr., "Black Literature and the White Aesthetic," in *The Black Aesthetic* (New York: Doubleday, 1972), p. 43.

11. William Van O'Connor has described the use of the grotesque mode in American fiction as "a reaction against the sometimes bland surfaces of bourgeois customs and habits." "The Grotesque Mode in Modern American Fiction," *College English* 20 (1959): 342. In a contemporary review of *The Bluest Eye* in *The New Yorker* (January 23, 1971): 94, L. E. Sissman argued that Morrison's framing her story by "the bland white words of a conventional school reader" was "unnecessary and unsuitable." Yet the novel derives its ironic force from its grotesque caricature of the bland clichés of the reader.

12. W. Keorapetse Kgositsile, "Towards Our Theater: A Definitive Act," in *Black Expression*, ed. Addison Gayle, Jr. (New York: Weybright, 1969), p. 147.

13. Toni Morrison, *The Bluest Eye* (New York: Simon and Schuster, 1970), p. 37. All further references to this work are cited in the text.

14. Philip Thomson, in *The Grotesque* (London: Methuen, 1972), argues that an "essentially divided" reader response and a refusal to resolve conflicts are distinguishing features of the grotesque mode (pp. 3, 21).

15. Philip Royster, "*The Bluest Eye*," *First World* 1, no. 4 (1977): 36.

16. For example, see Marco Portales, "Toni Morrison's *The Bluest Eye*: Shirley Temple and Cholly," *The Centennial Review* 30 (1986): 500.

17. Keith Byerman, "Intense Behaviors: The Use of the Grotesque in *The Bluest Eye* and *Eva's Man*," *CLA Journal* 25 (1982): 451.

18. Michael Steig, "Defining the Grotesque," *Journal of Aesthetics and Art Criticism* 29 (1970): 256.

19. Hoyt W. Fuller, "The New Black Literature: Protest or Affirmation," in *The Black Aesthetic*, p. 338.

20. Robert B. Stepto, "'Intimate Things in Place': A Conversation with Toni Morrison," in *Chant of Saints*, ed. Michael Harper and Robert B. Stepto (Chicago: University of Chicago Press, 1979), p. 219.

21. Amiri Baraka/LeRoi Jones, *Home: Social Essays* (New York: Morrow, 1966), p. 213.

22. Ibid.

23. So many readers have testified to the fact that *The Bluest Eye* aggravates rather than mitigates the reader's sense of anger with Pecola's experience. Raymond Hedin's "The Structuring of Emotion in Black American Fiction," *Novel* 16, no. 1 (1982): 49-50, contains one of most eloquent discussions of the discomfort produced by *The Bluest Eye*. Also see Joan Bischoff, "The Novels of Toni Morrison: Studies in Thwarted Sensibility," *Studies in Black Literature* 6, no. 3 (1975): 21; and Linda Wagner, "Toni Morrison: Mastery of Narrative," in *Contemporary American Women Writers: Narrative Strategies*, ed. Catherine Rainwater and William J. Scheick (Lexington, Ky.: University of Kentucky Press, 1985), p. 34.

24. See Philip Thomson, *The Grotesque*, p. 9.

25. Price M. Cobbs and William H. Grier, *Black Rage* (New York: Bantam, 1968), p. 34.

26. Madonne Miner, in "Lady No Longer Sings the Blues: Rape, Madness and Silence in *The Bluest Eye*," *Conjuring: Black Women, Fiction and Literary Tradition*, ed. Marjorie Pryse and Hortense Spillers (Bloomington: Indiana University Press, 1985), pp. 176-91, argues that all the male characters in *The Bluest Eye* contribute to the "depresencing of Pecola" (p. 180). In Miner's feminist reading, the novel allots the values of absence and presence along sexual lines (p. 181). Reading *The Bluest Eye* exclusively by its gender dynamics, Miner inevitably simplifies the novel, failing to account for those moments when racial dynamics ascribe absence to the black man and presence to the white woman.

27. Susan Willis, "Eruptions of Funk: Historicizing Toni Morrison," in *Black Literature and Literary Theory*, ed. Henry Louis Gates, Jr. (New York: Methuen, 1984), p. 267. I have little to add to Willis's astute analysis of the connotations of funk in *The Bluest Eye*. Mary O'Connor has recently observed that Willis's discussion of funk is remarkably evocative of Bakhtin's definition of the grotesque body. See O'Connor, "Subject, Voice, and Women in Some Contemporary Black American Women's Writing," in *Feminism, Bakhtin, and the Dialogic*, ed. Dale M. Bauer and S. Jaret McKinstry (Albany: SUNY Press, 1991), p. 201. O'Connor's suggestive (although undeveloped) comparison informs my brief discussion of funk in *The Bluest Eye*.

28. Barbara Christian, *Black Women Novelists: The Development of a Tradition* (Westport, Conn.: Greenwood Press, 1980), pp. 144-45.

29. For analyses of *The Bluest Eye* as an initiation novel, see Ruth Rosenberg, "Seeds in Hard Ground: Black Girlhood in *The Bluest Eye*," *Black American Literature Forum* 21 (1987): 435–46; Jane Bakerman, "Failures of Love: Female Initiation in the Novels of Toni Morrison," *American Literature* 52 (1981): 541–63; and Phyllis Klotman, "Dick-and-Jane and the Shirley Temple Sensibility in *The Bluest Eye*," *Black American Literature Forum* 13 (1979): 126–29. It is difficult

to agree with Klotman's assertion that, despite the novel's presentation of "a dichotomy between Black experiences and white culture," its use of the bildungsroman "points to the commonality of human experience" (p. 125).

30. Barbara Christian, *Black Women Novelists*, p. 143.

31. Barbara Christian, *Black Feminist Criticism* (New York: Pergamon Press, 1985), p. 57.

32. Bonnie Barthold, *Black Time: Fiction of Africa, the Caribbean and the United States* (New Haven: Yale University Press, 1981), p. 100.

33. Susan Gubar, "Mother, Maiden and the Marriage of Death: Women Writers and an Ancient Myth," *Women's Studies* 6 (1979): 308.

34. My reading of the black folk culture presented in *The Bluest Eye* is exactly contrary to Trudier Harris's affirmative evaluation of this culture as a vibrant, unifying force. See Harris, "Reconnecting Fragments: Afro-American Folk Tradition in *The Bluest Eye*," in *Critical Essays on Toni Morrison*, ed. Nellie McKay (Boston: Hall, 1988), pp. 68–76.

35. Johnanna Lucille Grimes, *The Function of Oral Tradition in Selected Afro-American Fiction*, Ph.D. diss. (Northwestern University, 1980), p. 139. In his essay detailing why some folklore should be discarded by nationalist writers, Eldridge Cleaver quotes this rhyme as a "prime example of 'self-hate' folklore." "As Crinkly As Yours," in *Mother Wit from the Laughing Barrel*, ed. Alan Dundes (Englewood Cliffs: Prentice-Hall, 1973), p. 10.

36. Elizabeth A. Schultz, "The Insistence upon Community in the Contemporary Afro-American Novel," *College English* 41 (1979): 184.

37. Leo Spitzer, cited in Dorritt Cohn, *Transparent Minds: Narrative Models for Presenting Consciousness in Fiction* (Princeton, N.J.: Princeton University Press, 1978), p. 33.

38. In his provocative reading of *The Bluest Eye*, Michael Awkward claims that the novel's double-voiced narration corresponds directly to the split, schizophrenic voice of Pecola, and that both Pecola's and the narrators' voices constitute instances of the double-consciousness theorized by W. E. B. DuBois. See Awkward, *Inspiriting Influences: Tradition, Revision, and Afro-American Women's Novels* (New York: Columbia University Press, 1989), pp. 11–12. While the DuBoisian notion of double-consciousness certainly offers a valuable intertext for Pecola's split voice, it is not clear to me, and Awkward does not explain, how the novel's double-voiced narration corresponds to DuBois's articulation of an internal struggle between two antithetical selves, one Negro and the other American. Awkward goes on to argue that, at the end of the novel, the "distinctive narrative voices . . . merge into a single voice" (p. 94), and that this "conflation of narrative voices" (p. 95) heals the earlier double-voicedness of the narrators' as well as of Pecola's discourses. I argue, instead, that the novel strongly refuses the notion of a unified, single voice, promoting instead a creative and dynamic exchange between different voices and languages.

39. Toni Morrison, "Rootedness: The Ancestor as Foundation," p. 343.

40. Ishmael Reed used the phrase "talking book" to describe his fiction, in *Shrovetide in New Orleans* (New York: Doubleday, 1978), p. 160.

41. Morrison, "Rootedness," pp. 339–40. The loss of a black oral tradition is usually figured in terms of spatial and temporal discontinuity in Morrison's fiction. The oral tradition, with its assumption of an intact black collectivity, is fictionally located in the rural South, in an era prior to the Northern urban migration. See Susan Willis's extensive analysis of this aspect of Morrison's fiction, in *Specifying: Black Women Writing the American Experience* (Madison: University of Wisconsin Press, 1987), pp. 84–88. Also see Donald Gibson, "Individualism and Community in Black History and Fiction," *Black American Literature Forum* 11 (1977): 128–29, who argues that, in the symbolic geography

of post-1960s black fiction, the rural South becomes the locus of community and cultural heritage.

42. Morrison, "Rootedness," p. 340.

43. My discussion of the novelistic as opposed to mythical treatment of time in *The Bluest Eye* is indebted to Bakhtin's distinction between mythical and fictional time in *The Dialogic Imagination*, trans. Caryl Emerson (Austin: University of Texas Press, 1981). Bakhtin writes that the genre of myth assumes "beginnings as the crystal clear, pure sources of all being, of eternal values and modes of existence" that belong to an ideal past (p. 148). With the novel, "the temporal model of the world changes radically: it becomes a world where there is no first word (no ideal word), and the final word has not yet been spoken. For the first time in artistic-ideological consciousness, time and the world become historical" (p. 30).

44. Morrison, "Rootedness," p. 341.

45. Bakhtin, *The Dialogic Imagination*, p. 294.

46. Morrison, "Rootedness," p. 344.

47. Audre Lorde, *Sister Outsider* (New York: Crossing Press, 1984), p. 111.

3. "No Bottom and No Top"

1. Jerry Bryant, Review of *Sula*, *The Nation* (July 6, 1974): 24.

2. Barbara Jean Varga-Coley, *The Novels of Black American Women*, Ph.D. diss. (SUNY, Stonybrook, 1981), p. 119.

3. Roseann Bell, "Judgement: Addison Gayle," in *Sturdy Black Bridges*, ed. Roseann Bell, Bettye J. Parker, and Beverly Guy-Sheftall (New York: Anchor, 1979), p. 213.

4. The quoted phrases are from Richard Barksdale's essay "Castration Symbolism in Recent Black American Fiction," *CLA Journal* 29 (1986): 401, 408.

5. Robert Stepto, "'Intimate Things in Place': A Conversation with Toni Morrison," in *Chant of Saints*, ed. Michael Harper and Robert Stepto (Chicago: University of Chicago Press, 1979), p. 219.

6. Toni Morrison, *Sula* (New York: NAL, 1973), pp. 82–83. All subsequent references to this work are included in the text.

7. Alvin Poussaint described the black man as "the number one object of racism," in "White Manipulation and Black Oppression," *The Black Scholar* 10, nos. 8–9 (1979): 55.

8. Susan Willis, "Black Women Writers: Taking a Critical Perspective," in *Making a Difference*, ed. Gayle Greene and Coppelia Kahn (New York: Methuen, 1985), p. 236.

9. Barbara Smith, "Toward a Black Feminist Criticism," 1977, rptd. in *But Some of Us Are Brave*, ed. Gloria T. Hull, Patricia Bell Scott, and Barbara Smith (New York: Feminist Press, 1982), p. 170.

10. For example, see Susan Willis, "Black Women Writers," p. 232; and Deborah McDowell, "New Directions for Black Feminist Criticism," in *The New Feminist Criticism*, ed. Elaine Showalter (New York: Pantheon, 1985), p. 190.

11. Barbara Smith, "Toward a Black Feminist Criticism," p. 165.

12. For a critique of Smith's definition of lesbian literature, see Bonnie Zimmerman, "What Has Never Been: An Overview of Lesbian Feminist Criticism," in *Making a Difference*, pp. 184–85.

13. Barbara Smith, p. 166.

14. Ibid., p. 165.

15. Maureen Reddy, "The Tripled Plot and Center of *Sula*," *Black American Literature Forum* 22 (1988): 43.

16. See Hortense Spillers, "A Hateful Passion, a Lost Love," in *Feminist Issues*

in Literary Scholarship, ed. Shari Benstock (Bloomington: Indiana University Press, 1987), p. 181; Jacqueline de Weever, "The Inverted World of Toni Morrison's *The Bluest Eye* and *Sula*," *CLA Journal* 22 (1979): 413; and Susan Willis, "Black Women Writers," p. 213.

17. Roseann Bell, Review of *Sula, Obsidian* 2, no. 3 (1976): 95. Also see Odette Martin, "Sula," *First World* 1, no. 4 (1977): 42.

18. Sara Blackburn, Review of *Sula, New York Times Book Review* (December 30, 1973): 3.

19. Barbara Christian, *Black Feminist Criticism* (New York: Pergamon Press, 1985), p. 76.

20. For a balanced discussion of the novel's ambivalent treatment of the maternal, see Marianne Hirsch, "Maternal Narratives: 'Cruel Enough to Stop the Blood,'" in *Reading Black, Reading Feminist*, ed. Henry Louis Gates, Jr. (New York: Meridian, 1990), pp. 425–26.

21. Faith Ringgold, "From Being My Own Woman," in *Confirmations*, ed. Amina Baraka and Amiri Baraka (New York: Morrow, 1983), p. 301.

22. Toni Morrison, "Rootedness: The Ancestor as Foundation," in *Black Women Writers*, ed. Mari Evans (New York: Anchor, 1984), p. 344.

23. Toni Morrison, too, shares Nel's and the narrator's regret about these changes: "I felt a sense of loss, a void. Things were moving too fast in the early 1960s–70s . . . it was exciting but it left me bereft." See Sandi Russell, "It's OK to Say OK" (An Interview Essay), 1986, rptd. in *Critical Essays on Toni Morrison*, ed. Nellie Y. McKay (Boston: Hall, 1988), p. 45.

24. Susan Willis, "Black Women Writers," pp. 218, 219.

25. Kimberley Benston, "I Yam What I Am: The Topos of (Un)naming in Afro-American Literature," in *Black Literature and Literary Theory*, ed. Henry Louis Gates, Jr. (New York: Methuen, 1984), p. 162.

26. Quoted out of context from Sherley Anne Williams, *Give Birth to Brightness: A Thematic Study of Neo-Black Literature* (New York: Dial, 1972), p. 92. This statement forms an important part of Williams's argument that even when it pits the individual against the community, the black literature of the 1960s posits a communal vision.

27. Adrienne Munich, "Notorious Signs, Feminist Criticism and Literary Tradition," in *Making a Difference*, p. 254.

28. Keith Byerman, *Fingering the Jagged Grain* (Athens, Ga.: University of Georgia Press, 1985), p. 196.

29. Edward Guerrero, in "Tracking 'The Look' in Toni Morrison's Novels," *Black American Literature Forum* 24 (1990): 761–73, describes Shadrack as a "proto-nationalist figure" (p. 768).

30. Toni Morrison, in Claudia Tate, *Black Women Writers at Work* (New York: Continuum, 1983), p. 128.

31. Mary Russo, "Female Grotesques: Carnival and Theory," in *Feminist Studies/Critical Studies*, ed. Teresa de Lauretis (Bloomington: Indiana University Press, 1986), p. 219.

32. See Mikhail Bakhtin, *Rabelais and His World*, trans. Helene Iswolsky (Bloomington: Indiana University Press, 1984), pp. 325, 367. The quoted phrase is from Peter Stallybrass and Allon White, *The Politics and Poetics of Transgression* (Ithaca, N.Y.: Cornell University Press, 1986), p. 21. My discussion of the grotesque mode in *Sula* is informed by Stallybrass and White's critical reconsideration and historicization of Bakhtin's concept of the grotesque body.

33. I am quoting Karen Stein, "Toni Morrison's *Sula*: A Black Woman's Epic," *Black American Literature Forum* 18 (1984): 148. Despite the novel's strong emphasis on absence and division, critics tend to read *Sula* as an affirmation of a whole, unified black subjectivity. For example, see Lynn Munro, "The Tattooed

Heart and the Serpentine Eye: Morrison's Choice of an Epigraph for *Sula*," *Black American Literature Forum* 18 (1984): 153; and Dorothy Lee, "The Quest for Self: Triumph and Failure in the Works of Toni Morrison," in *Black Women Writers*, ed. Mari Evans, p. 359. Even Susan Willis, who extensively analyzes lack and self-mutilation in *Sula*, argues that the novel ultimately achieves a "spontaneous re-definition of the individual not as an alienated cripple but as a new and whole person." *Specifying: Black Women Writing the American Experience* (Madison: University of Wisconsin Press, 1987), p. 104. The question of fragmented versus whole selfhood constitutes perhaps the most hotly disputed issue in criticism on *Sula*. For significant recent contributions to this critical debate, see Deborah McDowell, "Boundaries: Or Distant Relations and Close Kin," in *Afro-American Literary Study in the 1990s*, ed. Houston A. Baker, Jr., and Patricia Redmond (Chicago: University of Chicago Press, 1989), pp. 51–70, which is followed by the untitled responses of Hortense Spillers (pp. 71–73) and Michael Awkward (pp. 73–77). Also see Timothy Powell, "The Black Figure on the White Page," *Black American Literature Forum* 24 (1990): 754.

34. Robert Stepto, "'Intimate Things in Place,'" p. 216.

35. Valerie Smith, in *Self-Discovery and Authority in Afro-American Narrative* (Cambridge, Mass.: Harvard University Press, 1989), persuasively argues that the device of the split protagonist undercuts the notion of unified, self-sufficient individuality (pp. 133–34).

36. Barbara Christian, *Black Women Novelists: The Development of a Tradition* (Westport, Conn.: Greenwood Press, 1980), p. 155.

37. Claudia Tate, *Black Women Writers at Work*, p. 124.

38. Ibid., p. 125. In "Rootedness: The Ancestor as Foundation," Morrison describes the use of gaps in her fiction as an effort to recreate the collective reception situation of oral black culture (p. 341). Morrison's fictional adaptation of oral forms significantly modifies the notions of collectivity and identity invested in oral forms by Black Aesthetic theorists. Founded on gaps and absences, and offering the reader a difficult though active entry into the text, *Sula* does not assume the self-present and unified collective voice valorized by Black Aesthetic critics. For a different reading of the novel's use of the oral tradition, see Chikwenye Okonjo Ogunyemi, "*Sula*: 'A Nigger Joke,'" *Black American Literature Forum* 13 (1979): 130–33. According to Ogunyemi, the novel exactly replicates all the central features of a black folk narrative voice (p. 130).

39. For related discussions of Morrison's revaluation of binary oppositions, see Deborah McDowell, "Boundaries: Or Distant Relations and Close Kin," p. 60; and Linda Myers, "Perception and Power through Naming: Characters in Search of Self in the Fiction of Toni Morrison," *Explorations in Ethnic Studies* 7, no. 1 (1984): 51.

4. "A New World Song"

1. Toni Morrison, "Reading," *Mademoiselle* 81 (May 1975): 81.

2. Toni Morrison, "Rootedness: The Ancestor as Foundation," in *Black Women Writers*, ed. Mari Evans (New York: Anchor, 1984), p. 344.

3. In an interview with Roseann Bell, Jones drew attention to *Corregidora's* deviance from the functional reading norms of Black Aesthetic ideology. To Bell's question, "What does that novel . . . teach us?" Jones replied, "It is difficult to say what it should teach. I don't start off thinking of the writing itself as instructive, not in the sense of message." Roseann Bell, "Gayl Jones Takes a Look at *Corregidora*," in *Sturdy Black Bridges*, ed. Roseann Bell, Bettye J. Parker, and Beverly Guy-Sheftall (New York: Anchor, 1979), p. 286.

4. Gayl Jones, "About My Work," in *Black Women Writers*, ed. Mari Evans, p. 235.

5. Ibid.

6. Claudia Tate, *Black Women Writers at Work* (New York: Continuum, 1983), p. 95.

7. Larry Neal, "The Black Arts Movement," in *The Black Aesthetic*, ed. Addison Gayle, Jr. (New York: Doubleday, 1972), p. 271.

8. Ibid., p. 272.

9. Gayl Jones, *Corregidora* (Boston: Beacon, 1975), p. 22. Subsequent references to this work are included in the text.

10. Such an interpretation has, in fact, been presented by Faith Pullin, who writes that *Corregidora* "has a happy ending: Ursa and her husband come together again, after many years of separation." This reunion can occur only after Ursa is "able to disentangle her mother's/grandmother's/great-grandmother's lives from her own." See "Landscapes of Reality: The Fiction of Contemporary Afro-American Women Writers," in *Black Fiction*, ed. Robert Lee (London: Vision, 1980), p. 201. In Melvin Dixon's similar reading, Mutt frees Ursa from the "oppressive matrilineage that held men and women captive" and forces her "to come to new terms with her femininity." See "Singing a Deep Song: Language as Evidence in the Novels of Gayl Jones," in *Black Women Writers*, ed. Mari Evans, pp. 239, 240. The black man here becomes the agent of a "new" heterosexual femininity that liberates the black woman from the matriarchal past.

11. Keith Byerman, *Fingering the Jagged Grain* (Athens, Ga.: University of Georgia Press, 1985), p. 180.

12. I am using "seme" here in Roland Barthes's definition of the word as a semantic unit, a "connotative signifier" that occurs in several places in the text, a "shifting element which can combine with other similar elements to create characters, ambiences, shapes and symbols," *S/Z*, trans. Richard Miller (New York: Farrar, Straus, and Giroux, 1974), p. 17.

13. This has been established by several historians of slavery. See, for example, Angela Davis, *Women, Race and Class* (New York: Random House, 1981), p. 7.

14. Byerman, *Fingering the Jagged Grain*, p. 179.

15. I am referring here to Nancy Miller's essay, "Emphasis Added: Plots and Plausibilities in Women's Fiction," in *The New Feminist Criticism*, ed. Elaine Showalter (New York: Pantheon, 1985), pp. 339–60. Miller argues that the plots of women's fiction are often "italicized" at moments when the text negotiates the constraints of literary and social conventions. This added emphasis betrays the "extravagant wish for a story that would turn out differently" (pp. 349–52).

16. Gloria Wade-Gayles, *No Crystal Stair: Visions of Race and Sex in Black Women's Fiction* (New York: Pilgrim, 1984), p. 175.

17. Gloria Joseph and Jill Lewis, *Common Differences: Conflicts in Black and White Feminist Perspectives* (New York: Anchor, 1981), p. 189.

18. Ibid., p. 192.

19. Alexis DeVeaux, in Claudia Tate, *Black Women Writers at Work*, p. 52.

20. Bonnie Barthold, *Black Time: Fiction of Africa, the Caribbean and the United States* (New Haven: Yale University Press, 1981), pp. 125–26.

21. See Angela Davis, "Black Women and Music: A Historical Legacy of Struggle," in *Wild Women in the Whirlwind*, ed. Joanne M. Braxton and Andrée Nicola McLaughlin (New Brunswick, N.J.: Rutgers University Press, 1990), pp. 17–18; and Daphne Duvall Harrison, "Black Women in the Blues Tradition," in *The Afro-American Woman: Struggles and Images*, ed. Sharon Harley and Rosalyn Terborg-Penn (New York: Kennikat, 1979), p. 62.

22. Charles Keil, *Urban Blues* (Chicago: University of Chicago Press, 1966),

pp. 152, 185; Michele Russell, "Slave Codes and Liner Notes," in *But Some of Us Are Brave*, ed. Gloria T. Hull, Patricia Bell Scott, and Barbara Smith (New York: Feminist Press, 1982), p. 131; and Hazel Carby, "It Jus Be's Dat Way Sometime: The Sexual Politics of Women's Blues," in *Feminisms*, ed. Robyn Warhol and Diane Price Herndl (New Brunswick, N.J.: Rutgers University Press, 1991), p. 747.

23. Roger Abrahams, *Positively Black* (Englewood Cliffs: Prentice-Hall, 1970), p. 30. That the blues vision refuses the comforting closing gestures of resolution and transcendence is also emphasized throughout Gayl Jones's *Liberating Voices: Oral Tradition in African American Literature* (Cambridge, Mass.: Harvard University Press, 1991).

24. Claudia Tate, *Black Women Writers at Work*, p. 146.

25. Houston A. Baker, Jr., *Blues, Ideology and Afro-American Literature* (Chicago: University of Chicago Press, 1984), p. 7.

26. Ralph Ellison, *Shadow and Act* (New York: Random House, 1964), p. 189.

27. James Snead, "Repetition as a Figure of Black Culture," in *Black Literature and Literary Theory*, ed. Henry Louis Gates, Jr. (New York: Methuen, 1984), p. 67. Keith Byerman writes that the cut "marks a difference from European cultural notions of progress and resolution," in *Fingering the Jagged Grain*, p. 7. For this reason, novels that use the cut as a structuring device are incompatible with linear narrative models such as the one formulated by Peter Brooks in *Reading for the Plot* (New York: Knopf, 1984). In Brooks's Freudian masterplot, desire, at the beginning of a novel, is a mobile textual energy "aroused into expectancy and possibility"; the narrative middle attempts a "binding" of these energies that "allows them to be mastered by putting them into serviceable form, usable bundles, within the energetic economy of the narrative." The middle of a narrative also creates "a postponement in the discharge of energy," which is finally accomplished at the end (p. 101). The plot of *Corregidora* appears to follow this model. Desire is mobilized by Ursa's hysterectomy at the beginning, and then insufficiently bound by the two false choices represented by Tadpole and Catherine. The end of the novel literally enacts a phallic discharge of energy ("He came and I swallowed"). However, this phallic discharge displaces attention from the real impetus of the novel's plot—to release and to bind a nonreproductive feminine energy. The middle sections of the novel repeatedly offer and defer possibilities of clitoral sexuality and, even at the end, clitoral energy remains unreleased and unbound. The vacillating temporal movement of this plot is maintained up to the very end, and markedly withholds the ultimate culmination and release of Brooks's phallic masterplot.

28. Amiri Baraka/LeRoi Jones, *Home: Social Essays* (New York: Morrow, 1966), p. 106.

29. Amiri Baraka/LeRoi Jones, "The Changing Same (R&B and New Black Music)," in *The Black Aesthetic*, p. 117.

30. Ron Karenga, "Black Cultural Nationalism," in *The Black Aesthetic*, p. 36.

31. Houston A. Baker, Jr., *Long Black Song* (Charlottesville: University Press of Virginia, 1972), p. 18.

32. Ralph Ellison, *Shadow and Act*, p. 246.

33. Ibid., pp. 245, 246.

34. For example, see Keith Byerman, *Fingering the Jagged Grain*, p. 172; and George Kent, "The 1975 Literary Scene: Significant Developments," *Phylon* 37 (1976): 107.

35. Gayl Jones, *Liberating Voices*, p. 26.

36. I am alluding here to Walter Ong's discussion of the changed notions of audience and community produced by a novelistic appropriation of oral forms, in *Orality and Literacy* (London: Methuen, 1982), pp. 69, 74, 171. I would, how-

ever, like to distance my discussion from Ong's evolutionary analysis of the transition from orality to print. In *The Presence of the Word* (New Haven: Yale University Press, 1967), Ong invokes Freud's model of psychosexual development to analogize the development of societies from orality to literacy (pp. 93–106). Such a model constructs oral cultures as the primitive origins of a fully developed Western literate culture, and thus precludes an appreciation of the sophisticated use of orality—in black American and other residually oral cultures—to challenge the authority of literate culture.

37. Robert Hemenway, "Are You a Flying Lark or a Setting Dove?" in *Afro-American Literature: The Reconstruction of Instruction*, ed. Dexter Fisher and Robert Stepto (New York: MLA, 1978), p. 130.

38. See Barbara Bowen's highly suggestive essay, "Untroubled Voice: Call and Response in *Cane*," in *Black Literature and Literary Theory*, pp. 187–204. Bowen writes that "for the blues singer, the importance of the call and response pattern is its continual affirmation of collective voice" (p. 189).

39. Byerman, *Fingering the Jagged Grain*, p. 7.

40. See Catherine Belsey, *Critical Practice* (New York: Methuen, 1980), pp. 70–72, on the hierarchical privileging of the omniscient narrator's discourse in classic realist fiction; and Elizabeth Ermarth, "Fictional Consensus and Female Casualties," in *The Representation of Women in Fiction*, ed. Carolyn G. Heilbrun and Margaret R. Higonnet (Baltimore: Johns Hopkins University Press, 1983), p. 4, on the "absolute ontologizing power" of omniscient narration.

41. Claudia Tate, *Black Women Writers at Work*, p. 91.

42. In *Liberating Voices*, Jones observes that "the language of the blues is generally concrete, graphic, imagistic, immediate" (p. 196). Also see Sherley Anne Williams, "The Blues Roots of Contemporary Afro-American Poetry," in *Chant of Saints*, ed. Michael Harper and Robert Stepto (Chicago: University of Chicago Press, 1979), pp. 123–35. Williams describes blues language as "almost always literal, seldom metaphoric or symbolic except in sexual and physical terms" (p. 131).

43. Gayl Jones, *Liberating Voices*, pp. 93, 97.

44. My language here echoes Sherley Anne Williams's statement, "Michael Harper alludes to the communal nature of the relationship between blues singer and blues audience when he speaks of the audience which assumes 'we' even though the blues singer sings 'I,'" "The Blues Roots of Contemporary Afro-American Poetry," p. 124.

45. My analysis of the dialogic interaction between the blues and the fictional modes in *Corregidora* is informed by Bakhtin's discussion of the folk form of the grotesque as it was transformed into various literary genres. See *Rabelais and His World*, trans. Helene Iswolsky (Bloomington: Indiana University Press, 1984), pp. 34–58. In an attempt to historicize Bakhtin's remarkably suggestive analysis of the novelization of oral forms, I foreground the ideological intentions that motivated the varying constructions of oral and fictional forms in black nationalist discourse and in black women's fiction. Whereas oral forms were affirmed as communal origins and fiction devalued in Black Aesthetic discourse, black women writers exploited the tension between oral and fictional modes in order to articulate their sense of unease with the univocal oral collectivity of Black Aesthetic ideology.

46. Jones, *Liberating Voices*, p. 198.

5. "Don't You Explain Me"

1. Clarence Major was one of the very few contemporary black critics to give *Eva's Man* a favorable review. Major's review stands virtually alone in its

consideration of the novel's formal features rather than its ideology. See Major, Review of *Eva's Man, Library Journal* (March 15, 1976): 834–35.

2. Richard Stookey, Review of *Eva's Man, Chicago Tribune Book Review* (March 28, 1976): 3. The novel's exclusive emphasis on the sexual victimization of black women by black men was the feature most emphasized by contemporary reviewers. Like Stookey, Charles Larson praised *Eva's Man* for its exploration of sexual conflict, which, according to Larson, "is not exactly a Black issue." See Larson, Review of *Eva's Man, National Observer* (April 17, 1976): section 5, p. 27. Also see Jessica Harris, Review of *Eva's Man, Essence* 7 (1976): 87; and two unsigned reviews of *Eva's Man* in *Kirkus Reviews* 44 (1976): 90, and *Booklist* 72 (1976): 1164.

3. This argument is offered by Askia Toure, "Black Male/Female Relations: A Political Overview of the 1970s," *The Black Scholar* 10, nos. 8–9 (1979): 46; and Ron Karenga, "On Wallace's Myths: Wading through Troubled Waters," *The Black Scholar* 10, nos. 8–9 (1979): 36.

4. Loyle Hairston, "No Feminist Tract," *Freedomways* 15 (1975): 291; Hairston, "The Repelling World of Sex and Violence," *Freedomways* 16 (1976): 133.

5. Keith Mano, "How to Write Two First Novels with Your Knuckles," *Esquire* (December 1976): 66.

6. Ibid., p. 62.

7. Ibid.

8. Gayl Jones, *Eva's Man* (Boston: Beacon, 1976), p. 128. All further references to this work are included in the text.

9. Addison Gayle, Jr., "Blueprint for Black Criticism," *Black World* 1, no. 1 (1977): 44.

10. Gloria Wade-Gayles, *No Crystal Stair: Visions of Race and Sex in Black Women's Fiction* (New York: Pilgrim Press, 1984), p. 178.

11. The novel's reliance on stereotypical characterization provoked John Updike's comment that "the characters are dehumanized as much by [Jones's] artistic vision as by their circumstances." See Updike, Review of *Eva's Man, The New Yorker* (August 9, 1976): 75.

12. In its figuration of the black feminine subject as an absence, *Eva's Man* resembles *The Bluest Eye* (New York: Simon and Schuster, 1970). Like Pecola, Eva tries to understand black feminine sexuality by observing her mother's sexual relationship with her father. Like Pecola, who cannot imagine the black woman as the subject of desire because of the "no noise at all from her mother" (p. 49), Eva perceives black feminine sexuality as a matter of silence and absence: "I didn't hear nothing from her the whole time. I didn't hear a thing from her" (p. 37). Unlike *Sula* and *Corregidora*, which explore absence as a source of power and freedom, *Eva's Man* and *The Bluest Eye* present black women who suffer from a culturally imposed negation of identity.

13. Jerilyn Fisher writes that black women writers of the 1970s "avoid the cliché of sexist—or feminist—stereotypes of Black women," and prefer to expose the contradictions of black femininity. See Fisher, "From under the Yoke of Race and Sex: Black and Chicano Women's Fiction of the Seventies," *Minority Voices* 2, no. 2 (1978): 1. While seeming to differ from black feminist criticism that calls for positive images, Fisher, too, sets up a false opposition between complex, contradictory characterization and reductive, simplistic stereotypes. As *Eva's Man* illustrates, stereotypes can be the means of highly complex and contradictory explorations of black femininity.

14. Addison Gayle, Jr., "Blueprint for Black Criticism," p. 43.

15. June Jordan, Review of *Eva's Man, New York Times Book Review* (May 16, 1976): 36.

16. Ibid., p. 37.

17. Addison Gayle, Jr., "Black Women and Black Men: The Literature of Catharsis," *Black Books Bulletin* 4, no. 4 (1976): 50, 51.

18. John Leonard, in his review of *Eva's Man, New York Times* (April 30, 1976): C17, argues that the novel obliquely targets white racism as the source of the sexual black stereotype: "The whites took everything away from the Blacks but their sexuality, and the distortions of that sexuality are responsible for Eva."

19. Claudia Tate, *Black Women Writers at Work* (New York: Continuum, 1983), pp. 96–97. Six years after the publication of *Eva's Man*, Gayl Jones seemed to have capitulated to the Black Aesthetic critique of her novel. In an interview with Charles Rowell in 1982, Jones said that in her current writing, she finds herself "wanting to back away from some questions. . . . I should mention that the male characters in those early novels are unfortunate, like the sexual theme—in this society that looks for things to support stereotypes." See Rowell, "An Interview with Gayl Jones," *Callaloo* 5, no. 3 (1982): 51.

20. Larry Neal, "The Black Arts Movement," in *The Black Aesthetic*, ed. Addison Gayle, Jr. (New York: Doubleday, 1972), p. 267.

21. For a perceptive discussion of the reader's entrapment in the novel's structure, see Jerry R. Ward, "Escape from Trublem: The Fiction of Gayl Jones," in *Black Women Writers*, ed. Mari Evans (New York: Anchor, 1984), pp. 249–52.

22. See Keith Byerman, "Black Vortex: The Gothic Structure of *Eva's Man*," *MELUS* 7, no. 4 (1980): 93–101, for an extensive analysis of the sense of inevitability created by the "whirlpool" structure of the novel.

23. Roger Rosenblatt, *Black Fiction* (Cambridge, Mass.: Harvard University Press, 1974), p. 64.

24. Darryl Pinckney, Review of *Eva's Man, The New Republic* (June 19, 1976): 27.

25. Ann Allen Shockley argues that "the ideology of the sixties provided added impetus to the Black community's negative image of homosexuality"; the lesbian, in particular, posed a "threat to the projection of Black male macho." See "The Black Lesbian in American Literature: An Overview," *Conditions: Five* (1979): 85.

26. Unsigned review of *Eva's Man, Publishers Weekly* 209 (1976): 92.

27. Michael Cooke, "Recent Novels: Women Bearing Violence," *Yale Review* 66 (1976): 92.

28. Addison Gayle, Jr., "Black Women and Black Men," p. 50.

29. Roseann Bell, "Judgement: Addison Gayle," in *Sturdy Black Bridges*, ed. Roseann Bell, Bettye J. Parker, and Beverly Guy-Sheftall (New York: Anchor, 1979), p. 215.

30. Michael Harper, "Gayl Jones: An Interview," in *Chant of Saints*, ed. Michael Harper and Robert B. Stepto (Chicago: University of Chicago Press, 1979), p. 361.

31. Margo Jefferson, "A Woman Alone," *Newsweek* (April 12, 1976): 104; Larry McMurtry, Review of *Eva's Man, The Washington Post* (April 12, 1976): C5. Also see an unsigned review of the novel in *Choice* (September 1976): "The novel . . . is of interest only for its investigation into abnormal psychology. . . . It does not have the larger canvas and social perspective of her previous *Corregidora*" (p. 823).

32. Charles Rowell, "An Interview with Gayl Jones," p. 43.

33. Diane Johnson remarks that "Jones seems to record what people say and think as if it were no fault of hers. . . . Perhaps art is always subversive in this way." See "The Oppressor in the Next Room," *The New York Times Review of Books* (November 10, 1979): 7.

34. In eschewing the authority of realism, *Eva's Man* may be said to signify

upon one of the founding motives of early black American narrative—the struggle to establish a credible and morally reliable black narrative voice. The narrating "I" of the slave narratives was constructed as a representative, transparent reflector of reality in order to authenticate the often surreal accounts of the horrors of slavery. Richard Yarborough, in "The First Person in Afro-American Fiction," *Afro-American Literary Study in the 1990s*, ed. Houston A. Baker, Jr., and Patricia Redmond (Chicago: University of Chicago Press, 1989), pp. 105–21, writes that this same "abiding concern . . . with establishing the credibility of their literary voices and thus of their views of reality" motivated the avoidance of first-person narration in early black fiction (p. 111). *Eva's Man*, like several black novels published in the 1970s, employs an atypical, incredible first-person narrator as a gesture of revolt against the truth-telling imperative that was imposed on black writers by Black Aesthetic theorists.

35. Keith Byerman, "Black Vortex," p. 99.

36. Charles Rowell, "An Interview with Gayl Jones," p. 37.

37. Robert Stepto argues, in "Distrust of the Reader in Afro-American Narratives," *Reconstructing American Literary History*, ed. Sacvan Bercovitch (Cambridge, Mass.: Harvard University Press, 1986), pp. 300–22, that distrust of the reader and of literacy are primary reasons for the use of the oral storytelling model in black fiction (pp. 303–305). Stepto's persuasive claim that the storytelling paradigm schools readers into the role of responsive and responsible listeners, and thereby serves a didactic function (pp. 309–10) is belied by the unusual function of the storytelling model in *Eva's Man*. Eva's distrust of the reader entails neither a hidden didactic intention nor an absent listener who may be responsive to such an intention.

38. Claudia Tate, *Black Women Writers at Work*, p. 92.

39. John Wideman, "Defining the Black Voice in Fiction," *Black American Literature Forum* 1 (1983): 81.

40. Melvin Dixon, "Singing a Deep Song: Language as Evidence in the Novels of Gayl Jones," in *Black Women Writers*, ed. Mari Evans, p. 237.

41. My reading of black dialect in the novel diverges from Valerie Gray Lee's argument that black women novelists such as Toni Morrison and Gayl Jones use black folk talk as an effective medium for expressing the deepest feelings of their female protagonists. See "The Use of Folk Talk in Novels by Black Women Writers," *CLA Journal* 23 (1980): 266–72. *Eva's Man*, in particular, shows black folk talk to be unamenable to feminine intentions; if anything, the novel bears out Roger Abrahams's assertion that urban black dialect often displays a strong animosity toward and "rejection of the 'feminine principle.'" See *Deep Down in the Jungle* (Chicago: Aldine, 1970), p. 32.

42. Michael Harper, "Gayl Jones: An Interview," p. 359.

6. "To Survive Whole"

1. Charles Rowell, "An Interview with Gayl Jones," *Callaloo* 5, no. 3 (1982): 38.

2. Alice Walker, in John O'Brien, *Interviews with Black Writers* (New York: Liveright, 1973), pp. 207–208.

3. Alice Walker, *In Search of Our Mothers' Gardens* (New York: Harcourt, 1984), p. 137. Hereafter cited in the text as *Search* and followed by page numbers.

4. Walker, in O'Brien, p. 193.

5. "Everyday Use" is, of course, the title of one of Walker's best-known short stories from her collection *In Love and Trouble* (New York: Harcourt, 1973). My

discussion of Walker's use of quilting as a metaphor for functional art is indebted to Barbara Christian's perceptive analysis of quilting in "Alice Walker: The Black Woman Artist as Wayward," in *Black Women Writers*, ed. Mari Evans (New York: Anchor, 1984), pp. 462–63.

6. Alice Walker, *The Third Life of Grange Copeland* (New York: Simon and Schuster, 1970), p. 342. All subsequent references to this work are included in the text.

7. Addison Gayle, Jr., "Blueprint for Black Criticism," *Black World* 1, no. 1 (1977): 44.

8. Michael Harper, "Gayl Jones: An Interview," in *Chant of Saints*, ed. Michael Harper and Robert B. Stepto (Chicago: University of Chicago Press, 1979), p. 361.

9. Falvia Plumpp, Review of *The Third Life*, in *Black Books Bulletin* 1, no. 1 (1971): 26. Robert Coles, who reviewed *The Third Life* for *The New Yorker*, predictably applauded the novel precisely for its refusal of a clear didactic or political function. Coles's comments, "Miss Walker is a storyteller. . . . She does not exhort," assume a dichotomy between good fiction and didacticism. See Coles, "To Try Men's Souls," *The New Yorker* (February 27, 1971): 104.

10. Loyle Hairston, "Work of Rare Beauty and Power," *Freedomways* 15 (1971): 177, emphasis mine.

11. Walker, in Claudia Tate, *Black Women Writers at Work* (New York: Continuum, 1983), p. 177.

12. Addison Gayle, Jr., in Roseann Bell, "Judgement: Addison Gayle," in *Sturdy Black Bridges*, ed. Roseann Bell, Bettye J. Parker, and Beverly Guy-Sheftall (New York: Anchor, 1979), p. 214.

13. Hairston, "Work of Rare Beauty and Power," p. 177.

14. The quoted phrase is from Toni Morrison's *Sula* (New York: NAL, 1973), p. 14.

15. John O'Brien, *Interviews with Black Writers*, p. 192.

16. Mary Helen Washington, "An Essay on Alice Walker," in *Sturdy Black Bridges*, p. 134; and Bettye Parker-Smith, "Alice Walker's Women: In Search of Some Peace of Mind," in *Black Women Writers*, p. 480.

17. The quoted phrase is taken from Karen Gaston, "Women in the Lives of Grange Copeland," *CLA Journal* 24 (1981): 276. Also see Barbara Christian, *Black Women Novelists* (Westport, Conn.: Greenwood Press, 1980), p. 195.

18. Mary Helen Washington, "An Essay on Alice Walker," p. 147.

19. Chikwenye Okonjo Ogunyemi, "Womanism: The Dynamics of the Contemporary Black Female Novel in English," *Signs: Journal of Women in Culture and Society* 11 (1985): 64, 68, 74.

20. Molefi Kete Asante, *The Afrocentric Idea* (Philadelphia: Temple University Press, 1987), p. 185.

21. Ogunyemi, "Womanism," pp. 68–69.

22. Alice Walker, *Living by the Word* (New York: Harcourt, 1988), p. 62.

23. Dianne F. Sadoff, "Black Matrilineage: The Case of Alice Walker and Zora Neale Hurston," *Signs: Journal of Women in Culture and Society* 11 (1985): 22–24.

24. Faith Ringgold, "From Being My Own Woman," in *Confirmations*, ed. Amina Baraka and Amiri Baraka (New York: Morrow, 1983), p. 301.

25. See, especially, Harold Hellenbrand's excellent discussion of how Grange "plays mother" to Ruth, in "Speech, After Silence: Alice Walker's *The Third Life of Grange Copeland*," *Black American Literature Forum* 20 (1986): 125.

26. See, for example, Amiri Baraka/LeRoi Jones, *Home: Social Essays* (New York: Morrow, 1966), p. 224; and Eldridge Cleaver, *Soul on Ice* (New York: Dell, 1968), pp. 13–14.

27. Many of Walker's essays celebrate the Southern Civil Rights movement

from a womanist perspective. In "Coretta King: Revisited," Walker praises Martin Luther King, Jr., because "although [he] was constantly harassed and oppressed by the white world he was always gentle with his wife and children" (*In Search of Our Mothers' Gardens*, p. 151). In another essay, "Choosing to Stay at Home," Walker contends that the sexism of the black nationalist movements in the North represented "a movement backward from the equalitarian goals" of the Civil Rights movement (*Search*, p. 169). That *The Third Life* should locate its vision of political transformation in the rural South of the Civil Rights movement rather than in the urban North, which was the locale privileged by the various black nationalist movements, is itself significant. As Barbara Christian has observed in "Alice Walker: The Black Woman Artist as Wayward," Walker's fictional reclamation of the South sets her outside the mainstream of militant black writers of the 1960s and 1970s, whose fictional representations of political change were largely situated in the urban North (p. 459). Also see Walker's own discussion of the symbolic significance of the South in her fiction, in "The Black Writer and the Southern Experience," in *Search*, pp. 15–21.

28. Claudia Tate, *Black Women Writers at Work*, p. 176.

29. Susan Willis, *Specifying: Black Women Writing the American Experience* (Madison: University of Wisconsin Press, 1987), p. 118.

30. Susan Willis, "Black Women Writers: Taking a Critical Perspective," in *Making a Difference*, ed. Gayle Greene and Coppelia Kahn (New York: Methuen, 1985), pp. 221–22.

31. Elliott Butler-Evans argues that, in *The Third Life*, "the racial historical discourse becomes increasingly marginalized and is often displaced by alternative narratives of feminist desire," *Race, Gender, and Desire* (Philadelphia: Temple University Press, 1989), p. 126. Setting up race and gender as "two contending discourses" (p. 126), Butler-Evans tends to place the black woman exclusively in the feminist discourse of gender and black men in the discourse of race. I would argue that the point of a term like *womanism* is to disclose the simultaneous operation of racial and gender dynamics in the lives of black women. My reading of *The Third Life* emphasizes Walker's attempt to integrate the discourses of nationalism and feminism.

32. Trudier Harris, "Folklore in the Fiction of Alice Walker: A Perpetuation of Historical and Literary Traditions," *Black American Literature Forum* 11 (1977): 7.

33. Lawrence Levine's extensive account of black folk thought is motivated by a similar impulse to correct "the popular formula which has rendered black history an unending round of degradation and pathology," *Black Culture and Black Consciousness: Afro-American Folk Thought from Slavery to Freedom* (New York: Oxford University Press, 1977), pp. x–xi.

34. Alice Walker, in John O'Brien, *Interviews with Black Writers*, p. 206.

35. Walker, *Living by the Word*, p. 32.

36. Gayl Jones, *Liberating Voices: Oral Tradition in African American Literature* (Cambridge, Mass.: Harvard University Press, 1991), pp. 151, 157.

37. I am drawing upon Lawrence Levine's discussion of the folk figure of the badman, in *Black Culture and Black Consciousness*, pp. 407–20.

38. Keith Byerman, *Fingering the Jagged Grain* (Athens, Ga.: University of Georgia Press, 1985), p. 129.

39. Robert B. Stepto, *From Behind the Veil: A Study of Afro-American Narrative* (Urbana: University of Illinois Press, 1979), p. 167. Stepto's influential formulation of the central tropes of the Afro-American narrative tradition has recently been critiqued for its gender-blindness. Michael Awkward challenges the "sexist biases" of Stepto's tropes of immersion and ascent, in *Inspiriting Influences* (New York: Columbia University Press, 1989), p. 47; and Valerie

Smith, in "Gender and Afro-Americanist Literary Theory and Criticism," *Speaking of Gender*, ed. Elaine Showalter (New York: Routledge, 1989), pp. 56–70, argues that Stepto's emphasis on the quest for literacy in the Afro-American narrative tradition establishes a "specifically masculine legacy" (p. 61). Although Stepto does not explicitly consider novels written by black women (with the exception of Hurston's *Their Eyes Were Watching God*), his tropes can be immensely suggestive if refigured and applied to black women's fiction. Stepto's trope of immersion and ascent (which falls outside the thematic scope of this study) might inspire powerful rereadings of novels as diverse as *Their Eyes Were Watching God*, Nella Larsen's *Quicksand* and *Passing*, Morrison's *The Bluest Eye*, *Song of Solomon*, and *Tar Baby*, and Walker's *Meridian*, all of which play upon the tensions between the desire for ascendence and the opposing impulse toward cultural immersion. Stepto's discussion of the quest for literacy in Afro-American narrative informs my analyses of *The Bluest Eye* and *The Third Life*; both novels valorize literacy as an empowering cultural skill that alone can enable black Americans to read critically and to displace the authoritative master-texts of white U.S. culture.

40. Harold Hellenbrand, "Speech, after Silence," p. 124.

41. Gayl Jones, in Charles Rowell, "Gayl Jones: An Interview," p. 137.

42. See Catherine Belsey, *Critical Practice* (New York: Methuen, 1980), pp. 70–72; and Elizabeth Ermarth, "Fictional Consensus and Female Casualties," in *The Representation of Women in Fiction*, ed. Carolyn G. Heilbrun and Margaret R. Higonnet (Baltimore: Johns Hopkins University Press, 1983), pp. 1–18, for discussions of the hierarchical privileging and the unquestionable authority of the omniscient narrator's discourse in classic realist fiction.

43. Walker, in Claudia Tate, *Black Women Writers at Work*, p. 176.

44. Ogunyemi argues, in "Womanism," that the womanist novel finds its resolution only "when the black woman's communion with the rest of society is established" (p. 74). Ogunyemi's discussion of *The Third Life* diverges from mine in its assertion that the novel achieves the "womanist objective" of establishing "the integration of the Ruths into the Black world" (p. 73).

7. "A Crazy Quilt"

1. Alice Walker, in Claudia Tate, *Black Women Writers at Work* (New York: Continuum, 1983), p. 176.

2. Gayl Jones uses this phrase in Charles Rowell, "An Interview with Gayl Jones," *Callaloo* 5, no. 3 (1982): 38.

3. See Robert Stepto, "After the 60's: The Boom in Afro-American Fiction," in *Contemporary American Fiction*, ed. Malcolm Bradbury and Sigmund Ro (London: Edward Arnold, 1987), p. 101; and Bettye Parker-Smith, "Alice Walker's Women: In Search of Some Peace of Mind," in *Black Women Writers*, ed. Mari Evans (New York: Anchor, 1984), p. 480.

4. Alice Walker, *In Search of Our Mothers' Gardens* (New York: Harcourt, 1984), p. 381. Hereafter cited in the text as *Search*, and followed by page numbers.

5. Karen Stein argues that Walker criticizes the Civil Rights movement because "it failed to acknowledge women's selfhood and thus perpetuated the counterrevolutionary values of a destructive society." See Stein, "*Meridian*: Alice Walker's Critique of Revolution," *Black American Literature Forum* 20 (1986): 129. Stein correctly describes the novel's critique of the black nationalist movement, but overlooks the novel's sharp distinction, based on feminist grounds, between the nationalist and the Civil Rights movements.

6. Alice Walker, *Revolutionary Petunias* (New York: Harcourt, 1973), pp. 45, 33.

7. Alice Walker, *Meridian* (New York: Simon and Schuster, 1976), p. 188. All further references to this work are cited in the text.

8. Alice Walker, in Claudia Tate, *Black Women Writers at Work*, p. 184.

9. Walker's presentation of Saxon College is strongly reminiscent of Naxos, the black middle-class educational institution satirized in Nella Larsen's *Quicksand*. Aside from the obvious resemblance of their names, Saxon and Naxos are similar in their suppression of sexuality and their goal of producing black ladies and gentlemen cast in a white middle-class mold.

10. Chikwenye Okonjo Ogunyemi, "Womanism: The Dynamics of the Contemporary Black Female Novel in English," *Signs: Journal of Women in Culture and Society* 11 (1985): 68–69.

11. Walker, *Living by the Word* (New York: Harcourt, 1988), p. 95.

12. Marie Buncombe, "Androgyny as Metaphor in Alice Walker's Novels," *CLA Journal* 30 (1987): 423–26.

13. Failing to appreciate the novel's androgynous vision, the black writer David Bradley criticized Walker's fiction on the Black Aesthetic grounds that it does not affirm black men unless they are "feminized." See Bradley, "Novelist Alice Walker Telling the Black Woman's Story," *New York Times Magazine* (January 8, 1984): 35.

14. See Eldridge Cleaver, *Soul on Ice* (New York: Dell, 1968), p. 208; and Robert Staples, "The Myth of the Black Matriarchy," 1970, rptd. in *The Black Woman Cross-Culturally*, ed. Filomina Chioma Steady (Cambridge, Mass.: Schenkman, 1981), p. 346.

15. Toni Morrison, *Sula* (New York: NAL, 1973), p. 92.

16. Margaret Homans argues that Louvinie's silencing results from her racial rather than sexual subjection. "'Her Very Own Howl': The Ambiguities of Representation in Recent Women's Fiction," *Signs: Journal of Women in Culture and Society* 9 (1983): 198. My reading emphasizes the inextricable entanglement of race and gender in the episode of Louvinie's silencing, which occurs because Louvinie abuses the maternal role imposed upon her by her slavemaster. Overlooking the central significance of reproduction in the Louvinie narrative, Homans sets up a distinction between racial and gender-based silencing (p. 198) that is rather difficult to sustain in a womanist novel like *Meridian*.

17. See Martha McGowan, "Atonement and Release in Alice Walker's *Meridian*," *Critique* 23, no. 1 (1981): 35; and John Callahan, *In the African-American Grain* (Urbana: University of Illinois Press, 1988), p. 226.

18. See Larry Neal, "The Black Arts Movement," in *The Black Aesthetic*, ed. Addison Gayle, Jr. (New York: Doubleday, 1972), p. 272.

19. Dianne F. Sadoff, "Black Matrilineage: The Case of Alice Walker and Zora Neale Hurston," *Signs: Journal of Women in Culture and Society* 11 (1985): 9.

20. Sadoff, "Black Matrilineage," p. 11.

21. See Richard Wright, "Blueprint for Negro Writing," 1937, rptd. in *The Black Aesthetic*, pp. 315–16; James Baldwin, "Everybody's Protest Novel," in *Notes of a Native Son* (New York: Bantam, 1964), p. 17; and Ralph Ellison, "The Art of Fiction: An Interview," in *Shadow and Act* (New York: Random House, 1964), pp. 168, 170. However, it would only be fair to point out that Ellison has criticized the oedipal metaphor of literary influence because it "misnames a complicated relationship." See Michael Harper and Robert Stepto, "Study and Experience: An Interview with Ralph Ellison," in *Chant of Saints*, ed. Michael Harper and Robert Stepto (Chicago: University of Chicago Press, 1979), p. 451. Ellison mocks the Bloomian model in an extended and intentionally absurd

comparison of the masculine writer to "an unwedded mother [who] gives her unwanted baby [her talent] over for adoption" (p. 451).

22. Amiri Baraka/LeRoi Jones, *Home: Social Essays* (New York: Morrow, 1966), p. 105.

23. Addison Gayle, Jr., "The Function of Black Literature at the Present Time," in *The Black Aesthetic*, p. 393.

24. Hoyt W. Fuller, "The New Black Literature: Protest or Affirmation," in *The Black Aesthetic*, p. 327.

25. Sadoff, "Black Matrilineage," p. 11.

26. Roseann Bell, "Judgement: Addison Gayle," in *Sturdy Black Bridges*, ed. Roseann Bell, Bettye J. Parker, and Beverly Guy-Sheftall (New York: Anchor, 1979), p. 214.

27. Walker, *Living by the Word*, p. 98.

28. Alan Nadel, "Reading the Body: Alice Walker's *Meridian* and the Archeology of Self," *Modern Fiction Studies* 34 (1988): 56.

29. Walker, *Living by the Word*, p. 67.

30. Claudia Tate, *Black Women Writers at Work*, p. 176.

31. Barbara Christian writes that the circular structure of the novel "is itself a visual representation of the term *revolution*, the moving backward to move forward beyond the point at which you began." *Black Women Novelists: The Development of a Tradition* (Westport, Conn.: Greenwood Press, 1980), p. 207. John Callahan, too, observes that the novel's "elliptical pattern of continual change figures revolutionary process," *In the African-American Grain*, p. 224.

32. Sherley Anne Williams, in Claudia Tate, *Black Women Writers at Work*, p. 208.

33. Roseann Bell, "Gayl Jones Takes a Look at *Corregidora*," in *Sturdy Black Bridges*, p. 285.

34. Roger D. Abrahams, "Introduction" to *Afro-American Folktales* (New York: Pantheon, 1985), pp. 24, 29.

35. Ibid., p. 3.

36. Ibid.

37. Alice Walker, in John O'Brien, *Interviews with Black Writers* (New York: Liveright, 1973), p. 204.

38. Susan Willis, *Specifying: Black Women Writing the American Experience* (Madison: University of Wisconsin Press, 1987), p. 114; and John Callahan, *In the African-American Grain*, p. 218.

39. Alan Nadel, "Reading the Body," pp. 56, 60.

40. Mikhail Bakhtin, *Rabelais and His World*, trans. Helene Iswolsky (Bloomington: Indiana University Press, 1984), p. 355.

41. The novel's mysticism seems to derive from many different cultural traditions. Meridian's experiences of mystical ecstasy are explicitly located within the frame of Native Indian culture in the chapter "Indians and Ecstasy," but elements of Native Indian culture somewhat incoherently coexist with the Christian rhetoric of mysticism as an ascetic scourging of the body. In an interview with John O'Brien, Walker traced her mystical vision to yet another source—animism, which Walker believes is the "one thing African-Americans have retained of their African heritage," *Interviews with Black Writers*, p. 193. The diverse cultural origins of Meridian's mysticism are typical of the novel's crazy quilt form, which takes bits and pieces from different sources with little concern for an overarching unity or coherence.

42. Sadoff, "Black Matrilineage," p. 23.

43. Deborah McDowell, "The Self in Bloom: Alice Walker's *Meridian*," *CLA Journal* 24 (1981): 263.

44. Bernard Bell discounts a reading of *Meridian* as a political novel, arguing

that the novel's social and political context "resound[s] with personal self-indulgence. . . . The Civil Rights movement, in short, provided a means of spiritual and moral redemption from a guilty past for individuals like Meridian, not a radical new social order in which all could realize their full potential." *The Afro-American Novel and Its Tradition* (Amherst: University of Massachusetts Press, 1987), pp. 262–63.

45. See, especially, Walker's "Really, Doesn't Crime Pay," in *In Love and Trouble* (New York: Harcourt, 1973), and "The Girl Who Died #2," in *Revolutionary Petunias*.

Conclusion

1. Toni Morrison, "Rootedness: The Ancestor as Foundation," in *Black Women Writers*, ed. Mari Evans (New York: Anchor, 1984), p. 341.

2. Charles Rowell, "An Interview with Gayl Jones," *Callaloo* 5, no. 3 (1982): 43.

3. Alice Walker, *In Search of Our Mothers' Gardens* (New York: Harcourt, 1984), p. 137; Alice Walker, *The Third Life of Grange Copeland* (New York: Simon and Schuster, 1970), pp. 342–45. Subsequent references to this work are parenthetically cited in the text.

4. Toni Morrison, *The Bluest Eye* (New York: Simon and Schuster, 1970), p. 160.

5. Toni Morrison, *Sula* (New York: NAL, 1973), p. 147. Subsequent references to this work are parenthetically cited in the text.

6. Gayl Jones, *Corregidora* (Boston: Beacon, 1975), p. 59. Subsequent references to this work are parenthetically cited in the text.

7. Gayl Jones, in Claudia Tate, *Black Women Writers at Work* (New York: Continuum, 1983), p. 92.

8. The quoted phrase is from Charles Rowell, "An Interview with Gayl Jones," p. 38.

9. Alice Walker, *Meridian* (New York: Simon and Schuster, 1976), p. 19. Subsequent references to this work are parenthetically cited in the text.

10. Toni Cade Bambara, in Claudia Tate, *Black Women Writers at Work*, p. 21.

11. Ann Allen Shockley, *Loving Her* (New York: Bobbs-Merrill, 1974), p. 31. Subsequent references to this work are parenthetically cited in the text.

12. Carlene Hatcher Polite's *Sister X and the Victims of Foul Play* (New York: Farrar, Straus and Giroux, 1975) includes a letter from a black male nationalist character named Black Will (pp. 100–104) that closely echoes Eldridge Cleaver's affirmation of heterosexuality in his "Letter to All Black Women, from All Black Men," *Soul on Ice* (New York: Dell, 1968), pp. 205–10. Subsequent references to *Sister X* are parenthetically cited in the text.

13. The end of Rosa Guy's *Ruby* (New York: Viking, 1976) writes off the lesbian affair that constitutes the novel's central theme as a passing adolescent phase. This containment is supported by Ruby's reconciliation with her father (who had strongly objected to her lesbian relationship) and with heterosexuality. In the last scene of the novel, Ruby eagerly anticipates a date with Orlando, a minor character who is awkwardly ushered into the final pages of the novel to effect Ruby's return to heterosexuality.

14. Although *Zami* (New York: Crossing Press, 1982) is subtitled "A Biomythography," Audre Lorde claims that the book "is really fiction." See Claudia Tate, *Black Women Writers at Work*, p. 115.

15. The quoted phrase is from Alice Walker's *Meridian*, p. 188.

16. Alice Childress, *A Hero Ain't Nothin' but a Sandwich* (New York: Coward,

1973), p. 89. Subsequent references to this work are parenthetically cited in the text.

17. Zora Neale Hurston, *Dust Tracks on a Road* (1942; Urbana: University of Illinois Press, 1970), p. 215.

18. Ibid., p. 218.

19. Margaret Wade and Melvin Wade, "The Black Aesthetic in the Black Novel," *Journal of Black Studies* 2 (1972): 394–99.

20. All these novels manipulate typography to achieve their intention, using different type faces, for example, to convey the demarcations between various, competing social languages. Playful juxtapositions of print and orality recur in *Sister X*; see, for example: "My word! aqwsxedcrftvgbyhnujimklo (Now how does that sound in the light of day?)" (p. 65).

21. Toni Morrison, in Claudia Tate, *Black Women Writers at Work*, p. 126.

22. Alexis DeVeaux, *Spirits in the Street* (New York: Doubleday, 1973), p. 80. Subsequent references to this work are parenthetically cited in the text.

23. The quoted phrase is from Alice Walker's *In Search of Our Mothers' Gardens*, p. 138.

24. Carlene Hatcher Polite, *The Flagellants* (Boston: Beacon, 1967), p. 57. Subsequent references to this work are parenthetically cited in the text.

25. The quoted phrase is taken from Polite, *The Flagellants*, p. 86.

26. Toni Morrison, "Rootedness," p. 339.

27. Toni Morrison, in Claudia Tate, *Black Women Writers at Work*, p. 123.

28. I am drawing upon Raymond Williams's discussion of periodicity in terms of residual, dominant, and emergent strains, in *Marxism and Literature* (Oxford: Oxford University Press, 1977), pp. 121–27. Williams's use of these terms encourages a conception of literary periods as dynamic and processual, rather than static and unified.

29. See, for example, Sherley Anne Williams's preface to *Dessa Rose* (New York: Berkley, 1987): "I loved history as a child, until some clear-eyed young Negro pointed out, quite rightly, that there was no place in the American past I could go and be free. I now know that slavery eliminated neither heroism nor love; it provided occasions for their expression" (p. x).

30. I am quoting from Ntozake Shange, *Sassafras, Cypress and Indigo* (New York: St. Martin's Press, 1982), p. 28.

31. This trend is also visible in other 1970s black women's novels. For example, in *The Third Life of Grange Copeland*, Ruth's grandfather teaches her the "untaught history" (p. 190) of her ancestors, and in Louise Meriwether's *Daddy Was a Number Runner* (New York: Feminist Press, 1970), Francie's father teaches her that black Americans are proud "Yoruba's children" (p. 82) rather than the disinherited descendants of slaves. *Eva's Man*, too, hints at the redemptive possibilities of ancestral heritage in Eva's memories of her great-grandmother. However, in all these novels, the transformative potential of the ancestral past remains undeveloped, and is frequently choked by a strong opposing sense of the past and of generational continuity as nothing but burdensome legacies of oppression.

32. In *Dessa Rose, Beloved*, and *Mama Day*, motherhood plays a crucial role in black women's political resistance: Dessa leads a slave rebellion while she is pregnant, Sethe chooses to kill her daughter rather than subject her to slavery, and Mama Day exercises all her powers of conjuring in order to safeguard the survival of Baby Girl, the only remaining female child in the Day family. This kind of political reclamation of motherhood is unthinkable in 1970s black women's fiction, which can imagine political resistance only against the imposed reproductive definition of black women's political function in nationalist discourse.

INDEX

MADHU DUBEY is Assistant Professor in English at Northwestern University.